OUTLINES
OF
THE HISTORY OF RELIGION

OUTLINES
OF
THE HISTORY OF RELIGION

TO THE
SPREAD OF THE UNIVERSAL
RELIGIONS

BY C. P. TIELE

Translated from the Dutch

by

J. ESTLIN CARPENTER, M.A.

GYAN

Published by

Gyan Publishing House
5, Ansari Road
Daryaganj, New Delhi-110002
Phone: 011-47034999, 9811692060
E-mail: books@gyanbooks.com

Distribution Network
gyanbooks.com
India, USA, Canada, UK, Australia, France

ISBN : 978-81-212-6103-6 (PB)
First Published, 1877

2nd Impression 2021

Printed at: Gyan Press, Delhi.

Outlines of The History of Religion
Author: C. P. Tiele

OUTLINES

OF

THE HISTORY OF RELIGION

TO THE

SPREAD OF THE UNIVERSAL RELIGIONS.

By C. P. TIELE,

Translated from the Dutch

BY

J. ESTLIN CARPENTER, M.A.

1877.

TO

P. H. W.

WITHOUT WHOSE AID

This Translation

COULD NOT HAVE BEEN

ACCOMPLISHED.

PREFACE BY THE AUTHOR

TO

THE ENGLISH EDITION.

WHAT I give in this little book are outlines, pencil-sketches, I might say,—nothing more. In the present state of our knowledge about the ancient religions, this only can be reasonably expected from the students of this branch of science, this only can be attempted with some hope of success. The time for writing an elaborate History of Religion, even of Religions, has not yet come. Not a few special investigations must be instituted, not a few difficult questions elucidated, before anything like this can be done. But it is useful, even necessary, from time to time to sum up the amount of certain knowledge, gathered by the researches of several years, and to sketch, be it here and there with an uncertain hand, the draught of what may at some time become a living picture. This is what I propose to do. The interest of what is called by the unhappy name of Science of Religions, let us say of Hierology, is increasing every day. Now, I think there is great danger that so young a science may lose itself in abstract speculations, based on a few facts and a great many dubious or erroneous statements, or not based on any facts at all. For the philosopher who wishes to avoid this danger, for the theologian who desires to compare Mosaism and Christianity with the other religions of the world, for the specialist who devotes all his labours and all his time to one single department of this vast science, for him who studies the history of civilisation—none of whom have leisure to go to the sources themselves, even for him who intends to do so, but to whom the way is as yet unknown, a general survey of the whole subject is needed, to serve as a kind of guide or travelling-book on their journey through the immense fairyland of human faith and hope. My book is an attempt to supply what they want. In a short paragraph-style I have written down my conclusions, derived partly from the sources themselves, partly (for no man can be at home everywhere) from the study of what seemed to me the best authorities: and I have added some explanatory remarks and bibliographical notices on the literature of the subject—very short where such notices could easily be found elsewhere, more extensive and as complete as possible where nothing of the kind, so far as I knew, yet existed.

I am the more anxious to state this character of my work as one of my critics (my friend and colleague Dr. H. Oort, in his interesting notice of my work in the Dutch Review *de Tijdspiegel*) seems to have wholly forgotten it.

He sets up an ideal of a History of Religion, and then tries my simple and modest outlines by that elevated standard. Of course they are not able to fulfil such great expectations, and they were not intended to do so.

I know that even this slight sketch is incomplete, and it is so on purpose. I have limited myself to the ancient religions, those which embrace a tribe, a people, or a race, or have grown into separate sects, and I have left out the history of the universal religions, Buddhism, Christianity, and Islâm. Only the origin of these religions is mentioned, as they form a part of the history of the religions out of which they sprang, and which culminate in them. A thorough study of this more modern religious history would have occupied me for several years, and would have deferred the publication of my little book for a long time. So I have narrated the History of Religion "till the spread of the universal religions," of Buddhism in Eastern, Islâm in Western Asia, and of Christianity in the Roman Empire. As Buddhism only reigned supreme in Hindostân and Dekhân now and then for a while, and was finally driven out from both parts of the Indian peninsula, with the sole exception of Ceylon, I could not break off the history of Brâhmanism at the foundation of the great rival church, but had to relate what became of it in the centuries after that event. I confess that this part of my sketch leaves much to be desired, the sources being still very defective, and the conclusions of Lassen, whom I have followed in the main, being still very uncertain. Perhaps I may find occasion some time to give a better and more trustworthy account of this period.

Not only the universal religions, but even some ancient religions are passed over altogether. I have not said a word on the old Keltic and the national Japanese religions. This, too, is an intentional omission. What is commonly regarded as the history of those two religions seems to me so very dubious and vague that I preferred to leave them out entirely rather than to be led astray myself, or to propagate mere conjectures, which might prove errors after all.

But though mere outlines, my history is one of religion, not of religions. The difference between the two methods is explained in the Introduction. It is the same history, but considered from a different point of view. The first lies hidden in the last, but its object is to show how that one great psychological phenomenon which we call religion has developed and manifested itself in such various shapes among the different races and peoples of the world. By it we see that all religions, even those of highly civilised nations, have grown up from the same simple germs, and by it, again, we learn the causes why these germs have in some cases attained such a rich and admirable development, and in others scarcely grew at all. Still I did not think it safe to found my history on an *a priori* philosophical basis. Dr. Oort is of opinion that I ought to have started from a philosophical definition of religion. In this I do not agree with him. Such a definition, quite different from that which I give in my first paragraph, ought not to be the point of issue, but must be one of the results of a history of religion. It forms one of the principal elements of a philosophy of religion; in a history it would be out of place.

Lastly, I may add a few words on this English edition. It is thoroughly revised and corrected. Some of these corrections I owe to my friend and colleague Dr. H. Kern, who knows all, or nearly all, about ancient India, and who has made such a profound study of German mythology (see his kind notice of my work in the Dutch Review *de Gids*). My own continued study of the religions of Western Asia and Northern Africa has led to other corrections and additions.

C. P. TIELE.

LEIDEN, *September* 1877.

CONTENTS.

CHAPTER II.

CHAPTER III.

CHAPTER IV.

CHAPTER V.

INTRODUCTION.

Literature.—Of the older works on the general history of religion, the following may still be named: MEINERS, *Allgemeine kritische Geschichte der Religionen*, 2 vols., Hanover, 1806–7 (neither general nor critical): BENJ. CONSTANT, *De la Religion considerée dans sa source, ses formes et ses dêveloppements*, 5 vols., Paris, 1824–31. The doctrines of ancient religion are treated by F. CREUZER, *Symbolik und Mythologie der alten Völker*, 4 vols., with Atlas, Leipzig and Darmstadt, 1819–21, and F. C. BAUR, *Symbolik und Mythologie, od. die Naturrel. des Alterthums*, 2 vols., 3 parts, Stuttgart, 1824–25. (Both works are now antiquated. Their speculations are for the most part founded on very imperfect or incorrect data.) L. NOACK, *Mythol. und Offenbarung. Die Religion in ihrem Wesen, ihrer geschichtl. Entwickel.*, &c., 2 vols., Darmstadt, 1845, more systematic than historic. A. VON CÖLLN, *Lehrb. der vorchristl. Religionsgeschichte*, Lemgo & Detmold, 1853, still useful in some parts. J. H. SCHOLTEN, *Geschiedenis der Godsd. en Wijsbegeerte*, Leiden, 1863. O. PFLEIDERER, *Die Religion, ihr Wesen und ihre Geschichte*, 2 vols., Leipzig, 1869. Comp. also F. MAX MÜLLER, *Chips from a German Workshop*, vols. i. and ii., London, 1867.

1. The history of religion is not content with describing special religions (*hierography*), or with relating their vicissitudes and metamorphoses (the history of religions); its aim is to show how religion, considered generally as the relation between man and the superhuman powers in which he believes, has developed in the course of ages among different nations and races, and, through these, in humanity at large.

The definition of religion as the relation between man and the superhuman powers in which he believes is by no means philosophical, and leaves unanswered the question of the essence of religion. The powers are designedly not described as supersensual, as visible deities would thus be excluded. They are superhuman, not always in reality, but in the estimation of their worshippers.

2. The hypothesis of development, from which the history of religion sets out, does not determine whether all religions were derived from one single prehistoric religion, or whether different families of religions sprang from as many separate forms, related in ideas, but independent in origin—a process which is not improbable. But its fundamental principle is that all changes and transformations in religions, whether they appear from a subjective point of view to indicate decay or progress, are the results of natural growth, and find in it their best explanation. The history of religion unfolds the method in which this development is determined by the character of nations and races, as well as by the influence of the circumstances surrounding them, and of special individuals, and it exhibits the established laws by which this development is controlled. Thus conceived, it is really history, and not a morphologic arrangement of religions, based on an arbitrary standard.

Compare J. I. DOEDES, *De Toepassing van de Ontwikkelingstheorie niet aantebevelen voor de Geschiedenis der Godsdiensten*, Utrecht, 1874. On the opposite side, C. P. TIELE, "De Ontwikkelingsgeschiedenis van den Godsdienst en de hypotheze waarvan zij uitgaat," *Gids*, 1874, No. 6. In reply, J. I. DOEDES, "Over de Ontwikkelingshypotheze in verband met de Geschiedenis der Godsdiensten;" *Stemmen voor Waarheid en Vrede*, 1874. Further, O. PFLEIDERER, "Zur Frage nach Anfang und Entwickelung der Religion," *Jahrbücher für Protest. Theologie*, 1875, Heft i. In reply, C. P. TIELE, "Over den Aanvang en de Ontwikkeling van den Godsdienst. Een verweerschrift," *Theol. Tijdschrift*, 1875, p. 170, *sqq*. On the laws which control the development of religion, see C. P. TIELE, "Over de Wetten der Ontwikkeling van den Godsdienst," *Theol. Tijdschrift*, 1874, p. 225, *sqq*.

3. It is on various grounds probable that the earliest religion, which has left but faint traces behind it, was followed by a period in which Animism generally prevailed. This stage, which is still represented by the so-called Nature-religions, or rather by the polydæmonistic magic tribal religions, early developed among civilised nations into polytheistic national religions resting upon a traditional doctrine. Not until a later period did polytheism give place here and there to nomistic religions, or religious communities founded on a law or holy scripture, and subduing polytheism more or less completely beneath pantheism or monotheism. These last, again, contain the roots of the universal or world-religions, which start from principles and maxims. Were we to confine ourselves to a sketch of the abstract development of the religious idea in humanity, we should have to follow this order.

The polytheistic religions include most of the Indo-Germanic and Semitic religions, the Egyptian, and some others. The nomistic religions comprise Confucianism, Taoism, the Mosaism of the eighth century B.C., and the Judaism which sprang from it, Brâhmanism, and Mazdeism. The universal religions are Buddhism, Christianity, and Mohammedanism. The pre-Islâmic religion of the Arabs was certainly not a nomistic religion, but without Judaism, to say nothing of Christianity, Islâm would never have been founded.

4. But in actually describing the general history of religion, we are compelled to take into account, also, the genealogical connection and historical relation of religions, which gave rise to different streams of development, independent of each other, whose courses in many instances afterwards met and joined. It is inexpedient, for the sake of a systematic arrangement, to divide these historic groups.

By genealogical connection we mean the filiation of religions, one of which has obviously proceeded from the other, or both together from a third, whether this be known to us historically or must be referred to prehistoric times. Thus the Vedic and old Erânian religions sprang from the Aryan, Confucianism and Taoism from the ancient Chinese religion, Buddhism from Brâhmanism, &c. In the course of history, moreover, religions which are not allied by descent come into contact with each other, and if their mutual influence leads to the adoption by one of them of customs, ideas, and deities belonging to the other, they are said to be historically related. This is the case, for example, with the north Semitic religions in reference to the Akkadian, with the Greek in reference to the north Semitic, and with the Roman in reference to the Greek.

5. For these reasons we divide our history in the following manner:—

(1.) From the polydæmonistic magic tribal religions of the present day we shall endeavour to become acquainted with Animism, this being the form of religion which must have preceded the religions known to us by history, and served as their foundation. The example of the more civilised American nations (Mexicans and Peruvians) and of the Finns will show us what an advanced development may be attained under favourable circumstances by an animistic religion, even where it is left to itself. This forms the transition to the proper history of religion, which will be treated in the ensuing order:—

(2.) Religion among the Chinese:

(3.) Among the Egyptians, the Semites proper, and the northern Semites or Mesopotamians, in connection with whom the Akkadian religion, which dominates all the north Semitic religions, will be discussed:

(4.) Among the Indo-Germans who came little, or not at all, into contact with the Semites, the Aryans, Hindûs, Erânians, Letto-Slavs, and Germans:

(5.) Among the Indo-Germans in whose religion the national elements were supplemented and blended with others of north Semitic or Hamitic origin, viz., the Greeks and Romans.

The history of the internal development of the universal religions and their mutual comparison lie beyond our plan; they require separate study, and are too vast to be included here. The third division, however, will trace the development of Islâm out of the Semitic religion; the fourth, that of Buddhism from Brâhmanism; and the fifth will indicate how European Christianity arose out of the fusion of Semitic and Indo-Germanic religions.

A description of the so-called nature-religions, which belongs to ethnology, is excluded from our design for obvious reasons. They have no history; and in the historic chain they only serve to enable us to form an idea of the ancient prehistoric animistic religions of which they are the remains, or, it may be said, the ruins. It must suffice, therefore, to recount here a few of their chief features. Of the Japanese no mention is made, because the history of the present form of their religion belongs to that of Buddhism, and the investigation of the old national religion (designated by a Chinese name, *Shinto,* the way or doctrine of spirits, and perhaps itself derived from China) has not yet led to any sufficiently satisfactory results. The latter remark also holds good of the religion of the Kelts, which we have also left out of consideration for the same reason.

6. The question whether religion is as old as the human race, or whether it is the growth of a later stage, is as little open to solution by historical research as that of its origin and essence; it can only be answered by psychology, and is a purely philosophical inquiry. The statement that there are nations or tribes which possess no religion, rests either on inaccurate observation, or on a confusion of ideas. No tribe or nation has yet been met with destitute of belief in any higher beings; and travellers who asserted their existence have been afterwards refuted by the facts. It is legitimate, therefore, to call religion in its most general sense a universal phenomenon of humanity.

CHAPTER I.

RELIGION UNDER THE CONTROL OF ANIMISM.

I.

ANIMISM IN ITS INFLUENCE ON RELIGION IN GENERAL.

Literature.—TYLOR, *Primitive Culture*, 2 vols., London, 1871, and *Researches into the Early History of Mankind*, London, 1865; Sir JOHN LUBBOCK, *Origin of Civilisation*, London, 1874; FRITZ SCHULTZE, *Der Fetischismus, ein Beitrag zur Anthropologie und Religionsgeschichte;* THEOD. WAITZ, *Anthropologie der Naturvölker*, vol. i., "Ueber die Einheit des Menschengeschlechtes und den Naturzustand des Menschen," Leipzig, 2d ed., 1877; OSCAR PESCHEL, *The Races of Man*, translated from the German, London, 1876, a book of the highest importance, and written in attractive style. Much useful material may be found in CASPARI, *Die Urgeschichte der Menschheit mit Rucksicht auf die natürliche Entwickelung des frühesten Geisteslebens*, 2 vols., Leipzig, 1873, 2d ed. ibid., 1877, and in (RABENHAUSEN) *Isis. Der Mensch und die Welt*, 4 vols., Hamburg, 1863. The notions of GEORG GERLAND, in his "Betrachtungen über die Entwickelungs- und Urgeschichte der Menschheit," in *Anthropologische Beiträge*, i., Halle, 1875, are altogether peculiar, often hypothetical, but not always to be rejected. ADOLF BASTIAN, of whose numerous works we only name under this head *Der Mensch in der Geschichte*, 3 vols., Leipzig, 1860, and *Beiträge zur vergleichenden*

Psychologie ("Die Seele und ihre Erscheinungsweisen in der Ethnographie"), Berlin, 1868, and whose ideas deserve consideration, heaps up an ill-arranged mass of examples, from all periods and nations, and nowhere names a single authority, which almost prevents his writings from being used. To this, however, his *Besuch an San Salvador* makes a favourable exception. Compare further M. CARRIÈRE, *Die Anfänge der Cultur und das Oriental. Alterthum*, 2d ed., 1872; L. F. A. MAURY, *La Magie et l'Astrologie dans l'Antiquité et au Moyen Âge*, Paris, 1860, and C. P. TIELE, *De Plaats van de Godsdiensten der Natuurvolken in de Godsdienstgeschiedenis*, Amsterdam, 1873.

7. The belief that the religions of savages, known to us from the past or still existing, are the remains of the religion which prevailed among mankind before the earliest civilisation flourished, and are thus best fitted to give us an idea of it, rests on the following grounds:—

(1.) The most recent investigations indicate that the general civilisation had then reached no higher stage than that of the present savages, nay, it had not even advanced so far; and in such a civilisation no purer religious beliefs, ideas, and usages are possible, than those which we find among existing communities.

(2.) The civilised religions whose history ascends to the remotest ages, such as the Egyptian, the Akkadian, the Chinese, still show more clearly than later religions the influence of animistic conceptions.

(3.) Almost the whole of the mythology and theology of civilised nations may be traced, without arrangement or co-ordination, and in forms that are undeveloped and original rather than degenerate, in the traditions and ideas of savages.

(4.) Lastly, the numerous traces of animistic spirit-worship in higher religions are best explained as the survival and revival of older elements. We must not, however, forget that the present polydæmonistic religions only imperfectly reproduce those of prehistoric times; since even they have not stood still, but have to some extent outgrown their earlier form, which has consequently not been preserved unimpaired.

8. Animism is not itself a religion, but a sort of primitive philosophy, which not only controls religion, but rules the whole life of the natural man. It is the belief in the existence of souls or spirits, of which only the powerful—those on which man feels himself dependent, and before which he stands in awe—acquire the rank of divine beings, and become objects of worship. These spirits are conceived as moving freely through earth and air, and, either of their own accord, or because conjured by some spell, and thus under compulsion, appearing to men (*Spiritism*). But they may also take up their abode, either temporarily or permanently, in some object, whether living or lifeless it matters not; and this object, as endowed with higher power, is then worshipped, or employed to protect individuals and communities (*Fetishism*).

Spiritism, essentially the same as what is now called Spiritualism, must be carefully distinguished from Fetishism, but can only rarely be separated from it. It is difficult to determine which of the two appears first: in history they are equally old. Fetishism comes from *feitiço*, agreeing not with *fatum, chose fée* (De Brosses), but with *factitius*, "endowed with magic power," from which come the Old French *faitis*, and the Old English *fetys*, *i.e.*, well-made, neat (Tylor). Both are only different aspects of the same thing, and to express their unity I have chosen the word Animism, which is elsewhere generally employed to indicate what I call Spiritism. The derivation of the two last terms is sufficiently plain.

9 The religions controlled by Animism are characterised, first of all, by a varied, confused, and indeterminate doctrine, an unorganised polydæmonism, which does not, however, exclude the belief in a supreme spirit, though in practice this commonly bears but little fruit; and in the next place, by magic, which but rarely rises to real worship. Yet,—or rather precisely from this cause, the power possessed by the magicians and fetish priests is by no means small, and in some cases they are even organised into hierarchies. Moreover, among races the most widely separated, the Negroes, Polynesians, and Americans, there exist certain secret associations, types of the later mysteries and sacred orders, which exercise a most formidable influence.

Magic may be said to prevail where it is the aim of a cultus not to worship the spirits, although homage may also be offered to appease them, but to acquire power over them by spells, and thus cripple their dreaded influence. As higher conceptions are formed of the divine beings, these enchantments give way to efforts to propitiate them, or to calm their wrath. Among the Brâhmanic Hindûs, however, the old conception may still be traced in the well-known doctrine that it is possible for man by violent and continuous penances to force the devas into obedience to his will, and to strip them of their supremacy. The *tapas* (literally, "fire," "heat," and thence the glow of self-renunciation and self-chastisement) has here taken the place of magic, with which it was at first confounded. It is a striking example of the way in which a very primitive conception has survived in an otherwise highly-developed religion.

Secret associations both of men and women exist in great numbers among the Negroes. Among the North American Indians the three secret societies Jossakied, Meda, and Wabeno, seem, like the Greek mysteries, to transmit a certain doctrine of immortality; their members, at any rate, are regarded as born again. See WAITZ, *Anthropologie der Naturvölker*, iii. p. 215, *sqq.* The Areoi of Tahiti are of a peculiar constitution—a body of distinguished men who preserve and propagate the old traditions; they are regarded already as gods upon earth, and are supposed to be elevated above all the laws of morality. See Gerland in Waitz, *op. cit.*, vi. pp. 363–369.

10. In the animistic religions fear is more powerful than any other feeling, such as gratitude or trust. The spirits and their worshippers are alike selfish. The evil spirits receive, as a rule, more homage than the good, the lower more than the higher, the local more than the remote, the special more than the general. The allotment of their rewards or punishments depends not on men's good or bad actions, but on the sacrifices and gifts which are offered to them or withheld. With morality this religion has little or no connection, and the doctrine of immortality consists almost entirely in the representation that the earthly life is continued elsewhere (theory of continuance), while of the doctrine that men will receive hereafter according to their works (theory of recompense), only the first beginnings are to be traced.

II.

PECULIAR DEVELOPMENTS OF ANIMISTIC RELIGION AMONG DIFFERENT RACES.

Literature.—General sources: TH. WAITZ, *Anthropologie der Naturvölker*, vol. i., 2d ed., Leipzig, 1877; vols. ii.–v. part i., Leipzig, 1860–65; vols. v. (part ii.) –vi., continued by G. Gerland, 1870–72, an indispensable work, evincing great industry and clear-sightedness. The data, including those relating to religion, are always to be trusted; not so constantly, the theories founded on them by the writer. In this respect Waitz is far surpassed by Gerland, especially in vol. vi. FRIED. MÜLLER, *Allgemeine Ethnographie*, Vienna, 1873, very brief, but generally to be trusted in everything concerning religion. PESCHEL, *Races of Man*, London, 1876, p. 245, *sqq.*

Separate races:—The Australians. GERLAND–WAITZ, vi. pp. 706–829. GEORGE GREY, *Journals of Two Expeditions of Discovery in North-Western and Western Australia*, 2 vols., London, 1841; *cf.* TYLOR, *Primitive Culture*, i. p. 320, *sqq.*

Papuans and Melanesians. GERLAND–WAITZ, vi. pp. 516–705; see the literature, *ibid.*, p. xix., *sqq.* A. GOUDZWAARD, *De Papoewa's van de Geelvinksbaai*, Schiedam, 1863. VAN BOUDIJCK BASTIAANSE, *Voyages Faits dans les Moluques, à la Nouv. Guinée*, &c., Paris, 1845.

Malays. Malays proper, WAITZ, v. part i.; Micronesians and North-West Polynesians, *ibid.*, v. part ii.; Polynesians, *ibid.*, vi. pp. 1–514. Literature, *ibid.*, v. pp. xxvi–xxxiv; and vi. pp. xix–xxii. OBERLÄNDER, *Die Inseln der Südsee*, Leipzig, 1871, gives a good summary. C. SCHIRREN, *Die Wandersagen der Neuseeländer und der Mauimythos*, Riga, 1856; and Sir GEORGE GREY (see above under *Australians*), *Polynesian Mythology and Ancient Traditional History of the New Zealand Race*, London, 1855; both works much to be recommended. See also W. W. GILL, *Myths and Songs from the South Pacific*, with preface by MAX MÜLLER, London, 1876.

Negro Races and allied peoples. WAITZ, vol. ii.; literature, *ibid.*, pp. xvii–xxiv. A. KAUFMANN, *Schilderungen aus Central Afrika*, Brixen, 1862. An excellent summary will be found in ED. SCHAUENBURG, *Reisen in Central Afrika von Mungo Park bis auf Dr. Barth und Dr. Vogel*, 2 vols., 1859–65; while Vogel's travels are described by H. WAGNER, *Schilderung der Reisen und Entdeckungen des Dr. Ed. Vogel*, Leipzig, 1860. W. BOSMAN, *Nauwkeurige Beschrijving van de Guinese Goud- tanden slavekust*, 2d ed., 1709; very instructive and characteristic. J. LEIGHTON WILSON, *History and Condition of Western Africa*, Philadelphia, 1859, excellent. Much useful material in BRODIE CRUICKSHANK, *Eighteen Years on the Gold Coast*, London, 1853. Important for the knowledge of the priestly hierarchy, T. E. BOWDITCH, *Mission to Ashantee*, London, 1819. J. B. DOUVILLE, *Voyage au Congo et dans l'Intérieur de l'Afrique Équinoxiale*, 3 vols., Paris, 1832, not to be trusted in the least. The travels of Barth, Speke and Grant, and Sir Samuel Baker, contain very few notices of religion. Comp. also CAMERON, *Across Africa*, 2 vols., London, 1877.

On the Kaffirs, Hottentots, and Bosjesmans, the first authority is the admirable work of G. FRITSCH, *Die Eingeborenen Süd-Afrika's, ethnograph. und anatom. beschrieben*, Breslau, 1872. E. CASALIS, *Les Bassoutos*, Paris, 1860, attractive.

American Races. WAITZ, vols. iii. and iv.; literature,

ibid., iii. pp. xix–xxxii; and iv. pp. vii, viii. The much-used work of J. G. MÜLLER, *Geschichte der Amerikanischen Urreligionen*, Basel, 1855, contains abundance of material, and ideas and explanations which are sometimes very just; but the writer's abortive attempt to distinguish everywhere a northern belief in ghosts or spirits from a southern sun-worship, leads him occasionally to place the facts in a false light. D. G. BRINTON, *The Myths of the New World*, New York, 1868, original, but one-sided. The works of BRASSEUR DE BOURBOURG, CATLIN, and SCHOOLCRAFT (see the literature in WAITZ, to which may be added CATLIN, *A Religious Ceremony of the Mandans*) still deserve to be consulted. H. H. BANCROFT, *The Native Races of the Western States of America*, 5 vols., London, 1873–75. For Ethnology, see further, H. E. LUDEWIG, *The Literature of American Aboriginal Languages*, with additions by TURNER, edited by N. TRÜBNER, London, 1857.

On the religion of the FINNS, see M. ALEX. CASTRÉN, *Vorlesungen über die Finnische Mythologie, aus dem Schwed. mit Anmerkk. von* A. SCHIEFNER, St. Petersburg, 1853. Id., *Kleinere Schriften, herausgegeben von* SCHIEFNER, St. Petersburg, 1862 (containing an essay "Ueber die Zauberkunst der Finnen," and also "Allgemeine Uebersicht der Götterlehre und der Magie der Finnen während des Heidenthums"). Compare further, A. SCHIEFNER, *Heldensagen der Minussinschen Tataren, rythm. bearbeitet*, St. Petersburg, 1859. The most complete edition of the Kalevala is by EL. LÖNROTT in 1849 (under the sanction of the University of Helsingfors. The second edition contains 50 Runes, as against 32 in the first edition of 1835); translated by A. SCHIEFNER, *Kalewala, das National-Epos der Finnen, nach der 2ten Ausg. ins Deutsche übertr.*, Helsingfors, 1852.

11. The question of the relation in which the religions of savages stand to the great historic families of religions, has only just been opened; and not till it has been solved with some degree of certainty, will it be possible for the separate nature-religions to take their proper places in the history of religion. At present they only serve to give some idea of the religions which preceded those of civilised nations, and their description does not belong to this place. But while animistic religion is, in its nature, and even in its ideas and usages, with slight modification everywhere the same, it is necessary to point out the special causes which have led to its development among different races in such different forms and degrees. Of these the principal are (1) the different characters of these races, (2) the nature of their home and occupations, and (3) the historic relations in which some of them stood to their neighbours.

The question of the relation of the religions of savages to those of the great historic families of religions, amounts briefly to this:—Are the former entirely independent, or is there reason for regarding them as the backward and imperfectly-developed members of larger groups, to which the recognised families of religion (such as the Semitic or Indo-Germanic) belong? There is real agreement between the civilisation and religion of the Negroes, and those of the Egyptians. Similar correspondences exist between the Red Indians and Turanians. The Polynesians and Indo-Germans, also, exhibit so many points of contact, that Bopp even endeavoured, however fruitlessly, to prove the original unity of their languages. Gerland (*Anthropolog. Beiträge*, i. p. 396) has lately combined all the African nations, Negroes, Bantu tribes (Kaffirs), Hottentots,

Berbers, Gallas, &c., together with Egyptians and Semites into one great race, which he names the Arabic-African. Were this conjecture to be established, we should have to incorporate all the African religions with those of the Egyptians and Semites. Without going so far as this, R. Von Hartmann, *Die Nigritier*, vol. i., 1877, endeavours to prove the unity of all the African races, but he marks off the Semites from them very decidedly. His demonstration rests at present chiefly on physical grounds, but in the second volume, which has not yet appeared, he promises to establish the unity of these races in language and religion as well. But the inquiry is still in its first stage, and it must be carried to much more assured results before we may venture to make use of it in the history of religion.

12. The joyous careless disposition of the sensual Negro is reflected in his religion as clearly as the sombre melancholy character of the American Indian in his. If the latter is endowed with much more poetic feeling than the former, whose mythology is of the poorest order, and in this resembles that of the Semites, he is surpassed by the poetic genius of the Polynesian, which displays itself in his rich mythology. The great influence of national character on religion is specially apparent among peoples, which, though living in the same climate and engaged in the same occupations—like the Papuans, the Melanesians, and Polynesians—stand at such different stages of development: while the religion of the Americans, on the other hand, though they are spread over a whole quarter of the globe, and diverge so widely in civilisation, exhibits everywhere the same character, and is everywhere accompanied by the same usages.

13. The influence of the locality and the occupation of the different peoples must also be taken into account. Lowest in the scale stands the religion of the root-digging Australians, who do, indeed, engage in hunting, but show little skill in it, and that of the Bosjesmans, who live largely by plunder. The religion of the Koikoin or Hottentots, and of the Kaffirs, who are both for the most part pastoral tribes, is mild, that of some of the war-loving Negro tribes sanguinary and cruel; while among those Negroes who are engaged chiefly in industry and commerce, without neglecting cattle-breeding and agriculture, a much more humane and civilised worship prevails, in which however the spirit of trade shows itself in a certain cunning towards the spirits. The myths of the Polynesians at once betray that they have sprung up among a people of husbandmen and fishermen, and their religious customs correspond entirely to the beneficent nature which surrounds them.

14. Even at this point of development, the mingling, or even simply the mutual intercourse of nations, brings about a transfer of religious ideas and institutions from the one to the other. The mixed race of the Melanesians may still be distinguished in many respects from the Polynesians, but they adopted the religion of the latter, though in a very degraded form. The Abantu or Kaffirs, who are very near to the Negroes, but are only distantly related to the Koikoin or Hottentots, borrowed from the latter various religious conceptions.

That the Melanesians derived their religion from the Polynesians is denied by Gerland in Waitz, vi. p. 675. The statement is not strictly accurate, but the Melanesians are a mixed race of Polynesians and Papuans, among whom the religion of the former maintained the ascendant and was independently developed. Their supreme god Ndengei is only a degenerate form of Tangaloa, the god universally worshipped by the Polynesians, though the Melanesians apply to him their own peculiar myths, which are unknown to the Polynesians. From these they are distinguished by their greater rudeness, and want of poetic capacity, while on the other hand they are less luxurious and unchaste. Their customs correspond much more with those of the Papuans.

The religion of the Kaffirs bears a greater resemblance in character and conceptions to that of the Hottentots than to that of the Negroes. The myth of Unkulunkulu, "the great-grandfather," the Creator, does not in fact differ from that related by the Hottentots of their chief deity, the Moon-god *Heitsi-eibib*. The word *Utixo*, moreover, the Kaffir designation of the highest god, has been adopted from the Hottentots.

15. The original religions of America exhibit religious Animism at every stage of development. In one and the same race, whose religions possess everywhere the same distinctive character, and have certain peculiar usages in common, the richest variety of religious development may be found. Among some tribes, such as the Shoshonee and Comanches in North America, the Botokuds and Otomaks, the Pampas Indians, some of the Brazilian savages, and the Terra-del-Fuegians of South America, hardly anything more than the first germs of a cultus is to be traced. A higher stage has been reached by the tribes of the north-west of North America, by the Caribbees of Central America, and, among the closely-allied Hyperboreans, by the Esquimaux. But they are far surpassed by the savages of North America, on the east of the Missouri, and the south of Canada. In mythology, religion, and usages, these have attained about the same point of development as the Polynesians; their worship is directed for the most part towards spirits of a lower rank, especially towards those which they fear, yet they all acknowledge a great Spirit, Creator of everything which exists. The Natchez, a small tribe at the confluence of the Mississippi and Red River, had even founded a theocracy, based on sun-worship, and appear to have exerted great influence by their religion on the neighbouring tribes.

The character of the American with his sombre earnestness, his sagacity and silence, his passionateness combined with a self-mastery which expresses itself outwardly in gravity and at least apparent indifference, and enables him to endure the most terrible torments with a smile, is reflected in his religion. This is characterised by severe self-tortures and bloody ceremonies, which do not give way even before a higher civilisation. The myth of the hero who is worshipped as the founder of this civilisation (originally a sun-god) appears alike among savage tribes and among peoples already settled, and the national heroes everywhere resemble one another. The following usages may be regarded as universal: the use of the steam-bath for producing ecstasy, the sacred game at ball, and enchantment with a rattle. The most widely-separated peoples retain the practice of drawing blood out of certain parts of the body, which are regarded as the seat of the soul, a custom which probably served as a substitute for human sacrifices, and among the Cherokees, Aztecs, Mayas, and Peruvians, baptism accompanies the naming of children. This large agreement renders the differences in development more remarkable, especially when it is remembered that the nearest connections of the highly-civilised Aztecs in Mexico are the Shoshonee and Comanches, tribes which stand "nearer to the brutes than probably any other portion of the human race" (*Report of the Comm. of Indian Affairs*, 1854, p. 209).

The great Spirit, who is *primus inter pares*, is unquestionably of native origin.

The religion of the Natchez is raised by its organisation alone above that of their neighbours, but it is nothing more than an organised Animism. The absolute sovereign was the brother of the sun and high priest, and to all fire, even to that which served for household purposes, but especially to that which was always kept burning in the temple, a special sanctity was attached. In this case also religious progress seems to be connected with the introduction of agriculture.

16. The mingling of various races by migration and conquest, the transition from the wandering life of hunters and fishermen to the settled tasks of agriculture, and the establishment of regular states, resulted among the Muyscas or Chibchas (of New Granada) and the Mayas (of Central America, particularly Yucatan), but above all among the Peruvians and Mexicans, in a great advance, which did not leave religion behind; an advance which cannot be ascribed, as some writers have endeavoured to prove, to the influence of foreign colonists. The beings whom these nations worship, are as yet no gods in the strict sense, *i.e.*, supernatural beings, they are hardly more than spirits: they are, however, the representatives of the higher powers and phenomena of nature. Their usages, also, their cultus and their doctrine of immortality, are, in reality, animistic. Yet in their conception of the higher powers, and in the relation in which they imagined themselves to stand to them, it is impossible not to recognise the beginnings of a purer and more rational view. There were even princes, both in Peru and Mexico, who ventured to introduce important reforms, a sign of great activity of thought. However imperfect their success may have been at first, they would probably have become after a time the bases of a new order of things, if the course of the independent development of these nations had not been checked by the Spanish conquest. The religions of Mexico and Peru certainly reached, if they did not pass beyond, the extreme limits of Animism.

That the Mexican and Peruvian civilisation owed its origin to foreign colonists, has been asserted by many writers. The foolish suppositions that the Ten Tribes of Israel, or Welsh princes, or Phœnician merchants, may have wandered off to America, deserve no refutation. More likelihood attaches to the conjecture that East Asiatics may have landed in Mexico. This was suggested by Humboldt, *Ansichten der Natur*, i. p. 214. From the Chinese work *Nan-ssu*, *i.e.*, "History of the South," De Guignes, Paravey, and Neumann inferred that the Chinese were acquainted with America about 458 A.D.; but this conclusion is disputed by Klaproth, *Nouvelles Annales des Voyages*, 1831. All the material for the discussion of the question is given by Ch. G. Leland, *Fusang; or, The Discovery of America by Chinese Buddhist Priests in the Fifth Century*, London, 1875. The statements about this land Fusang, however, are for the most part not applicable to America, while they are altogether appropriate to Japan. The proofs adduced by G. d'Eichthal, *Étude sur les Origines Bouddiques de la Civilisation Américaine*, 1e partie, 1865, are also extremely feeble.

The names by which these nations designate the gods in general, *teotl* among the Mexicans, *guacas* among the Peruvians, signify nothing more than spirits. These feed on human flesh, and are drunken with blood, the human sacrifices in Mexico being counted by thousands. The mild deity of the Toltecs, Quetzalcoatl, to whom no human sacrifices were offered, forms an exception. Some expressions have been supposed to indicate the beginnings of monotheism, but they are extremely uncertain. But it is remarkable that the sun-spirit was called simply *teotl*, "the spirit" *par excellence*. It is also said that all the spirits die when he appears. The splendid addresses made, according to some writers, on solemn occasions by official speakers, and which teach a fairly pure morality, inspire no great confidence, especially when it is reflected that the Mexican hieroglyphics are of a very indefinite kind, and give scope for arbitrary explanations. Attempts at reform, however, were not wanting. Various noble princes, the Toltecs in Mexico, Netzalcuatl in Tezcuco, and the Incas in Peru, attempted to set limits at all events to the grossest licentiousness, and to human sacrifices. In 1440 A.D. the Inca Tupac Yupanqui, at the consecration of a temple of the sun at Cuzco, proclaimed a new deity, Illatici-Viracocha-Pachacamac, to whom the sun-god was subordinated, and he founded a temple to him at Callao containing no images, in which no human sacrifices might be offered. A similar advance was made by Netzalcuatl, prince of Tezcuco; he built a temple nine stories in height, which contained no image and might be polluted by no blood, in honour of the deity who, as cause of causes, was enthroned above the nine heavens. But neither this deity, nor that of the Inca, whose triple name is a combination of the terms for the three vital principles thunder-cloud (*i.e.*, the hidden receptacle of the thunder), sea-foam (*i.e.*, the fire hidden in the waters), and the earth-soul, ever became national gods, and the temple of the latter soon had its images and horrible paintings.

17. Over a large extent of Asia and Europe the Aryans, and perhaps also the Semites, were preceded by Turanian peoples, and the oldest civilisation which we can trace was derived if not from them, at any rate from a race very closely connected with them, of which the Akkadians in Mesopotamia are the chief representatives. Most of their religions have been supplanted by Buddhism, Islâm, or Christianity; but the remarkable religion of the Finns, compared with that of the kindred Siberian tribes and of the Tatars, proves how high a development they were capable of attaining. Their mythology and cultus were, it is true, completely under the influence of the belief in magic, and they are thus purely animistic. All the spirits which they worship, even the highest, are nature-beings of more or less might, but chiefly eminent for their magical power, and rarely endowed with moral qualities—a sort of independent patriarchs, differing in power, not in rank. High above all the other spirits, however, stands Ukko (the old man, father, grandfather, the venerable), the Creator (*luoya*) and deity (*yumála*) *par excellence*, the ancient one in heaven, mightier than the mightiest enchanter, whose

aid is invoked by all heroes and spirits. Only one step remained for the Finns to take in order to rise from polydæmonism to polytheism. Their epic poems, collected under the name of Kalevala, the subject of which is not a moral or national conflict, but simply the contest of the powers of nature personified, affords proof of their great poetic gifts.

The ethical element is almost entirely deficient. Even in the representation of Ukko I have not succeeded in discovering it. Evil spirits and good cry to him for help, and he grants it, alike when the powers of darkness are being resisted, and when the nine spirits which plague mankind are born. He is the highest and mightiest of the spirits, but not even the lesser are dependent on him.

Yumála, which signifies, according to Castrén, "the place of thunder," *i.e.*, the sky (?), was originally, in his opinion, the name of a distinct god of the sky. It is, however, an appellative of the divine beings in general, used parallel with *luoya*, but often employed to designate the highest god, and subsequently applied to the god of the Christians.

The worship of spirits (the chief of whom are called Haltia) and the doctrine of immortality are not developed any further among the Finns than among the Nature-peoples.

The three great heroes of the Kalevala, Wäinamöinen, Ilmarinen, and Lemminkäinen, are certainly ancient spirits of heaven, fire, and earth, and correspond to Odhinn, Loki, and Hunir, the German triad of gods, although the working out of their character and the description of their deeds have a character entirely their own.

CHAPTER II.

RELIGION AMONG THE CHINESE.

Literature.—General; J. E. R. KÄUFFER, *Geschichte von Ost-Asien*, 3 vols., Leipzig, 1858–60; id., *Das Chinesische Volk*, Dresden, 1850. GÜTZLAFF, *Geschichte des Chines. Reichs*, herausgegeben von K. F. Neumann, Stuttgart, 1847. A number of essays by J. H. PLATH, in the *Sitzungsberichte der Baierischen Akademie*, of which the following deserve to be named here: "Chronol. Grundlage der alten Chines. Geschichte," 1867, ii. 1; "Ueber die Quellen der alten Chines. Geschichte," 1870, i. 1; "China vor 4000 Jahren," 1869, i. 2, 3, ii. 1; "Ueber Schule und Unterricht bei den alten Chinesen," 1868, ii. 1. G. PAUTHIER, *Chine, ou Description historique, géographique, et littéraire*, &c.; id., *Chine moderne, ou Description*, &c., Paris, 1853. In *The Origin of the Chinese*, London, 1868, J. CHALMERS loses himself in very hazardous conjectures.

Religion of the Old Empire. J. H. PLATH, *Die Religion und der Cultus der alten Chinesen*, München, 1862, in two parts, (1) *Die Religion*; (2) *Der Cultus*. ED. BIOT, *Le Tcheou-li, ou Rites des Tcheou*, 2 vols., Paris, 1851.

Confucianism. J. H. PLATH, *Confucius und seiner Schüler Leben und Lehren*, (i.) *Histor. Einleitung*, München, 1867; (ii.) *Leben des Confucius*, i., ibid., 1870; (iii.) *Die Schüler des Confucius*, ibid., 1873; (iv.) *Sämmtliche Aussprüche des Confucius und seinen Schülern, systematisch geordnet*, i., ibid., 1874. Absolutely indispensable, J.

LEGGE, *The Chinese Classics, with a Translation, Critical and Exegetical Notes, Prolegomena, and copious Indexes*, Hongkong and London, 1861, and following years; in 7 vols., of which there have appeared—vol. i., Life of Confucius, and the first three classical books; vol. ii., the works of Mencius; vol. iii., i. and ii., the Shu-king; vol. iv., i. and ii., the Shi-king, and other poetical pieces. Vols. i. and ii. have been published without the text in a small edition, *The Life and Teachings of Confucius*, third ed., London, 1872, and the *Life and Works of Mencius*, ibid., 1875. The *Lün-yü* has been translated into German by W. SCHOTT, vol. i., Halle, 1829; vol. ii., Berlin, 1832. PAUTHIER, *Les Livres Sacrés de l'Orient*, Paris, 1840, contains a translation of the Shu-king and of the classical books. Other translations are enumerated in the Notices Bibliographiques, Pauthier, *op. cit.*, p. xxviii, and in the history of Käuffer named above, i. p. 83, *sqq.*, and ii. p. 17. As samples of the profane literature of the Confucianists we may specify, D'HERVEY DE ST. DENYS, *Le Li-sao, poème du 3me siècle avant notre ère*, Paris, 1870. STANISL. JULIEN, *Contes et Apologues Indiens suivis de Fables et de Poésies Chinoises*, 2 vols., Paris, 1860.

Taoism. *Lao tseu Tao te King, Le Livre de la Voie et de la Vertu, trad. &c., par* STANISL. JULIEN, Paris, 1842. *Laò-tsè's Taò tĕ King, übersetzt u. s. w. von* V. VON STRAUSS, Leipzig, 1870, follows Julien closely. Only an arbitrary paraphrase will be found in *Lao-tse Táo-tĕ-king, übers. und erklärt von* R. VON PLÄNCKNER, Leipzig, 1870. *Le Livre des Récompenses et des Peines, trad. par* A. RÉMUSAT, Paris, 1816. A. PFIZMAIER, *Die Lösung der Leichname und Schwerter, ein Beitr. zur Kenntniss des Taoglaubens*, Vienna, 1870; id., *Die Taolehre von den wahren Menschen und den Unsterblichen*, ibid., 1870. W. ROTERMUND, *Die Ethik*

Lao-tse's mit besonderer Bezugnahme auf der Buddhistischen Moral, Gotha, 1874.

18. The religion of the old Chinese Empire, as it existed certainly from the twelfth century B.C., and probably at a much earlier period, is best described as a purified and organised worship of spirits, with a predominant fetishist tendency, combined into a system before it was possible for a regular mythology to develop out of it. The sole objects of worship are the spirits (*shin*), which are divided into heavenly, earthly, and human, and, as a rule, are still closely connected with the objects of nature. Heaven (*Thian*), who, when conceived as a personal being, is called the supreme emperor (*Shang-ti*), stands at the head, and in co-operation with the earth has produced everything. His will is fate, and he rewards and punishes. He is one; but he has five emperors beside him, and an innumerable multitude of spirits beneath him, among which those of the sun, moon, stars, and constellations are pre-eminent. The spirit of the earth (*Heu-thu*), though not sharply personified, is for the most part conceived as of female nature. The spirits of the mountains, streams, &c., belong to her realm. Besides these, the spirits are without number. They are perceived, but are neither heard nor seen, though they reside in visible objects, and for the most part assume the forms of animals. It may be regarded as a great advance that there is no mention of essentially evil spirits, that all spirits are exalted servants of Shang-ti, and in their intercourse with men esteem moral qualities above everything else.

The twelfth century B.C. is the era of the establishment of the Tshow dynasty, whose cultus we know from the book *Tshow-li.* Plath objects to the conception of the joint working of heaven and earth as a marriage, and describes the earth as a male feudal prince. But the great power which they exert is called "generation" (*seng*), and in the *Yi-king* they are frequently represented as husband and wife, as father and mother. The same idea occurs also in the *Shu-king.* See the passages cited by Plath himself, *Rel. der alten Chinesen*, pp. 36–38 and 73. To treat this as a type of parental care is inappropriate. The two original principles *Yang* and *Yin*, which Plath regards as the fruit of later philosophical reflection, make their appearance as early as 1100 B.C. in the *Tshow-li*, *op. cit.*, vii. 3, and ix. 10, 11; and in the same work it is not the chief vassal of the empire, but the principal wife of the emperor who is named after the earth. The old and generally diffused myth of the marriage between heaven and earth certainly lies at the foundation of Chinese mythology also, though the philosophers afterwards disguised it past recognition.

19. The doctrine of continued existence after death among the Chinese entirely accords with that of the Nature-peoples. Man has two souls, one of which ascends after death to heaven, while the other descends into the earth, after vain attempts have been made to recall them both. Of the doctrine of retribution no certain traces are to be found, but we do find the idea that it is possible by sacrificing life to save a sick person. The souls of ancestors were worshipped with great pomp and earnestness, and were, it was supposed, present at the sacrifices.

Though no distinct traces of the doctrine of retribution after death can be discovered among the ancient Chinese, it must be remembered in this connection that all the books which are the sources of our knowledge of their religion before Kong-tse, have passed through the hands either of himself or his followers, and he always refused to express an opinion on souls and their destiny. The doctrine of retribution was held by the sect of the *Tao-sse*, and reached among them a very elaborate form, so that it may be regarded as probable that it was not unknown to the religion of the old empire.

20. The Chinese are remarkable for the complete absence of a priestly caste. Their worship, which was regulated down to its minute details, was entirely a civil function. It was placed under the control of one of the six ministers who directed all the officials connected with religion, including the musicians and dancers. To Thian, the spirit of heaven, only the emperor might sacrifice; to the spirits of the earth and the fruits of the land, only the emperor and the feudal princes; to the five house spirits, only the high officials, and so on in strict order. Of the sacrifices, which originally included also human victims, that part was presented which was regarded as the seat of the soul or of life. The greater number of the temples were consecrated to the dead, while the emperor himself performed his sacrifices under the open sky. Prayer, even when addressed to Thian, was permitted to all, but at the court, regular officials were appointed for the purpose. Even the magicians, soothsayers, and spirit-charmers, though numbered among the state functionaries, formed no priestly order. Great value, however, was attached to the oracles procured by their instrumentality, especially to those obtained by means of the plant *Shi*, and by the burning of furrows on a tortoise-shell (*pu*).

The most important source of our knowledge of the early worship of the Chinese is the book *Tshow-li*, written in the twelfth century B.C. by *Tshow-kung*, brother of the founder of the Tshow dynasty. From his family, six centuries later, came Kong-tse.

21. A reform of this religion was carried out in the sixth century B.C. by *Kong-fu-tse* (Master Kong, Confucius), though he himself did not wish to be regarded as doing anything more than transmit and preserve the doctrine of the Ancients. Born in 550 (or 551) B.C. in the principality of Lu, of a distinguished family, he began at the age of two-and-twenty years to give instruction as a teacher or sage. Labouring sometimes as an official, and once appointed to a high civil post, but for the most part living without office, and often compelled by the disturbances in his native country to go into exile, he saw himself always surrounded by a large number of disciples, consulted by the most eminent personages, and highly honoured even during his life. He died in the year 478.

Kong-tse had a high sense of his calling, and attached great value to purity of morals, though he detested the life of the hermit. Accused without cause of insincerity, he hated all false show, but he was inordinately punctilious about all forms, and perhaps not wholly free from superstition. If he thus appears somewhat narrow-minded, whoever judges him by the age in which he lived and the nation to which he belonged, notes the powerful impression which he made upon friends and foes, and observes, above all, his intercourse with his disciples, will recognise in him a man of rare qualities, endowed with a noble heart and a penetrating spirit.

22. The religious doctrine of Kong-tse is ethical naturalism, founded on the state religion of the Tshow. He engaged in supernatural questions with as much reluctance as in practical affairs, and expressed himself very cautiously and doubtfully on religious points. Even of heaven he preferred not to speak as a personal being, but he quoted its example as the preserver of order, and he would allude to its commands, ordinances, and purposes. But the actions of men also help to determine their destiny. The doctrine that good and evil are rewarded on earth by prosperity and adversity was firmly maintained by him. To prayer he ascribed no great value. He did not believe in direct revelations, and he regarded forebodings and presentiments simply as warnings. Rather than express an opinion on the nature of spirits and souls, he insisted that they should be worshipped faithfully and the old usages maintained; but he laid the greatest stress on reverence, and urged that the spirits should not be served in barbarous fashion, and that, in times of scarcity, for instance, honour should not be paid to the dead at the expense of the living.

I speak of the state-religion of the Tshow, having in view the book named Tshow-li already quoted, which appears to have established a new order of things, and with the prescriptions of which Kong-tse always perfectly accords. That this book does not reproduce the old popular religion, and that Kong-tse only retained a portion of the earlier doctrines of his nation, will become apparent by and by, on the consideration of Taoism. In ancient times he was always worshipped next to Tshow, which proves that the connection between their reforms continued to be felt.

23. Kong-tse devoted much attention to religious literature. He studied zealously the *Yi-king*, an obscure book of magic. The *Shu-king*, an historical work, was perhaps recast by himself, it is certainly written in his spirit. The *Shi-king* is a collection of songs chosen by him out of a large number, from which all mythological expressions have probably been eliminated. The *Li-ki*, a ritual work, was enlarged by him. These books, with the addition of a chronicle written entirely by him, entitled *Tshün tsiew*, and not of a religious nature, constitute the five *Kings*, regarded by the followers of Kong-fu-tse as the canonical books. In the *Lün-Yü* ("Arranged Conversations;" Legge, "Analects") the remarkable utterances of the Master addressed to his followers were collected by his disciples' disciples. Others attempted in the *Ta-hio* ("the Great Instruction;" Legge, "the Great Learning") and the *Tshung-yung* ("the Doctrine of the Mean") to supply a philosophical basis for his doctrine. These works form three of the four *Shu*, or classical books. The fourth, comprising the works of the sage Meng-tse (§ 24), was added to the collection at a much later period.

Yi-king signifies "Book of Changes." *Shu* means writings, and the *Shu-king* is regarded as the Book of books. It is commonly assumed that this work was put into its present form by Kong-tse, or at any rate modified by him in accordance with his views, but this is questioned by Legge. It is certain that it has been revised by some one belonging to his school. This is plain from a comparison of it with the so-called Bamboo-books found in the grave of King Seang of Wei, who died in 295 B.C.; these books contain a dry chronicle, with numerous fabulous additions, giving a totally different representation of the history. The object of the *Shu-king* is not so much to narrate a history, as to impart moral and political instruction, based on historical facts. *Shi* are poems, of which the *Shi-king* contains about three hundred, chosen out of several thousand. The source of the *Li-ki* ("rituum commemoratio") is the *Tshow-li*. *Tshün-tsiew*, signifying "Spring-Autumn," is a chronicle of the principality of Lu from the year 723 to 479 B.C. The *Ta-hio* is ascribed to the sage *Tsang-sin*, or his disciples, or also, like the *Tshung-yung*, to Kong-tse's grandson Tsze-sse.

From the word *Shu*, "writings," is derived the term *Shu-kiao*, the name of the doctrine or sect of Kong-tse.

24. Immediately after Kong-tse's death, a temple was erected to him by the Prince of Lu, and his worship, though not yet recognised on the part of the Government, at first increased. Towards the commencement of the fourth century B.C., during the serious disturbances which led to the fall of the Tshow dynasty, new doctrines of all kinds arose. These threatened to undermine the authority of the Master. This tendency was resisted with great emphasis by the learned Meng-tse (Mencius, 371–288 B.C.) In his teaching, which was principally political and moral, or, more accurately, perhaps, anthropological, the religious element retires still further into the background than in that of Kong-tse. Less modest and disinterested, he was more independent in character, and a more powerful reasoner. By his instruction and writings he acquired great influence, triumphing over all the opponents of Kong-tse, who was in his eyes the most eminent of men. It is probably owing to his labours that even the great persecution under the Ts'in dynasty (212 B.C.), and the favour displayed by some emperors of the Han dynasty (after 201 B.C.) towards the followers of Lao-tse (§ 26), did not succeed in eradicating Confucianism. From the year 57 of our era the worship of Kong-tse by the side of Tshow was practised by the emperors themselves as well as in all the schools; and since the seventh century Kong-tse has been worshipped alone. For the great majority of the Chinese he is the ideal of humanity, which even the adherents of other systems may not despise.

The persecution, begun in 212 B.C., lasted only a short time; but it seems to have been very severe. Orders were issued for the burning of all the canonical books with the exception of the Yi-king, and on one occasion, even, four hundred and sixty *literati* were buried alive in pits. The persecutor was the founder of the Ts'in dynasty himself, called Hoang-ti, like the great Emperor so much revered by the Taoists. It was he who replaced the feudal system by a more centralising government; he was the first proper Emperor of China, and he was checked in his reforms by the opposition of the Confucian sages, who stood up for the old institutions. The occasion of the persecution was political rather than religious, although between these two spheres no sharp distinction can be made in China. The stern emperor, however, died within three years, and his dynasty also was soon replaced by that of the Han. Confucianism was exposed to more danger through the many new doctrines, alike those of the pessimist *Yang-tshu*, and those of *Mih-teih*, the preacher of universal love, and others, which found acceptance with many. They were obstinately resisted by Meng-tse.

25. The humane but prosaic Confucianism might satisfy the majority of cultivated Chinese, but it did not meet all wants. This not only becomes apparent at a later date through the introduction of Buddhism, but it is also clearly proved by the permanence of the ancient sect of the Tao-sse, which constantly endeavoured to vie with the ruling religion. This religious community represents rather the spiritist side of Animism. As a religious tendency it existed from the earliest times, and even tried to derive its origin from the ancient Emperor Hoang-ti, whose name is erased from the canonical books of the Confucians. It owed its rise as an association, however, to the necessity of offering vigorous resistance to the teaching of Kong-tse, and to the influence of the teaching of his great rival Lao-tse, whom it reveres as its saint. It enjoyed the temporary favour of some emperors, and it is even now very widely diffused. But it did not succeed in gaining the ascendency in the empire, or in making its way among the ranks of learning and distinction. The cultivated Chinese now regard it with unmixed contempt.

Although the history of Hoang-ti, the Yellow Emperor, is obscured by all kinds of myths, so that we might be disposed to consider him as a mythical being, the majority of Sinologues regard him as an historical personage. In fact, similar myths are related of persons indisputably historic, such as Lao-tse himself. The Bamboo-books supply many details about him; in the Shu-king his name is designedly omitted. He was connected with Lao in the same way as Tshow with Kong. Taoism is even called "the doctrine" or "the service of Hoang-Lao."

26. Lao-tse, born in the principality of Thsu, 604 B.C., was highly renowned even in his lifetime as a profound philosopher. Kong-tse visited him in order to consult him as an older and celebrated sage, and esteemed him highly, but the tendency of Lao was entirely different from his own, leading to mystic reflection and the contemplative life. Not much is known of his history, but the story of his journey to India must be rejected as unworthy of belief. He wrote the famous *Tao-te-King*, which became the most sacred book of the sect, although its adherents, at any rate at the present day, certainly do not understand it. *Tao*, a term in use with Kong-tse's followers also, and employed by the Chinese Buddhists in the sense of wisdom or higher enlightenment (*bodhi*), possesses among the Tao-sse, who derive their name from it, a mystic significance, and is even worshipped by them as a divine being. Lao-tse distinguishes in his book between the nameless, supreme Tao, which is the ultimate source, and the Tao which can be named, and is the mother of everything. To this, and to the power or virtue proceeding from it (*te*=*virtus*), the highest worship, according to him, is due, and in this does the sage find his ideal. To withdraw entirely into himself and free himself from the constraints of sense, in order, thus, without action or speech, to exercise a blessed power, must be his aim.

This is the best philosophy of life and the best policy. The often obscure system developed in the *Tao-te-King* is purely Chinese, and is incorrectly derived from the influence of Indian philosophy, with which it agrees rather in form than in spirit. From the Buddhist doctrine it is essentially different. It is marked by a morbid asceticism, and takes up an attitude of hostility towards civilisation and progress, but it is distinguished by a pure and sometimes very elevated morality.

It is altogether erroneous to regard Tao, with Rémusat, as the primeval Reason, the λόγος, and worse still to call the Tao-sse the Chinese rationalists. This character fits them least of all, and they do their utmost to be as unreasonable as possible. The name would be much more appropriate to their opponents. The ordinary meaning of the word is "way," in the literal and the metaphorical sense, but always "the chief way." In the mysticism of Lao the term is applied to the supreme cause, the way or passage through which everything enters into life, and at the same time to the way of the highest perfection.

27. The later writings of the Tao-sse, among which the Book of Rewards and Punishments occupies a prominent place, show that they did not maintain this morality at the same elevation, but gradually lost themselves in confused mysticism and an unreasoning belief in miracles. To gain long life and immortality by means of self-chastisement, prayer, and watching, as well as by the use of certain charms, was their highest endeavour. But many remains of the ancient Chinese mythology, banished by Kong-tse, and transformed by Lao-tse into philosophical reflections, were preserved nearly unaltered in their dogmas.

28. The ancient Chinese religion, which, with vast differences in character, stands at the same point of development as the Egyptian, in some respects took a higher flight than the latter. By Tshow and Kong-tse it was purified from many superstitions, which in Egypt lasted till the fall of the Empire. The feudal system, as it prevailed in China, amid all its faults possessed one virtue, in that it permitted a much more independent development of personality and a freer influence on the part of the sages, than the theocratic absolutism which in Egypt crippled all intellectual movement.

When the feudal system in China was obliged to give way before another form of government, the two sects were too firmly rooted to be involved in the ruin of the old polity, yet they proved too purely national for either of them to become a universal religion. It was only when Chinese civilisation made its way complete, as in Corea and Japan, that the Chinese religion, especially the doctrine and worship of Kong-tse, was adopted with it.

CHAPTER III.

RELIGION AMONG THE HAMITES AND SEMITES.

Compare F. LENORMANT, *Les Premières Civilisations*, tom. i., "Archæol. préhistorique," Égypte; tom. ii., "Chaldée et Assyrie, Phénicie," Paris, 1874. G. RAWLINSON, *The Five Great Monarchies of the Ancient Eastern World*, 3 vols. (3d edition), London, 1873. OPPERT, *Mémoire sur les Rapports de l'Égypte et de l'Assyrie dans l'Antiquité*, Paris, 1869, "Progrès des Études relatives à l'Égypte et à l'Orient." *Études Égypt.*, par E. DE ROUGÉ; *Déchiffr. des Écrit. cunéif.*, par DE SAULCY; *Études Sémitiques*, par MUNK; *Langue et Litt. Arab.*, par REYNAUD, &c., 1867. *Transactt. of the Soc. of Bibl. Archæology*, London, 1872, *sqq.* P. PIERRET, *Mélanges d'Archæol. Égypt. et Assyr.* (in continuation of DE ROUGÉ'S *Recueil de Travaux*, &c., of which one part appeared in 1870), Paris, 1872, *sqq.* LEPSIUS' *Zeitschrift* (see below) also contains Assyrian studies.

I.

RELIGION AMONG THE EGYPTIANS.

Literature.—A. General Works.—The great collections of plates after the monuments, inscriptions, and ancient texts, such as those of Champollion, Rosellini, Leemans, Lepsius, Sharpe, Dümichen, Mariette, Pleyte, are only accessible to those who are familiar with the writing and language of the Egyptians. An accurate general survey of the history of the decipherment of hieroglyphics and of Egyptian literature is given by J. P. MAHAFFY, *Pro-*

legomena to Ancient History, London, 1871. Compare CHAMPOLLION LE JEUNE, *Précis du Système hiéroglyphique des Anciens Égyptiens*, 2d ed., with a vol. of plates, Paris, 1828, systematised in his *Grammaire Égyptienne*. *Horapollinis Niloi Hieroglyphica*, ed. C. Leemans, Amsterdam, 1835. Strongly to be recommended, H. BRUGSCH, *Hieroglyph. Grammatik zum Nutzen der studirenden Jugend*, Leipzig, 1872. A useful *Egyptian Grammar* has been published by P. LE PAGE RENOUF, London, 1875. Unfinished, E. DE ROUGÉ, *Chrestomathie Égyptienne, Abrégé grammatical*, fasc. 1, Paris, 1867; fasc. 2, 1868. H. BRUGSCH, *Hieroglyph.-demotisches Wörterbuch*, 4 Bde., Leipzig, 1867–68. C. C. J. BUNSEN, *Aegyptens Stelle in der Weltgeschichte*, 6 vols.: i.-iii., Hamburg, 1844–45; iv.–vi., Gotha, 1856–57. Of the English translation, *Egypt's Place in Universal History*, vols. i.–v., London, 1848–67, the fifth volume, translated by C. H. COTTREL, is indispensable; it contains numerous additions by S. BIRCH, among them being a *Translation of the Book of the Dead*, a *Dictionary of Hieroglyphics*, and a *Grammar*. Sir G. WILKINSON, *Manners and Customs of the Ancient Egyptians*, 1st series, 3 vols., London, 1837 (2d ed. of vol. i., 1842); 2d series, 2 vols., with one vol. of plates, London, 1841. Valuable contributions will be found in the *Revue Archéologique*, and in the *Zeitschrift für Aegypt. Sprache und Alterthumskunde*, edited by LEPSIUS and BRUGSCH, Leipzig, 1863, *sqq.* The following catalogues may be consulted with profit: C. LEEMANS, *Description Raisonnée des Monumens Égyptiens du Musée d'Antiquités des Pays-basà Leide*, Leiden, 1840. E. DE ROUGÉ, *Notice des Monuments Égyptiens du Musée du Louvre* (1re éd., 1849), 5me éd., Paris, 1869. H. BRUGSCH, *Uebersetz. und Erklär. Aegypt. Denkmäler des Mus. zu Berlin*, Berlin, 1850. TH. DEVÉRIA, *Notice des Antiquités Égypt. du Musée de Lyon*, Lyons, 1857.

A. MARIETTE-BEY, *Notice des Principaux Monuments du Musée à Boulaq, Paris*, 1869. TH. DEVÉRIA, *Catal. des Manuscr. Égypt. au Musée Égypt. du Louvre*, Paris, 1874.

B. Travels. — CHAMPOLLION, *Lettres Écrites d'Égypte et de Nubie en* 1828 *et* 1829, Paris, 1833. Compare the same author's *Notices Descriptives conformes aux Manuscr. Autogr.*, Paris, 1844. R. LEPSIUS, *Briefe aus Aegypten*, Berlin, 1852. W. GENTZ, *Briefe aus Aegypt. und Nub.*, Berlin, 1853. H. BRUGSCH, *Reiseberichte aus Aegypten*, Leipzig, 1855. G. A. HOSKINS, *A Winter in Upper and Lower Egypt*, London, 1863. J. J. AMPÈRE, *Voyage en Egypte et Nubie*, Paris, 1867. A. MARIETTE-BEY, *Itinéraire de la Haute-Égypte*, Alexandrie, 1872. H. BRUGSCH, *Wanderung nach den Türkis-Minen und der Sinai-Halbinsel*, 2d ed., Leipzig, 1868.

C. History.—R. LEPSIUS, *Königsbuch*, Berlin, 1858. H. BRUGSCH, *Histoire d'Égypte dès les Premiers temps de son existence jusqu'à nos jours*, 1re partie (to Nectanebos), Leipzig, 1859; 2de éd., 1re partie (to the end of the seventeenth dynasty), Leipzig, 1875. A complete German edition by the author has appeared, 1877. It contains some additions and corrections, but the proper names are given in transcription only. E. DE ROUGÉ, *Recherches sur les Monuments qu'on peut attribuer aux six premières Dynasties*, Paris, 1866. LEPSIUS, "Ueber die zwölfte Aegypt. Königsdynastie" (*Akad. der Wiss.*, Berl., Jan. 5, 1852). F. CHABAS, *Les Pasteurs en Égypte*, Amsterdam, 1868. Id., *Recherches pour servir à l'Histoire de la XIXe Dyn.*, Chalons et Paris, 1873. M. BÜDINGER, *Zur Aegyptische Forschung Herodots*, Vienna, 1873. S. SHARPE, *History of Egypt*, 2 vols., 6th ed., London, 1876, must be used with caution in regard to Egyptian religion. Compare M. DUNCKER, *Geschichte des Alterthums*, vol. i. F. LENORMANT, *Manual of the Ancient History of the East*, London,

1869, vol. i. PHILIP SMITH, *The Ancient History of the East*, London, 1871, vol. i. G. MASPÉRO, *Histoire Ancienne des Peuples de l'Orient*, 2de éd., Paris, 1876.

On Chronology.—R. LEPSIUS, *Einleit. zur Chronol. der Aegypt.*, Berlin, 1848. J. LIEBLEIN, *Aegypt. Chronol.*, Christiania, 1863. F. J. C. MAYER, *Aegyptens Vorzeit und Chronol.*, Bonn, 1862. J. DÜMICHEN, *Die erste sichere Angabe über die Regierungszeit eines Aegypt. Königs aus dem alten Reich*, Leipzig, 1874. Unsatisfactory, C. PIAZZI SMITH, *On the Antiquity of Intellect. Man*, Edinburgh, 1868.

D. Texts with translation, and translated texts.—R. LEPSIUS, *Das Todtenbuch der Aegypter, nach dem hierogl. Pap. in Turin*, Leipzig, 1842; translated by BIRCH in Bunsen's *Egypt's Place*, &c., see above; by BRUGSCH in the *Zeitschr. für Aegypt. Sprache*, 1872, *sqq.* (not yet finished); and quite erroneously by G. SEYFFARTH in *Theol. Schriften der alten Aegypter*, Gotha, 1855. Compare PLEYTE, *Études Égyptologiques*, Leiden, 1866, *sqq.* EUG. LEFÉBURE, *Traduction comparée des Hymnes au Soleil compos. le xve chapitre du Rit. fun. Égypt.*, Paris, 1868. LEPSIUS, *Aelteste Texte des Todtenbuchs nach Sarkofagen des altaegypt. Reichs*, Berlin, 1867. F. CHABAS, *Le Papyrus magique Harris*, publ. et trad., Chalons, 1860. Id., *Mélanges Égyptologiques*, 1e–3e série, Chalons et Paris. 1862, *sqq.* Id., *Le Calendrier des Jours fastes et néfastes (Pap. Sallier IV.), trad. compl.*, ibid., no date. G. MASPÉRO, *Essai sur l'inscript. dédic. du temple d'Abydos*, Paris, 1867. Id., *Hymne au Nil, publ. et trad.*, Paris, 1868. *Records of the Past*, vols. ii. and iv., containing Egyptian texts, London, 1874–75. C. W. GOODWIN, *The Story of Saneha, an Egypt. Tale, transl. from the hieratic Text*, London, 1866. W. PLEYTE, "Een lofzang aan Ptah" (*Evangeliespiegel*, and "De Veldslag van Ramses den Groote tegen de Cheta," *Theol. Tijdschr.*, 1869, p. 221, *sqq.*

LOUIS MÉNARD, *Hermès Trismégiste*, trad. compl., Paris, 1866.

E. Religion.—C. P. TIELE, *Vergel. Geschiedenis der Egypt. en Mesopot. Godsdd.*, Amsterdam, 1869–72; first book, *Egypte.* CHAMPOLLION'S *Panthéon Égyptien* remains unfinished. *Plutarch, Ueber Isis und Osiris*, edited by G. PARTHEY, Berlin. LEPSIUS, *Ueber den ersten Aegypt. Götterkreis und seine geschichtlich-mythologische Entstehung*, Berlin, 1851. Id., *Ueber die Götter der vier Elemente bei den Aegypt.*, Berlin, 1856. PLEYTE, *Lettre sur quelques monuments relatifs au dieu Set*, Leiden, 1863. Id., *Set dans la barque du Soleil*, ibid., 1865. ED. MEYER, *Set-Typhon, eine relig.-geschichtl. Studie*, Leipzig, 1875. BRUGSCH, *Die Sage von der geflügelten Sonnenscheibe*, Göttingen, 1870. (Comp. E. NAVILLE, *Textes relatifs au Mythe d'Horos dans le temple d'Edfou*, Geneva and Basle, 1870.) Sir CH. NICHOLSON, "On the Disk-Worshippers of Memphis," in the *Transactt. of the Roy. Soc. of Literature*, 2d ser. vol. ix. pt. ii. p. 197, *sqq.* M. UHLEMANN, *Das Todtengericht bei den alten Aegyptern*, Berlin, 1854. P. PIERRET, *Le Dogme de la Résurrection chez les anciens Égyptiens*, Paris, no date. G. PARTHEY, *Das Orakel und die Oase des Ammon*, Berlin, 1862. EUG. PLEW, *De Sarapide*, Koningsberg, 1868. BRUGSCH, *Die Adonisklage und das Linoslied*, Berlin, 1852. DÜMICHEN, *Ueber die Tempel und Gräber im alten Aegypt.*, Strassburg, 1872. Id., *Bauurkunde der Tempel-anlagen von Dendera*, Leipzig, 1865. Id., *Der Aegypt. Felsentempel von Abu-Simbel*, Berlin, 1869. BRUGSCH, *Die Aegypt. Gräberwelt*, Leipzig, 1868. The treatise of O. BEAUREGARD, *Les Divinités Égyptiennes*, Paris, 1866, must be regarded as a complete failure.

F. Egyptian Religion in relation to other religions.—PLEYTE, *La Religion des Pré-Israëlites, Recherches sur le Dieu Seth*, Utrecht, 1862. W. G. BRILL, *Israël en Égypte*,

Utrecht, 1857. UHLEMANN, *Israëliten und Hyksos in Aegypt.*, Leipzig, 1856. F. J. LAUTH, *Moses der Ebräer, nach Aegypt. Papyrus-Urkunden*, Munich, 1868. A. EISENLOHR, *Der grosse Papyrus Harris, ein Zeugniss für die Mosäische Religionsstiftung enthaltend*, Leipzig, 1872. (The results in all these treatises are still very uncertain.) G. EBERS, *Aegypten und die Bücher Mose's*, vol. i. (publication not continued), Leipzig, 1868, thoroughly scientific. SHARPE, *Egyptian Mythology and Egypt. Christianity*, London, 1863, deficient in its treatment of the ancient Egyptian religion, yet not without value for the relation of its later forms to Christianity. E. RÖTH, *Die Aegypt. und Zoroastr. Glaubenslehre als die ältesten Quellen unserer speculativen Ideen* (the first part of the *Geschichte unser. Abendl. Philosophie*), Mannheim, 1862, rendered useless, in spite of its learning, by wrong method. It has been imitated and outdone by J. BRAUN, *Naturgeschichte der Sage, Ruckführung aller relig. Ideen u.s.w. auf ihren gemeinsamen Stammbaum*, two vols., Munich, 1864.

29. Among the sources of our knowledge of the ancient Egyptian religion, the first and principal place belongs to the so-called Book of the Dead, or "Book of the going forth on the Day," a collection of texts partly ancient, and partly of later date, intended by their magic power to secure the victory for the soul on its journey to the abodes of eternity. To the same class belong certain magic papyri, except that these were to serve in the contest against evil spirits upon earth. All these books, on which fresh light is being constantly thrown, are inexhaustible mines for Egyptian mythology. Further, both these and others include religious hymns of the highest importance. The historical and literary works, also, the numerous inscriptions on temples, tombs, and other monuments, contain not a little bearing on religion. Though much yet remains to be investigated and explained, all this material, when compared with the statements of the Greeks, enables us to form a very fair conception of the belief and the worship of the ancient Egyptians. The history of this religion, however, can only be sketched in its main outlines.

30. In Egypt the old elements were not replaced by those of later growth, but always remained standing by their side. Thus through every period of Egyptian history we find different usages of animistic origin retained, though perhaps with changed significance, along with very elevated religious ideas, which are by no means in accord with them. Among these may be ranked the cultus of the dead, the deification of the kings, and the worship of animals, which reached the same height among no other people. The dead were worshipped in sepulchral chapels and temples; the kings, even in their lifetime, were regarded as the deity upon earth; and certain animals, among which the sacred bulls occupied the most prominent place, originally no doubt worshipped as fetishes, received homage as the incarnations of a higher being. Fetishism also was the root of the custom by which the innermost sanctuary of the temple contained no image, but only a symbol of the chief god. That the Egyptian religion, like the Chinese, was originally nothing but an organised animism, is proved by the institutions of worship. Here, too, existed no exclusive priestly caste. Descendants sacrificed to their ancestors, the officers of state to the special local divinities, the king to the deities

of the whole country. Not till later did an order of scribes and a regular priesthood arise, and even these as a rule were not hereditary.

The worship of animals is said to have been introduced by Kaiechos (Kakau, of the second dynasty); but if this statement deserves any credit, and is not founded on his name, which may signify "the bulls," it can only be referred to an official recognition of the animal-worship as a state institution. Such usages cannot be imposed by authority: they grow up among the people. The bull-gods chiefly honoured were the black Apis (*Hapi*, to be distinguished from the Nile-god *Hâpi*) of Memphis, and the white or yellow Mnevis (*Mena*) of Heliopolis. Of the first, Chamûs, son of Ramses II., the builder of the Serapeum, was an ardent worshipper. Even centuries later the people were so deeply attached to this cultus that the gift of a new Apis by Darius Hystaspes reconciled them for a time to the hated Persian rule.

The absence of an image in the inmost sanctuary of the temple, sometimes regarded as an evidence of a certain spirituality, is only a proof of the devotion of the Egyptians to ancient customs. There were images everywhere, but in the naos only the ancient fetish, dead or living, now perhaps, though this cannot be affirmed with certainty, regarded as a symbol.

31. It is altogether erroneous to regard the Egyptian religion as the polytheistic degeneration of a prehistoric monotheism. It was polytheistic from the beginning, but it developed in two entirely opposite directions. On the one hand, the world of gods, through the addition of the local religions and the adoption of foreign deities, grew richer and richer. On the other hand, a gradual

and tentative approach was made to monotheism, without attaining clear and unequivocal expression of it. The scribes harmonised the two, by representing the plurality of deities as the manifestations of the one uncreated hidden god—as his members, created by himself.

32. The Egyptian mythology reproduces in varying forms two leading ideas. The first is the belief in the triumph of light over darkness, and of life over death. This is exhibited by the sun-myths. The victory of light, conceived for the most part physically, is represented in the conflict of Râ, the god of Heliopolis (An) and the chief god of Egypt, with the serpent Apap. The triumph of life over death is rather the subject of the myth of Osiris, the other chief god of the empire, specially worshipped in Thinis-Abydos. Osiris, slain by his brother Set—lamented by his wife and sister Isis and Nephthys—endowed by Thut, the god of science and literature, with the power of the word—is avenged by his son Horos, and, while himself reigning in the kingdom of the Dead, lives again in him on earth. This mythic representation of the death and reawakening of the life of nature which was observed in the succession of day and night and of the seasons, was very early, and more closely than the myth of Râ, brought into connection with the doctrine of the resurrection. Each man, at his death, became identified with Osiris. As with the body of the god, his also was mourned, embalmed, and buried. As the soul of the god shines in Orion in the sky, so that of the departed lives likewise among the stars. As the shade of the one conquers in the world of the

Dead, so that of the other sustains there a series of trials in order at last to pass in and out freely with the god of light, and be united with him for ever.

The belief in the victory of light and life was expressed in the very name, *nuteru*, "those who renew themselves," which is the general designation of the gods, and in the constantly recurring triads of father, mother, and son. That the son is no other than the father himself alive once more, appears from the formula, "husband of his mother (*ka mut-f*)," which is applied to several Egyptian deities.

Though certainly regarded originally as independent gods, the other chief gods of Heliopolis must be viewed as forms of Râ. Such were the visible Harmachis (*Râ Harmachuti*, Ra-Horos on the two horizons), the hidden Tum (*Atum*, the nightly sun-god), Chepra, the creator, "he who continually renews himself," symbolised by a beetle. Less closely connected with him was his ally Shu, of whom two varying representations exist, founded on two different meanings of his name. As the "outspread" or "out-stretching," he is the god of the sky; as the "consuming," he is the god of the scorching heat of the sun.

The meaning of the names of Osiris (*Asar*, *Asiri*), Set (*Set* or *Suti*), and Thut (*Thuti*) is uncertain. The two first are the two hostile sun-gods, whom we find among the Semites. The last was once a moon-god, and then became the god of numbers, of weights and measures, and subsequently of literature and science. Isis (*As*) is the "ancient," the "venerable," or better, the "exalted;" Nephthys (*Nebt-ha*) the "mistress of the house," goddess of the underworld. Horos (*Her*, the "uppermost," "he who is above") is the god of the sun by day, and has a number of forms. It would seem that it was not till the myth of Osiris was so closely united with the belief in the resurrection, that Anubis (*Anup* or *Anpu*), the conductor of souls, was taken into it. In the oldest tombs it is with his image that we generally meet, and not with that of Osiris, as at a later date.

33. The other leading idea is that of creation by the supreme uncreated god with his assistant spirits, of which the eight personified cosmic powers are the chief. The work of creation is ascribed, indeed, to all the principal deities, but especially to the gods of fire and the element of moisture. At the head of the first stands Ptah, the god of Memphis, who himself personifies the cosmic fire, as the soul of the universe; just as his "great beloved" Sechet represents its destroying and purifying power, and Neith of Sais—often united with him—its mysterious hidden operation, while his form Bes with his consort Bast symbolise its beneficent warmth and cheering glow. That Chnum the architect, god of the waters—originally the wind which moves and fertilises them—and consequently the soul of the universe, and Hâpi the Nile-god, should also be regarded as creative deities, needs no further explanation.

The eight cosmic powers (*Sesmenu* or *Sesennu,* from whom the city of Thut, Hermopolis, derived its Egyptian name), always united with Thut, but nevertheless to be distinguished from his seven assistants, constitute four pairs: *Nun* and *Nunt,* the celestial ocean, the abyss; *Ḥeḥ* and *Ḥeḥt,* time (without end); *Kek* and *Kekt,* darkness; *Neni* and *Nenit,* breath, spirit, or wind. These are the four personifications of the ideas embodied in the well-known doctrines of creation, "In endless duration" (or "in the beginning") "was darkness on the abyss, and the waters of the primeval ocean were moved by the wind, the breath of the deity," *cf.* Gen. i. The myth, if not adopted from Semites, is clearly another form of the later Semitic representation.

Ptah (from *patāḥu*) signifies "former," "sculptor," an appropriate name for the god of fire. Sechet, a name generally transcribed Pacht (Pechet), denotes "kindling fire" (causative of *chet*, "flame"); Pechet is "the devourer," especially the lion. Neith (*Net* or *Nit*) is the Egyptian virgin mother, yet in a purely cosmogonic-theological sense. Bes is the ascending flame; he has a twofold nature as god of joy, music, and dancing, and as warrior. His consort Bast, the beneficent, is the gentle counterpart of the violent Sechet.

Chnum is the deity who was formerly, under the name of Kneph, regarded by some scholars as the supreme god of the Egyptian pantheon. He is one of the oldest gods, and his worship remained very sensual. By his side stand *Sati*, the generative power, and *Anuka*, "the embracing." These three personify the wind, flowing water, and the earth.

34. It is not surprising that in the earliest history of Egyptian religion much still remains obscure. When, however, we note that the Egyptians themselves called the prehistoric period the age of the Horus-followers, and that there was no place of importance which had not its Horus and its Hathor, we are justified in concluding that the chief gods adored above all others in the earliest period were these two gods of the light of heaven.

Under the first six dynasties, besides Osiris and Râ Ptah of Memphis was chiefly worshipped, as the deity who effected the union of the two divisions of the kingdom under one sceptre. It was probably in this period that the cultus of animals was raised to a state institution. The deification of the kings was carried, in the days of the builders of the pyramids, to the greatest extreme; and the three worships, of Osiris, Râ, and Ptah, were blended, perhaps imperceptibly, together. Such are the gradual stages of ascent from the visible gods to the higher and invisible. The simplicity of the tombs in this period is worthy of note. Rarely are the gods represented in them; and though the deceased already bear religious titles, the walls of the sepulchral chapels exhibit only the scantiest allusions to theological subjects. Religious feeling appears to have been vivid and deep, but the power of priests and scribes was certainly still small.

"Horus-followers" or "Horus-worshippers" seems the best translation of the often-recurring *Har-shesu*. The name Horus has been already explained. In later times this name also was employed as a general designation for the deity: was it so originally? It is not improbable. Hathor (Hathar) would signify literally "the house of Horus;" but she is without doubt the same as the Assyrian Istar, the Phenician Ashtoreth (*cf.* the South Arabian A*th*tar), and the only question is on which side lies the priority. Is the Egyptian Hathar a corruption of Istar, or the reverse? This point deserves further investigation. The great antiquity, however, to which the cultus of Hathor may be traced in Egypt, long before the time when there was any possibility of Semitic influence, renders only two interpretations tenable—either that Istar is the Egyptian Hathor in Semitic guise, or that both are forms, modified in accordance with varying national genius, of a goddess originally invoked under a similar name by the common forefathers of the Hamites and Semites.

35. The gods worshipped under the Middle Empire (the Eleventh to the Fourteenth Dynasties) correspond altogether to the character of the period, which was distinguished both by conquests and by the flourishing condition of agriculture and the arts of peace. Now that the centre of gravity of the kingdom was transferred from Memphis in Lower Egypt to the Thebais in Upper Egypt, the gods of this latter region, as so often happened in antiquity, were elevated to the highest rank. The principal deities are Munt, the god of war; Chem or Min, the god of fertility and agriculture, with whom must also be named, even at this early period, Amun, the god of the city of Thebes, as yet but slightly different from Chem, and far from being the great king of the gods, which he was only destined to become in later years. These three are in fact only different forms of the same divine being. It is not surprising that in an age so rich as this in the products of industry, Ptah, the former, and Chnum, the architect, were the objects of special veneration; and it is equally natural that a prince of the Thirteenth Dynasty, to whom Egypt owed a new canal system, and who by this means added a whole province to his dominions, should be zealously devoted to the Nile-god Sebak, god of the water which at once served for drinking and fertilised the land. Thus do the forms of religion undergo modification with the progress of civilisation. The kings of this period promote external religion, but as uncontrolled masters and not as yielding obedience to priests. Their inscriptions exhibit an

ethical tone. Literature is mostly secular, but the scribes are already beginning to apply themselves to the explanation of ancient texts. The tombs of this period indicate as yet no great development of the belief in immortality. It is brought, indeed, into closer connection with religion than under the Old Empire, but the future life is still regarded only as the continuation of the present, without reference to the doctrine of retribution.

If the history of Egypt is divided into two parts, the Middle Empire must be classed along with the Old. It forms the transition between the Old and the New.

That Min (also named Chem, "the ruler"), whose chief temple was at Koptos, Munt of Hermonthis, and Amun of Thebes, are essentially the same, appears (among other reasons) from their names, which are all derived from the same root, and originally indicated their character as gods of fertility. Chem is often named simply Amun-Râ. Subsequently, the meaning of the name Amun was modified.

Sebak, who was probably derived from Ethiopia, was no god of evil. This character was not ascribed to him till later, through a confusion with Set, to whom likewise the crocodile belonged. Sebak is the god of the inundation, and is sometimes interchanged with Hâpi. The crocodile was his body, since it was asserted to deposit its eggs every year just at the limit to which the inundation would that year extend.

36. Of the religious condition of the Egyptians under the sway of the Arab Shepherd-Princes (the Hyksos) we know nothing. The conquerors had combined the religion of Lower Egypt with their own, and worshipped Set whom they named Sutech, together perhaps with Ptah.

One of them even proposed to the contemporary Theban king, to elevate Sutech and Amun-Râ to be the sole gods of Egypt. After their fall Amun-Râ of Thebes became the chief god, to whom all the others were subordinated, and after whose type the rest of the chief gods were transformed. An attempt made by Amun-hotep IV. (Chunaten) to substitute the exclusive worship of Aten-Ra, the sun-disc, for that of Amun-Râ, had no permanent success. After his death the whole pantheon, with Amun-Râ at its head, was speedily restored.

Amun-Râ, the hidden creator, has now become the king of the gods, and the lord of the thrones of the world. In him the Egyptians expressed the most comprehensive and consequently the highest and most elevated religious conception which they were in a position to form. He unites in himself the nature of Min or Chem, the god of fruitfulness, and of the war-god Munt, but he possesses, besides, the characteristic qualities of all the principal deities. Sun-god and Nile-god, lord of the visible and the invisible worlds, he was the mysterious soul of the universe which reveals itself in light. His consort, Mat, "the mother," and Chonsu, his son, had the same composite character.

Among the many shapes peopling this world of deities, which was enriched just at this time with a number of strange forms, an endeavour was now made to introduce a certain order, whilst a monotheistic tendency was clearly gaining strength. The doctrine of immortality, now under the control of the dogma of retribution, becomes the centre of religion. Magic rises rapidly in importance, the influence and power of the priests increasing along with it; and the priests make themselves more and more independent, and finally occupy the place of the king. The high priest of Thebes seizes the sovereign power, and himself founds a dynasty.

The name Sutech, applied to Set, seems to me an attempt to reproduce in Egyptian form the Semitic divine name, Ṣedeq, "the righteous." At any rate, if the form Sutech is older, the reason why the Arabians made choice of this particular Egyptian god as their own, must be sought in the resemblance of this name to Ṣedeq.

Amun is, properly speaking, not the name of the Theban chief god, but the abbreviation of the formula, "He whose name is hidden" (Brugsch, *Wörterb.*, p. 71). Râ signifies "creator." As well as with the gods already named, he is chiefly identified with Chnum, and qualities of Ptah, Shu, Tum, Osiris, and others, are transferred to him. Mat, "the mother," is really a sort of abstraction of all Egyptian mother-goddesses, that is, the chief goddesses of the country. For this reason her worship was less actively pursued. Chonsu, whose name has not yet been explained, received so much the more homage. He seems to have been originally a moon-god.

37. The last period of Egyptian religion bears marks of profound decline. Lower Egypt throws off the yoke of the priest-kings of Thebes, who retreat to Ethiopia (Meroë). To this region, and also to the oasis of Ammon, they carry Egyptian civilisation and the worship of Amun; but they continually attempt, and occasionally for a time with success, to re-establish their authority, and with it the orthodox faith, over Egypt. The reign of the Saitic princes is a period of restoration. But the country is for the most part the prey of foreign conquerors

—Assyrians, Persians, and Greeks, whom the people only resist when they pay no reverence to the national religion. This religion lives on for centuries, but it subsists only upon the past. It undergoes, however, some modifications, which must be ascribed in part to the influence of the Greek spirit, and in part, perhaps at an earlier date, to that of the Persian. Thus it may have been the Persian type which imparted its ethical significance to the contest between Osiris and Set, until the latter, as a deity morally evil, was driven out of the pantheon. The Hathar of this period, whose splendid temple at Dendera was restored under the care of the Ptolemies, has not a few features in common with the Greek Aphrodite. One of these princes brought the Semitic god Serapis, already worshipped by many Greeks, to Egypt, where his worship was fused with that of Osiris-Apis. One circumstance in particular is a certain sign of decline, viz., that the goddesses now occupy a much higher position than the gods. At last, the equilibrium between the local worships is entirely broken; and of the remarkable Egyptian civilisation there remains nothing but monuments which are only destined once more to yield up their meaning when fifteen centuries have passed away.

The conflict of the Ethiopian priest-princes, such as Pianchi Meriamun, Sabako, Tahraka, with the North Egyptian dynasties which had subjugated Upper Egypt, was in part national, that of Ham with Shem, but in part, and indeed chiefly, religious. Thebes was always ready to receive them; nay, the prophets of this city invited Tahraka to advance as their liberator (De Rougé,

Mél. d'Archéol., i. p. 11, *sqq.*), while he declared that he fought against the blasphemers of Amun-Râ (Prisse, *Monum.*, pl. xxxi. a.) to deliver the god (ibid., pl. xxxii. d.) They were, however, driven out; and in Ethiopia itself Egyptian civilisation sank lower and lower, till beneath native additions the worship of Amun was no longer to be recognised.

Under the Saitic kings (Necho, Psamtik, Amasis) art flourished, and the chief objects of worship were Ptah and Neith. Homage was still paid to the Theban triad at Silsilis; but Thebes itself had fallen into such deep decline that one of its principal temples was already employed as a burial-place.

Darius Hystaspis was the only king who adopted a policy of reconciliation. Kambyses attempted the same course before his defeats. For their want of respect for the mysteries, Xerxes and his son were driven out of the palace at Sais (Brugsch, *Zeitschr.*, 1871, 1, *sqq.*) This intolerance resulted in the fall of the Persian supremacy in Egypt. The Ptolemies acted with much more prudence.

It is uncertain whether it was the first or the second Ptolemy who introduced the god Serapis from Sinope in Asia Minor. Plew (*op. cit.*) regards the deity as of Babylonian origin. The name signifies "serpent," and is the same as that of the Hebrew Seraphim. As the name can only be explained from the Indo-Germanic (*serpens*), the god was probably derived by the Semites from the Aryans.

By the edict of Theodosius, 381 A.D., the Egyptian religion was abolished.

38. It is not yet possible to enumerate with certainty all the elements which co-operated to lift the Egyptian religion out of Animism and place it on so lofty an eminence. African usages, such as circumcision, may be observed in it; the myth of the sun-god Râ has an Aryan character; and even the language contains not a few Aryan roots. The myths of Osiris, Amun, and Hathor, the cosmogony, and a number of customs, exhibit a large accordance with conceptions and practices like those which grew up in Mesopotamia out of the blending of the Semitic religion with that of the original inhabitants of the country, the Akkadians. The influence of the Semites in Egypt increases century by century, and the Semitic pushes the national element more and more into the background. Conversely, however, the Egyptian religion exerts a preponderating influence on the Canaanite races, though less upon the Hebrews than on the Phenicians. First by their means, and then directly, it reached the Greeks, made its way finally through the whole Roman Empire, and even furnished to Roman Catholic Christendom the germs of the worship of the Virgin, the doctrine of the Immaculate Conception, and the type of its theocracy.

The Semitic gods of light and fire contend with consuming and destroying sun-gods, as Osiris does with Set. Râ, like the Aryan gods of light, fights with the powers of darkness.

Parallelisms between Egyptian and Mesopotamian myths may be seen in (1) the abyss, from which everything proceeds, Egyptian *ṭûau*, Assyr. *tihavti;* (2) Osiris, Egypt. *Asar*, and Assyr. *Asar*, the under-world; (3) Isis, Egypt. *As*, *Ast*, and Assyr. *Asa*, *Asat*, also *As*, a surname of Istar, Accad. *Isi*, the earth; (4) *Hathar nehe-*

mau = Semit. *Ashtoreth nâamah;* (5) the doctrines of the god who is husband of his mother, and the god who is self-created, appear both in Egypt and in Babylonia, &c. The names of Thut and Nabu possess no resemblance, but their myths and their attributes are in remarkable agreement.

Astarte, Qadesh, Qen, Reshpu, Anith, and Tanith were introduced into Egypt at a later period.

II.

RELIGION AMONG THE SEMITES.

A. *The Two Streams of Development.*

Literature.—E. RENAN, *Histoire générale et système comparé des langues Sémitiques*, 1st part, 2d ed., Paris, 1858. Id., *Nouvelles considérations sur le caractère général des peuples Sémitiques et en particulier sur leur tendance au monothéisme*, Paris, 1859. (Criticised by C. P. TIELE, "De Oorsprong van het Monotheïsme bij de Israëlieten," *Gids*, Feb. 1862. From the supernatural standpoint, R. F. GRAU, *Semiten und Indogermanen in ihrer Beziehung zu Religion und Wissenschaft*, Stuttgart, 1864. Totally different, J. G. MÜLLER, *Die Semiten in ihrem Verhältniss zu Chamiten und Japhetiten*, Basel, 1872.) RENAN, *De la part des peuples Sémitiques dans l'histoire de la civilisation*, 5th ed., Paris, 1867. A sharp distinction is made between Indo-Germans and Semites by FRIED. MÜLLER, *Indogermanisch und Semitisch*, Vienna, 1870, although in his *Allgem. Ethnographie*, p. 437, *sqq.*, he places them, together with the Basques and Caucasians, in the family occupying the "Mediterranean Lands." D. CHWOLSON, *Die Semit. Völker; Versuch einer Charakteristik*, Berlin, 1872. See above all, E. SCHRADER, "Die Abstammung der Chaldäer und die Ursitze der Semiten," in *Zeitschr. der Deutsch. Morgenland. Gesellsch.*, xxvii., 1873, Hft. iii. p. 397, *sqq.*

On the ancient Arabian religion, CAUSSIN DE PERCEVAL, *Essai sur l'Histoire des Arabes avant l'Islamisme*, 3 parts, Paris, 1847. L. KREHL, *Ueber die Religion der Vorislamischen Araber*, Leipzig, 1863. OSIANDER, "Studien über die Vorisl. Relig. der Araber," *Zeitschr. der D. M. G.*, 1853.

On the Akkadian civilisation and religion see the works on Assyriology named further on. The following deal exclusively with the Akkadian language: F. LENORMANT, *Études Accadiennes*, vol. i. 1st part, "Introduction grammaticale;" 2d part, "Restitution des Paradigmes;" 3d part, "Répertoire des caractères:" vol. ii., "Choix de textes avec traductions interlin." (*Lettres Assyriologiques*, 2d series), Paris, 1873–74. Id., *La Magie chez les Chaldéens et les origines Accadiennes*, Paris, 1874, and *Études sur quelques Parties des Syllabaires cunéif.*, Paris, 1876. The existence of the Akkadian language is denied by J. HALÉVY, "Observations critiques sur les prétendus Touraniens de la Babylonie," in *Journ. Asiat.*, Juin 1874. Completely refuted (except on the point of the Turanian origin of the Akkadians) by F. LENORMANT, *La Langue primitive de la Chaldée et les idiomes Touraniens*, and by E. SCHRADER, "Ist das Akkad. der Keilinschriften eine Sprache oder eine Schrift?" in the *Zeitschr. der D. M. G.*, xxix. i. 1875.

On cuneiform writing in general, L. DE ROSNY, *Les Écritures Figuratives et Hiéroglyphiques*, Paris, 1860. J. MÉNANT, *Les Noms propres Assyriens*, Paris, 1861. Id., *Les Écritures Cunéiformes*, Paris, 1864. P. GLAIZE, *Les Inscriptions Cunéif. et les Travaux de M. Oppert*, Metz, Paris, 1867. J. MÉNANT, *Le Syllabaire Assyrien*, 1st part, 1869, 2d part, 1873. GEORGE SMITH, *The Phonetic Values of the Cuneiform Characters*, London, 1871. Of the highest value, E. SCHRADER, "Die Basis der Entzifferung der Assyrisch-Babylonischen Keilinschriften," in *Zeitschr. der D. M. G.*, xxiii. iii. 1869.

39. Among the Semites, who are closely connected with the Hamites, but are also, in the opinion of many scholars, more or less closely connected with the Indo-Germanic races, two streams of development may be clearly distinguished, alike in language and in religion, which may be designated as the Southern and the Northern. The common though not the most ancient home of the whole race was probably in the northern and central regions of Arabia. It must, however, have been abandoned at an early period by all the Semitic peoples, with the exception of the Arabs, who spread over the whole peninsula, and the Ethiopians, who subsequently crossed over to Africa. These form the group of the Southern Semites. With the exception of the Sabeans or Himyarites (see § 46), the Arabs, through the position of their country, remained the longest excluded from intercourse with civilised nations. From this cause they preserved the genuine Semitic family character and the national religion in their purest forms. It is from the little that we know of the latter that we must gather what was the nature of Semitic religion in its original simplicity. To the Northern Semites belong the Babylonians and Assyrians, the Arameans, Canaanites, Phenicians, and Israelites. Their amalgamation with the oldest civilised inhabitants of Mesopotamia produced important modifications in their religion, which developed with greater speed and richness. The study of religion among the Semites is of the highest consequence, because two of the three universal religions, Christianity and Islâm, proceeded from them.

That all the Semites once dwelt together in Northern Arabia, and that the Arabs preserved the Semitic character in the purest form, appears to me to have been convincingly proved by Schrader in the essay already cited. Against his main thesis, at any rate, there is little objection to be raised, however we may differ from him in detail. The vast difference in civilisation and religion existing between Northern and Southern Semites can be explained in no other way. Whether their original home is to be sought, as most scholars suppose, in the neighbourhood of that of the Indo-Germans, or as Gerland (*Anthropol. Beitr.*, p. 396, *sqq.*) maintains, in Africa, is a question which requires further investigation, but the answer to it is of only secondary importance for our present purpose.

40. The ancient religion of the Arabs rises little higher than animistic polydæmonism. It is a collection of tribal religions standing side by side, only loosely united, though there are traces of a once closer connection. The names Ilâh and Shamsh, the sun-god, occur among all the Semitic peoples; Allât, or Alilât and Al'Uzza, as well as the triad of moon-goddesses to which these last belong, are common to several, and the deities which bear them are reckoned among the chief. The names of the remaining Arab gods do not reappear among the other Semites. Sun-worship was practised by all the tribes, and the stars also, particularly the Pleiades (*Turayyâ*), were the objects of special homage, but there was no cultus of the planets as such, a fact which indicates that astronomy was but little developed. This cultus was in truth scarcely much more than Fetishism; and their worship of trees, and especially of stones and mountains, which were regarded as occupied by souls, belongs to precisely the same order, just as spiritism expressed itself also among them in the worship of ancestors. The

image-worship which prevailed among them at the time of Mohammed, was introduced, according to the Arabic writers, at a later period from Syria or Mesopotamia. It may very easily, however, have sprung out of the worship of stones. The few human sacrifices which they offered appear to have been of another kind from those which the Northern Semites borrowed from the Akkadians. The sanctuaries of the various spirits and fetishes had their own hereditary ministers, who, however, formed no priestly caste; but the Seers were generally regarded with great reverence, and were much consulted. But among the Arabs these last never became priests, as was the case among other Semites.

In that which constitutes the distinctive characteristic of a religion, the relation conceived to exist between man and the deity, they agreed entirely with their kindred. They, likewise, stood towards God as the servant (*'abd*) towards his master.

Ilâh, Assyr. *Ilu*, Hebr. and Canaanite, *Êl*. The later Allâh is a contraction of *al-ilâh*. Sprenger, *Leben und Lehre des Mohammad*, i. p. 286, *sqq.*, regards Allâh as made up of *lâh*, "mirage," "shining," with the article *al*, and thus as different from Ilâh.

The three moon-goddesses—Allât, the light moon; Manât, the dark moon; and Al'Uzza, the union of the two—re-appear among the Babylonians and Assyrians with partially-altered names. Some of the planets, such as Jupiter and Venus, the greater and the lesser fortune, were worshipped by the Arabs as by all Semites, but their movements were not distinguished from those of the fixed stars. The sacred number seven, applied among the Northern Semites to the five planets with the sun and moon, was derived among the Southern Semites from the Pleiades, to which, together with the Hyades (Aldabarân) and Sirius, they paid special veneration.

Very noteworthy is the absence of the chief myth of the Northern Semites, the so-called Adonis myth, among the Arabs. Krehl (*op. cit.*) and F. Lenormant (*Lettres Assyriol.*, ii. p. 241) have supposed that traces of it are, nevertheless, to be found among them also, but upon very insufficient grounds.

The only human sacrifices which are known with certainty to have existed among them, accord with those of savages. This was the offering of little girls at Mekka, against which Hanyf Zaïd vigorously contended. See Sprenger, *Leben und Lehre des Mohammad*, i. p. 120. The service of the idols was limited to particular families. The seers of the highest rank were called *Kahîn*, the same word as the Hebrew *Kohên*, priest. This last meaning, which the word never acquired among the Arabs, is regarded by Sprenger, i. p. 255, as the derivative; but other scholars (Fleischer, Von Kremer, Cheyne) declare this to be incorrect.

41. The Northern Semites advanced far beyond this standpoint. For this they were indebted without doubt to a longer or shorter sojourn in Mesopotamia, to which their own traditions point, and from which the majority of them again migrated to the north-west. In Mesopotamia they found an ancient non-Semitic civilisation, which had a decisive influence on their development. This civilisation belonged to a people classed by some with the Turanians, certainly related to the Elamites and non-Aryan Medes, and generally called Akkadians. They were the fathers of astronomy, the first beginnings of which developed themselves among them out of astrology, and the inventors of cuneiform writing, which was adopted from them by various other nations, and was employed by them not only for royal inscriptions, but also for daily use, and for the record of a rich, scientific, historic, poetic, and religious literature, which has been recovered partly in the original texts and partly in Assyrian translations.

For the Phenician tradition, see Herod., vii. 89; Strabo, vii. 98, &c. According to the Hebrew, Abram came from Ur-Kasdîm, the present Mugheir in Southern Chaldea. *Cf.* the author's *Vergelijk. Geschied. der Egypt. en Mesopot. Godsdd.*, p. 426, *sqq.* See, however, § 52, further on.

The name Turanian is here used to designate the so-called Ural-Altaic race, of which the Mongols, Turks, Magyars, Finns, and Samoyedes are the chief branches. Many scholars, among whom is Schrader, have expressed doubts whether the Akkadians are rightly classed with these, as Lenormant proposes. That they are closely related, however, with these peoples, and must certainly be placed among the "Mongoloid races" of Peschel, appears both from their language and their religion. They assuredly belong to the same race with the Elamites and non-Aryan Medes. They are generally called Akkadians on the supposition that in the constantly-occurring formula "king" or "land" "of the Sumirs and Akkadians," the Semitic population is designated by the first name, the non-Semitic by the second; J. Oppert (*Journ. Asiat.*, 1875, v. 2, p. 272, *sqq.*) maintains that the reverse is the truth. F. Delitzsch, also, in Smith's *Chald. Genesis, übersetzt von* H. Delitzsch, p. 291, *sq.*, proves on other grounds that the name Sumirs denotes the pre-Semitic population of Babylonia. The question is of subordinate importance.

Specimens of their astronomical knowledge may be found in the tablets published by A. H. Sayce in the *Transactions of the Soc. of Bibl. Archæol.*, iii. i. 1874, pp. 145–339. (Translation alone in *Records of the Past*, vol. i. p. 151, *sqq.*)

The cuneiform character is, like the Chinese, the modification of a hieratic character, of which a few characters still remain, and which in its turn must have arisen out of hieroglyphics. The two facts, that these have entirely disappeared, and that even on the oldest monuments the hieratic character only occurs here and there, prove the high antiquity of the Akkadian civilisation. The cuneiform character is also found among the Elamites, the non-Aryan Medes, and Armenians (Alarodians), and among the Persians, among whom, however, it was altogether modified. It is certain that both the last-named nations, and probable that the two first also, derived it from the Akkadians.

42. The religion of the Akkadians was the type of the richest and most complete development of the exclusive worship of the spirits and elements of nature. The host of spirits was innumerable. They were ranged in classes, and even the highest deities were classed with them. The ranks of these last included Ana, the highest heaven regarded as a divine being; Mulge and Ninge, the lord and lady of the hidden heaven beneath the earth, the abyss; and Êa or Hêa, the god of the atmosphere and of moisture, with his consort Dav-Kina, the lady of the earth. To this supreme triad corresponded a lower group, consisting of the moon-god Uru-ki, the sun-god Ud, and the wind-god Im. Nindar or Ninib, the lord of generation, the son of Mulge, was the god of the nightly or hidden sun, the Mesopotamian Herakles, a war-god like Nirgal, who finds a nearer representative in Mars. Mediating between Hêa and mankind, in which capacity he was regarded as the benefactor of the latter, stood Amar-utuki, the brightness of the sun, the great god of the city of Babylon. The system further included a goddess who corresponds to the Semitic Istar, and bears the hitherto-unexplained name Sukus. Fire played an important part among the Akkadians, and their worship consisted, though not exclusively, of magic. For it was chiefly concerned with combating the evil spirits, which were set in sharp dualistic contrast with the good. This confliot had, however, a very subordinate ethical significance; and the underworld, also, it would seem, was not yet, in the theology of the Akkadians, a place of recompense; but all encountered there the same destiny. The war of the gods of light with the powers of darkness had already furnished material for a rich epic literature, from which some important productions have been brought to light in Assyrian translations. The great importance of the investigation of this religion lies chiefly in the fact that it exercised so powerful an influence on the Semitic religion, and indirectly on that of the nations of the West.

The name of the highest class of spirits (*Anab*, abbreviated to *Ana, An*), almost equivalent to gods, seems to be derived from that of the heaven-god; at any rate it entirely accords with it. Êa or Hêa signifies "the house," "the abode." The triad of deities corresponds with the three worlds into which the Akkadians divided the universe.

The moon-god also bears various other names, such as Akû (perhaps from *aka*, to "lift up," to "exalt"); Enuzuna, "lord of growth" (the crescent moon), &c.; Uru-ki signifies "overlooker or protector of the earth;" Ud means "light;" and Im or Iv, "wind," "storm." Nir-gal (although the name as it is spelled could only signify "great-foot") signifies "great prince," and the full form of the name Nir-unu-gal, certainly means "prince of the great abode," by which the underworld is probably denoted. See *West. Asian Inscrr.*, ii. 59 rev., l. 37, *d* and *e*. The ingenious conjectures of Delitzsch, *Chald. Genesis*, p. 274, are therefore unnecessary. Amar-utuki, literally, "brightness with the sun," "light which accompanies the sun" (*ud*), is exactly the fitting mediator between God and men. As such, he is called Silik-mulu-chi, "He who ordains good (*chi*) for men (*mulu*)"; in the Akkadian texts he is designated almost exclusively by this epithet.

B. *Religion among the Babylonians and Assyrians.*

Literature.—Language.—Grammars by MÉNANT, 1868, and SAYCE, 1875; *Comparative Grammar* by SAYCE, 1872. *Assyrian Dictionary* by E. NORRIS, parts i.–iii. 1868–72, the best refutation of HITZIG'S doubts in his *Sprache und Sprachen Assyriens*, Leipzig, 1871. See in reply E. SCHRADER "Die Assyr.-Babyl. Keilinschriften," in the *Zeitschr. der Deutsch. Morgenl. Gesellsch.*, xxiv. i. and ii. 1872. *Texts:* without translation, RAWLINSON, NORRIS, and SMITH, *West. Asian Inscrr.*, and LENORMANT, *Choix*, &c.; with translation, OPPERT et MÉNANT, *Les Fastes de Sargon* ("Grande Inscr. des Salles du Palais de Khorsabad"), Paris, 1863. MÉNANT, *Inscrr. des Revers de Plaques du Palais de Khorsabad*, Paris, 1865. Id., *Inscriptions de Hammourabi, Roi de Babylone* (defective), Paris, 1863.

George Smith, *History of Assurbanipal*, London, 1871. E. Schrader, *Die Höllenfahrt der Istar, nebst Proben Assyr. Lyrik*, Giessen, 1874; also in his treatise *Die Keilinschriften und das Alte Testament*, Giessen, 1872. Translated texts in *Records of the Past*, vols. i. and iii. Essays on the inscriptions (including the Himyaritic) by Lenormant, *Lettres Assyriologiques et Épigraphiques*, vols. i. and ii., Paris, 1871–72.

Archæology.—Besides the larger collections of plates after the monuments by Botta, Layard, &c., and Oppert's *Expédition en Mésopotamie*, 2 parts, the following are of most importance for consultation: Layard, *Nineveh and its Remains*, London, 1848, and *Discoveries among the Ruins of Nineveh and Babylon*, London, 1853. Compare L. F. Janssen, *Over de ontdekkingen van Nineveh*, Utrecht, 1850. F. Finzi, *Ricerche per lo studio dell' Antichità assira*, Turin, 1872. George Smith, *Assyrian Discoveries; an Account of Explorations in 1873–74*, London, 1875.

History.—J. Kruger, *Geschichte der Assyrier und Iranier, vom* 13ten *bis zum* 5ten *Jahrh. v. C.*, Frankfort, 1856 (wholly untrustworthy). Rawlinson, *Outlines of Assyrian History, from the Inscriptions of Nineveh*, London, 1852. J. Oppert, *Histoire des Empires de Chaldée et d'Assyrie d'après les Monuments*, Versailles, 1865. W. Wattenbach, *Nineveh und Babylon*, Heidelberg, 1868. F. Lenormant, *Manual of the Ancient History of the East*, vol. i., London, 1869. J. Ménant, *Annales des Rois d'Assyrie*, Paris, 1874. Id., *Annales des Rois de Babylone*, ibid., 1875. G. Smith, *Assyria from the Earliest Times to the Fall of Nineveh*, London (1875). Compare F. Justi, *Ausland*, No. 30.

Religion.—F. Münter, *Religion der Babylonier*, Copenhagen, 1827. E. Hincks, *On the Assyrian Mythology*, Dublin, 1855 (*Transactions of the Roy. Irish Acad.*, Nov.

1854, vol. xxiii.) TIELE, *Vergelijk. Geschiedenis van de Egypt. en Mesopot. Godsdiensten*, 2e stuk., Amsterdam, 1870. F. LENORMANT, *Essai de Commentaire des Fragm. Cosmogon. de Bérose*, Paris, 1872. Id., *La Légende de Sémiramis*, ibid., 1873 (*Acad. de Belgique*, 8me Janv. 1872). Id., *Le Déluge et l'Épopée Babylonienne* (*Extr. du Correspondant*), Paris, 1873. (Compare G. SMITH, *Chaldean Account of the Deluge*, two photographs, with translation and text, London, 1872.) Id., *La Divination et la Science des Présages chez les Chaldéens*, Paris, 1875. OPPERT, *L'Immortalité de l'Âme chez les Chaldéens* (*Annales de Philosophie Chrétienne*, 1874), Paris, 1875. G. SMITH, *The Chaldean Account of Genesis*, London, 1875. (In accordance with the writer's own warning, his results, which are only provisional, must be used with caution. Compare A. H. SAYCE, *Academy*, 1st Jan. 1876.) German translation by H. Delitzsch, with annotations and additions by Fried. Delitzsch, Leipzig, 1867.

On the Sabeans, see the works cited in my *Vergelijk. Geschied.*, p. 400, *sqq.* HALÉVY has since discovered and published several more texts. See LENORMANT'S *Lettres Assyriol.*, ii., and the journals already referred to, *passim.*

43. Out of the amalgamation of Akkadians and Semites arose the Chaldean people, generally called Babylonians, after their most famous city and its province. The Assyrians, who derived their name from their ancient capital and their god Asur, were a Chaldean colony, which had established itself at an early period in the north of the land of the Two Rivers, and there gradually grew to a powerful monarchy. The two nations differed but slightly in language and religion; the difference was greater in civilisation and character. In arts and sciences the Babylonians were the predecessors and masters of the Assyrians, but their empire appears to have been rather a feudal theocracy than a compact monarchy, in which two states, Babylonia proper (Kardunyas ?) and Chaldea (Kaldu) on the Persian Gulf, took the lead. Involved in endless wars with Assyria, which had in the meantime become independent, it grew weaker and weaker, and was at last completely conquered. But the humiliated Babylon avenged itself. Nabupaluṣur (Nabopolassar), allied with the Medes, laid Nineveh in ruins, and founded the new-Babylonian empire, which derived its greatest glory from his son Nabu-kudur-uṣur (Nebukadreṣar), and through him ruled for a time the civilised world. Maruduk and Nabu, the local deities of Babylon, whose worship, however, had also spread long before into Assyria, now occupied the place at the head of the world of gods, which had been so long held by the chief god of the Assyrians, whose name now disappears entirely—a change exactly analogous to that which took place in Egypt.

The Babylonians were the teachers of the Assyrians, as the Akkadians had before taught them. The library of Sargina I. (placed conjecturally about 2000 B.C.) consisted, according to what we know of it through Asurbanipal, of a collection of texts, partly in Akkadian and partly translated from Akkadian. Extensive ruins bear witness to the great power of the oldest kings, and choicely-cut seals indicate the advance of art in early times. As artists, however, the Assyrians stood higher.

Nabupaluṣur was an Assyrian general, who, after having put down a rising in Chaldea, was appointed viceroy of Babylon.

44. The religion of the Babylonians and Assyrians, hitherto known only imperfectly from the statements of the ancients and the fragments of Berosus, has received new light through the decipherment of the cuneiform character. This has rendered the actual sources themselves accessible, and the monuments prove conclusively that the Mesopotamian Semites adopted the religion of the original occupants of the country almost entirely, and fused it with their own.

All the principal gods of the Akkadians reappear in the Babylonio-Assyrian pantheon, the original names being sometimes preserved, sometimes partially modified in accordance with Semitic idiom, and sometimes translated. Old-Semitic deities to which counterparts were found among the Akkadians, were amalgamated with the latter. Among these may be named Samas, the sun-god, among the Semites originally a goddess; Sin, the moon-god; and Nabu, the prophet, the god of revelation, of letters and arts. Others were simply placed by the side of the corresponding Akkadian deities, the three Semitic moon-goddesses, for example, unknown to the Akkadians, being set beside Sin, perhaps also Dagan, the god of fertility, beside Bel of the underworld. The origin of Istar lies in obscurity, but she likewise, though under another name, existed already as an Akkadian goddess, who played an important part in the old mythology. For the Akkadian generic names of the gods a Semitic parallel was found in Ilu (Êl), who at a later date, like the supreme Bel, was sometimes placed at the head of all. The Assyrians assigned this elevated position to their national god Asur.

Hêa and Nirgal passed almost without any change from the Akkadian system into the Semitic. Nisruk is probably, and Salmanu is certainly, a Semitic surname of Hêa. Ana, the heaven-god, becomes *Anu*, "the hidden," Amarutuki is contracted into *Marduk*. The transformation of Nindar, the god of the solar fire and of generation, into *Adar*, "the shining," "the exalted," would exhibit a greater change if this reading, which is almost universally adopted, were at all certain. The Semites named him *Ṣamdan*. The Semitic pronunciation of Yam or Yiv is uncertain; it is possibly Yav, according to others, Bin; the name which he bore among the Semites was *Ramanu*. Mul-ge and Nin-ge were translated into *Bel* and *Belit tihavit*, but the old characters were left unchanged. Sin and Nabu occur, apparently, in Sinai and Nebo, in North Arabia, and seem accordingly to be Semitic deities: their names have neither the sound nor the meaning of the corresponding Akkadian gods; they perhaps arose under Egyptian influence (Aah and Ṭhut). This is also true of Istar, whose worship, but little practised in Babylonia, was much more developed in Assyria, and who is certainly the same as Hathor. The agreement with the Bactrian *çtare*, "star" (dialectic *içtar*), on which I still laid stress in my *Vergelijk. Geschied.*, p. 348, seems to be accidental.

For the sign AN the Assyrians read *Ilu*, alike when it was employed for the Akkadian generic name of the gods, *Ana* or *Anab*, or for the name of the supreme god *Dingir* (in the full form *Dingira* and *Dingiri*). The correctness of the latter reading is doubted by Oppert without adequate grounds. See Syllabary, p. 14, *Transactions Soc. Bibl. Archæol.*, iii. 2, p. 508, and Norris, *Assyrian Dictionary*, s. v. AN.

45. Star-worship was not unknown to the Semites, but the highly-developed astrology and magic which we find among the Babylonians and Assyrians were derived from the Akkadians, and the more easily because their own religion was not wanting in points of connection. Of Akkadian origin also was the regularly-organised priesthood, to whose learning and moral influence the triumph of the religion of the conquered nation over that of the conquerors must certainly be in the first place ascribed. The Babylonians, moreover, built their temples on the model furnished by their instructors, namely, in the form of terraced pyramids such as were erected also in Elam and among the oldest inhabitants of Media and India, to which class belonged the famous tower of Babel. In Assyria temples were also built on another plan.

The majority of the Assyrian priestly titles are pure Akkadian, *Sakan* and *Sakannakku*, the "high priest;" *Patesi*, the "vicar" or "lieutenant of the gods;" *Emga* (literally, "the illustrious," "the glorious"), "the Magian," &c.

The principal sanctuaries everywhere were terraced temples of this kind, representations of the mountain of the gods in the north, *i.e.*, of the heavenly spheres. The number of terraces varied, being either three, as at Ur, after the second triad of gods or the three worlds; or five, as at Kalach, after the five planets; or seven, as at Barzipa (near Babylon), at Chorsabad (Dur-Saryukin), and elsewhere, after the five planets with the sun and moon. The terraces, like those also at Ecbatana in Media, were of different colours. At the top stood a square chapel, containing an image. The opinion of Lenormant, that the Assyrian *Zikurats*, as these structures were called, served not as temples, but for the observation of the stars, is contradicted by an inscription of the Assyrian king Raman-nirari, in which he says of the god Nabu that he dwells in the temple of Bit-Zida in the midst of Kalach, and this was a terraced temple. See *West. As. Inscrr.*, i. pl. 35, No. 2.

46. Our sources do not yet enable us to trace the internal development of the Babylonio-Assyrian religion, although it is possible to point out which were the dominant gods in each of the three great periods of its history. Even while it was subject to Assyria, Babylon remained the religious centre, the holy city *par excellence*; and whatever hostility might exist between the monarchs of the two provinces, the gods of the city, so far as they were still unknown to the Assyrians, were readily accepted by them, and received equal honour with their own highest deities. Outwardly, there was no more difference between their religion and the Babylonian than might be expected to result from their early migration to the north. Inwardly, however, there were varieties of development in the two kindred nations, because the Assyrians, with their rougher climate and on their barren soil, grew into a race quite unlike the highly-civilised but somewhat effeminate Babylonians who were bathed in abundance.

It is not surprising, therefore, that of the two chief sacrifices which their religion prescribed, and which were probably both practised among the Akkadians, the sacrifice of chastity was more in vogue in Babylon, and human sacrifices prevailed among the Assyrians. By the latter people the gods of war, by the former those of knowledge and civilisation, were the most zealously served. The same deity who was feared at Nineveh and Kalach especially on account of the destructive violence of his storms, Ramanu (Yav), the god of wind and spirit, was chiefly worshipped at Babylon as the god of understanding. In short, the Babylonian religion, being that of a people principally devoted to agriculture, industry, and learning, was distinguished by its luxurious character and influential hierarchy; the Assyrian, on the other hand, as that of a war-loving, conquering nation, by rude conceptions and cruel usages.

In the oldest times Ur, Uruch, Agane, and other cities were the principal royal residences of Chaldea. The greatness of Babylon, at any rate, as a Semitic city, does not begin till the reign of the famous 'Hammuragas, who established his residence there, probably in the eighteenth century B.C., and erected the great temple to Marduk. Neither this god nor Nabu appears on older Babylonian monuments, and for centuries after they are not found among the chief Assyrian gods, not even in the list of them given by Tuklat-palasar, 1130 B.C. It is not till 882 and 857 B.C. that they are named among the twelve or thirteen chief gods of Asurnazirpal and Salmanasar, and from that time onwards they were worshipped by the Assyrians with quite as much enthusiasm as by the Babylonians, especially after the marriage, about 800 B.C., of an Assyrian sovereign with a Babylonian princess. The kings of Assyria often offered sacrifices in the temples of Babylon, Barzippa, and other Chaldean cities.

The difference which we have noted in religious development between the two nations, must not, therefore, be conceived too sharply. It is only a matter of degree. Assur was constantly endeavouring to tread in the footsteps of Babylon. The luxurious worship of the Chaldeans proved full of attraction for the Assyrians, and Nineveh became a centre of it as early as the thirteenth century B.C., alternating after the tenth century with Kalach. The last but one of the Assyrian kings, Asurbanipal, was a protector of civilisation, science, and letters.

47. Largely, however, as the Mesopotamian Semites borrowed from their predecessors, their religion reached a really higher stage. What they adopted, they developed; and on all foreign elements they impressed the stamp of their own spirit. The nature-beings whom they invoked in imitation of the Akkadians, became among them real gods, raised above nature and ruling it, as they had never done before. Above the highest triads they placed a god whose commands all the others reverenced, as the head of an unlimited theocracy. If magic and augury remained prominent constituents of their ceremonial religion, they practised besides a real worship, and gave utterance to a vivid sense of sin, a deep feeling of man's dependence, even of his nothingness before God, in prayers and hymns hardly less fervent than those of the pious souls of Israel.

Such a supreme god was *Bilu-Bili*, "the Lord of Lords," at Babylon, and Asur in Assyria, both being sometimes called briefly Ilu, "god." The Akkadian Dingira, with whom he was identified, appears in general not to have occupied so high a position. The prefect of Kalach, under King Raman-nirari, even says in an inscription, "Put your trust in Nabu, and trust in no other god!"

Examples of Assyrian prayers and hymns may be

found in my *Vergelijk. Geschied.*, p. 391, *sqq.*, and in Schrader, *Die Höllenfahrt der Istar*, Nos. 2–9.

48. In the religion of the Sabeans of South Arabia, made known to us by the decipherment of the Himyaritic inscriptions, by the side of the national gods of a genuinely Arabic character—such as the principal god Al-makah ("the god who hearkens"), the female sun-deity Shamsh, and others—we meet with a number of purely Babylonio-Assyrian gods, but always under their Semitic names or surnames. Among these are included the supreme Bel, the moon-god Sin, the goddess Istar in two forms, the male A*th*tar and the female A*th*tareṭ, and Ṣimdan, which can only be the Assyrian name of Nindar. These instances of agreement, to which must be added others in the territory of art, may not be invoked as proof that the religion of the Sabeans is a branch of the Assyrian, but receive their best explanation from commercial relations between Chaldea and South Arabia, which were already at an early period, as is well known, exceedingly active.

It must not be forgotten that the Himyaritic inscriptions with which we are acquainted are all of a relatively late date, from the first centuries of our era. Whether the South Arabic god *Nasr*, the "eagle," is a modification of Nisruk, as Hêa was surnamed, is uncertain, and appears to me doubtful.

C. *Religion among the West Semites.*

Literature.—On the Phenicians, see the *Inscriptions* edited and translated by HAMAKER (antiquated), GESENIUS

(*Monumenta Phœn.*), RENAN (*Mission en Phénic.*), DE VOGÜÉ (*Inscrr. Sémit.*), MEIER (*Erklärung Phœniz. Sprachdenkmale*, 1860, and *Ueber die Nabat. Inschrr.*, 1863, neither of them deserving of much confidence), and others. M. A. LEVY, *Phönizische Studien*, 4 parts, Breslau, 1856–70 (the first part containing a translation of the great Sidonian inscription), indispensable. Id., *Siegel und Gemmen mit Aram. Phöniz., &c., Inschriften*, ibid., 1869. On the great Sidonian inscription, K. SCHLOTTMANN, *Die Inschrift Eshmunazars Kön. der Sidonier*, Halle, 1868, and the literature on the subject, ibid., p. 9, *sqq*. The essay by H. EWALD, in the *Abhandl. der Königl. Gesellsch. der Wissenschaften in Götting.*, 1856, leaves much to be desired. See further DE VOGÜÉ, *Mélanges d'Archæol. Orient.*, Paris, 1868.

On Sanchoniathon, BUNSEN, *Egypt's Place*, &c., v. p. 793, *sqq*. EWALD, *Abhandl. über die Phön. Ansicht von der Weltschöpfung und der geschichtl. Werth Sanchon.*, Göttingen, 1851. RENAN, "Mémoire sur l'Origine et le Caract. Vérit. de l' Hist. Phén. de Sanch.," *Mém. Acad. Inscr. et Belles Lettres*, xxiii. 1858, p. 241, *sqq*. W. W. GRAF BAUDISSIN, "Ueber die Relig. Geschichtl. Werth der Phönic. Geschichte Sanchoniathon's" in the *Studien*, cited below, pp. 1–46. *Sanchoniathon's Urgeschichte der Phönic.*, by WAGENFELD, Hanover, 1836, is a literary fraud.

The treatise of F. C. MOVERS, *Die Phönizier*, vol. i., *Untersuchungen über die Religion, und die Gottheiten der Phön.*, Bonn, 1841, vol. ii., *Das Phöniz. Alterth.*, 3 parts, Berlin, 1849-56, and his article "Phœnizien" in Ersch and Gruber's *Allg. Encyclopaedie*, xxiv. pp. 319-443, must still be consulted, in spite of his adventurous hypotheses. On the Phenician religion, see further MÜNTER'S *Religion der Karthager*, and *Der Tempel der Himmlischen Göttin zu Paphos*, Copenhagen, 1824. C. P.

TIELE, *Vergelijk. Gesch.*, p. 415, *sqq.* AL. MÜLLER, "Astarte" (*Sitzungs Berichte der Wiener Akad.*, April 10, 1861), and "Esmun" (ibid., February 24, 1864).

It is unnecessary to give a list here of the extensive literature on the ancient history and religion of Israel, which may easily be found elsewhere. Of the recent works on Hebrew mythology and polytheism, I name only H. OORT, *De Dienst der Baälim onder Israël*, Haarlem, 1864. Id., *Het Menschenoffer in Israël*, ibid., 1865. A. BERNSTEIN, *The Origin of the Legends of Abraham, Isaac, and Jacob*, transl. from the German, London (no date). W. G. COM. DE BAUDISSIN, *Jahve et Moloch, sive de ratione inter Deum Israelitarum et Molochum intercedente*, Leipzig, 1874. Id., *Studien zur Semit. Religionsgesch.*, part i., Leipzig, 1876. I. GOLDZIHER, *Mythology among the Hebrews*, transl. by Russell Martineau, M.A., London, 1877. M. SCHULTZE, *Handbuch der Ebräischen Mythologie*, Nordhausen, 1876, full of the most hazardous conjectures and the wildest combinations.

49. The religion of the Western branch of the Northern Semites, the Arameans, Canaanites, and Phenicians, bore quite a different relation to the Babylonio-Assyrian from that of the Sabeans. They did indeed occasionally adopt, even in historical eras, the worship of one or another deity from the Assyrians, but the resemblances between their mythology and the Mesopotamian date from prehistoric times, and confirm the tradition that they themselves also once dwelt in the land of the Two Rivers. They must have quitted it before the fusion of the religious system of the Akkadians with the Semitic was so complete, as we already find it among the early Babylonians. At any rate, neither the two triads nor the Akkadian deities belonging to them, neither Ṣamdan nor Marduk, occur among them. Only of the worship of Sin and Nabu do any clear traces present themselves around and in Canaan; but these deities appear to have been already the property of the Semites before their entry into Mesopotamia. The names Ba'al and Ba'alith, however, applied to their principal gods, 'Ashtoreth, perhaps also Asher and Ashera and 'Anath, can only have been brought by Canaanites and Phenicians from Chaldea.

That Ba'al and Ba'alith were generic names of the principal deities, or rather simple epithets, only occasionally applied in later times for brevity to a particular god, has been proved, in my judgment, in my *Vergelijk. Geschied.*, pp. 452–458. I have, indeed, seen it denied (for example, by Graf Baudissin in his *Jahve et Moloch*, p. 35), but not refuted. I observe with satisfaction that Dr. Matthes, in his article "Mythen in het O.T." in the *Theol. Tijdschr.*, 1877, No. ii., accords with my views. Further investigation has confirmed me in this belief. Schrader's correct observation that the Babylonian Bel and the Phenician Ba'al are not identical, I would rather express by saying that the principal deities of the Babylonians and Phenicians do not correspond, except in the circumstance that they both of them bore the title of Bel-Ba'al, "Lord."

'Ashtoreth is no other than Istar with a feminine termination, in accordance with the Phenician idiom. Asher and Ashera correspond tolerably well with the Assyrian Asir and Asirat, the first being probably the original form of the name of the god Asur (the "propitious," the "giver of prosperity"), and the second a surname of Istar. But I do not offer this as more than a conjecture.

50. The same remarks hold good in still higher measure of their cosmogony, and of many of their myths. Myths such as those of the fighting and dying sun-god (Melqarth, Samson), of the spring-god who likewise dies (Adonis, Tammuz), their legends of Paradise and the Flood, and several other of their ideas and usages, were all Akkadian in origin, and could only have attained their Semitic form in Mesopotamia. From the Akkadians, in like manner, were probably derived the cruel and unchaste forms of worship which distinguished them from the other Semites, as well as the consecration of the seventh day as a Sabbath or day of rest, the institution of which cannot therefore be ascribed to Moses.

On the myth of Samson, which was applied in Phenicia both to Melqarth and to Eshmun, see Kuenen, *The Religion of Israel*, i. p. 307. Schwartz, *Sonne, Mond und Sterne*, pp. 130, *sqq.*, 221, *sqq.* Steinthal, in the *Zeitschr. für Völkerpsych. und Sprachwissensch.*, ii., p. 129, *sqq.*, translated in the appendix to Goldziher's *Mythology among the Hebrews*, p. 392, *sqq.* Meyboom, *Raadselachtige Verhalen*, and *Godsd. der Noormannen*, p. 270. The god is no other than the Assyro-Akkadian Herakles, Nindar, or Ṣamdan, the dead sun-god, represented as a giant who strangles a lion. The Adonis myth, also, in which the youthful god of the spring, the beloved of Istar, dies, and is mourned by her, has now been discovered in the Akkado-Babylonian epos. See Lenormant, *Le Déluge*, pp. 25, 29. G. Smith, *Daily Telegraph*, Sept. 20, 1873. Schrader, in the *Zeitschr. der Deutsch. Morgenländ. Gesellsch.*, xxvii. p. 424, is of opinion that even the name Tammuz was not unknown in Mesopotamia. This view is also shared by Lenormant.

That the Sabbath, the rest-day, on the seventh day of the week, passed to the Semites from the Akkadians, was conjectured by Oppert and Schrader, and has now been proved from the texts by Sayce, *Academy*, Nov. 27, 1875, p. 554, *cf. Trans. Soc. Bibl. Archæol.*, 1874, p. 207. In the *West. Asian Inscrr.*, ii. 32, 16, the very word *sabatuv* occurs in a vocabulary, with the explanation, "a day of rest for the heart."

51. The development of this religion among the Phenicians possessed a special character of its own. An industrial, seafaring, and commercial people, they gave a national form to the Mesopotamian myths, and moulded the god Eshmun with the Kabiri, and Ba'al 'Hamman, the god of the solar fire, with his consort Tanith, into the representatives and propagators of Phenician civilisation. In many respects their theology agrees with that of the Israelites. In later times they seem to have been completely dominated by Egyptian influence, and, in their eagerness to imitate the Hamitic civilisation, to have brought even their religion, at any rate externally, into concord with it.

Perhaps even Eshmun and the Kabiri were derived from Egypt. These last I formerly regarded erroneously as the gods of the seven planets. They rather correspond with the seven helpers of the creative deities Ptah and Chnum, with whose functions we have become better acquainted through monuments recently deciphered. *Asmunu*, however, occurs in the Babylonian inscriptions.

52. The culminating-point of the religion of the

Northern Semites was reached in that of Israel. During the thirteenth century before Christ a considerable portion of Canaan was gradually conquered by this small nation. They entered the country on different sides, possessing a religion of extreme simplicity, though not monotheistic. It did not differ in character from the Arabian, and approached most nearly, it would seem, to that of the Qenites. Their ancient national god bore the name of El-Shaddai, but it is not without reason that their great leader Moses is supposed to have established in its place before this period the worship of Yahveh. To him also was ascribed the composition of a fundamental religious and moral law, the so-called Ten Words. Undoubtedly this deity, by whatever name they may have designated him, was the dreadful and stern god of the thunder, whose character corresponded to the nature which surrounded them and the life which they led.

The history of the development of the Israelite religion requires to be studied independently. I state here only what is necessary to bring out clearly the relation in which it stands to kindred forms of worship. Moreover, the brief summary here presented needs no detailed explanation, since ample expositions of the subject will be found in Kuenen's *Religion of Israel*, my own *Vergelijkende Geschiedenis*, and other recent works.

The latest discoveries in the field of ancient Babylonian literature give rise to the question whether the traditions of the Israelites about their origin really belonged to them, or whether they appropriated them from the Canaanites. Does the tradition of Abraham's migration from Ur of the Chaldees, and of the sojourn of the patriarchs in Canaan and Egypt, really furnish us with a preliminary history of the Israelites wrapped up in legends, or did they find it in existence in Canaan and adopt it? In other words, were the tribes of Israel originally a branch of the Northern Semites, or were they a branch of the Southern Semites related to the Ishmaelites, who only mingled with the Northern Semites when settled in their new abode, and there became acquainted with the civilisation brought by their kinsmen from Mesopotamia? Before these questions are solved by further inquiry, all that we can say with certainty of the origin of the Israelites is that they belong to the Semitic race, and I have therefore been purposely silent on the subject in the text.

53. This religion they did not abandon in their new fatherland, although it was really sometimes in danger of being supplanted. At first the Israelites, or those of them, at least, who had settled on the west of the Jordan, placed their national god Yahveh by the side of the Canaanite deity of the country, whom they called briefly "the Baal," and whom most of them, after they had renounced their wandering shepherd-life and begun to devote themselves to agriculture, worshipped together with Ashera, the goddess of fertility, and other native deities. As the god of the conquerors, however, Yahveh was still commonly placed above the others. Even his ardent worshippers, such as some of the judges, and especially Samuel, only maintained his supremacy; and such zealous champions of Yahvism as Saul and David named their children after the Baal. Solomon, who erected a splendid temple for Yahveh in his capital, saw no harm in building sanctuaries for other gods as well, which was regarded as a sin, indeed, by the later historians, but cer-

tainly not by his contemporaries. The Baal against which the stern Elijah contended so vigorously in the kingdom of Israel, was not the deity of the country; it was the Phenician Baal, introduced by the wife of Ahab, the Sidonián princess Jezebel. Elijah's disciple Elisha, and his follower Jehu, rooted out this foreign cultus with violence, but did not interfere with that of the native Ashera.

54. In the meantime, largely through the instrumentality, it would seem, of the prophetic schools, the stricter Yahvism had quietly, and even imperceptibly to itself, adopted a number of elements from the native religion, and brought them into harmony with its spirit and requirements. This appears especially in the cosmogony, the narratives of Paradise, of the Deluge, and others, the myth of Samson, the legend of the patriarch Jacob-Israel—particularly in that of his quarrel with his brother Esau, who plays a similar part in Phenician mythology, and is also named in the Assyrian inscriptions—and more of the same kind. To the conception of Yahveh, also, as the dreadful god of the desert, there were slowly added various traits borrowed from that of the beneficent Baal, the god of blessing and abundance. By this process the representation of Yahveh was gradually softened, without, however, losing its original character. There was now no longer any reason for supplementing his worship with that of the Canaanite god of agriculture; Yahveh was now sufficiently like the latter to be able, even alone, to satisfy the wants of the nation when it was civilised and settled.

55. This gradual modification of the conception of deity paved the way for the reforming work of the great prophets, who began in the eighth century before Christ to insist on the exclusive worship of Yahveh. To attain this end, they contended not only against the cruel worship of the god of fire, called by the Israelites briefly "the Molek," to whom in the Assyrian period, following probably the example of their neighbours, they sacrificed children and men, but also against the cultus of the native Baal, and even against the purely national worship dedicated to the sun, moon, and stars, to which not a few of the Israelites had always remained faithful. Some kings, such as Hezekiah and Josiah, devoted themselves to carrying out their doctrine; other princes, however, supported by the majority of the people, maintained the old and the new nature-gods. It was not till the establishment of a priestly state by the small section of the nation who returned to the fatherland after the captivity, that Yahveh was recognised as the only god, and there was no further mention of any Baal or Molek.

Molek is the old Akkadian fire-god, who was blended in Assyria partly with Anu, partly with Adar, and was worshipped in the same fashion by Phenicians, Moabites, Ammonites, and other kindred tribes. It is uncertain whether the prominence which his worship acquired in Israel after the ninth century, must be ascribed to Assyrian influence or to local causes.

56. The prophets, however, were not only the teachers of their people, but also the interpreters of whatever passed in the inmost heart of the nation. The monotheism which

was the last and ripest fruit of the preaching of the prophets before the captivity, grew slowly, and remained, besides, purely national. Out of the conception of Yahveh's supremacy over the other gods of the country sprang the idea of his sole lordship over Israel. Beyond this idea the first prophets of the reformed Mosaism made no great advance. Even the Book of Deuteronomy, which is written entirely in their spirit, still assigns to each people a deity of its own, while the Most High retains Israel for himself. It is not till Jeremiah that utterance is given to the thought that Yahveh is the eternal God, besides whom there exists no other, and in contrast with whom the other gods are nothing but emptiness, and the Babylonian Isaiah, with more emphasis and genius, develops the same conception. The pantheistic monotheism of the Aryans, which regards all deities simply as names of the One, the All-embracing and Infinite, remained unknown to them; and to the universalist monotheism of the Gospel, which has entirely broken down the bounds of nationality, not even the noblest of them was able to rise. The great value of the preaching of the prophets lies in its ethical character, and in the pure and elevated representation which it gave of their Yahveh. But even this conception of deity is still one-sided, and their universalism continues particularist. What they opposed to the religions of other nations was not a universal religion, but simply their own national religion, and they expected that every one would be converted to it, and would recognise the sole supremacy of their national god. This expectation is the highest expression of the theocratic belief which rules the whole Semitic life, the conclusion to which the reflective mind was necessarily impelled by progressive development, when it had once adopted as its point of departure the idea of the unlimited sovereignty of a God in contrast with whom man is nothing more than a slave.

57. This prophetic movement gave rise to a religious sect, or nomistic religion, the foundations of which were firmly laid before the captivity by the code prepared under Josiah, and during the captivity and after it by Ezekiel and the priestly legislation, and which was organised, chiefly by Ezra, as a priestly community. Out of the Mosaism of the prophets grew Judaism. Superficially considered, the period of Israelite religious history which now ensued, appears an era not of progress but of exclusion and petrifaction. In reality this is not the case. The Jewish mind took into itself new elements, which worked and fermented in silence till they produced a nobler thought. Before the gaze of Israel opened a world hitherto unknown. It came into contact with the Indo-Germans, first with the Persians, then with the Greeks, and lastly with the Romans. Pârsism attracted them by its ethical tendency, though they could make no terms with the dualism on which it rested, the doctrine of two Creators, one good and one evil; it even seems that the great prophet of the captivity denounced it (Isa. xlv. 7). But the prominence and the large development attained among them after the captivity by the doctrine of good and evil angels, can only be ascribed to Persian influence, and Persian representations may be recognised no less clearly in their eschatology.

The Greek polytheism, which it was sought to force upon them with violence, they resisted obstinately and successfully, and the Romans they hated. But Greek humanism and Greek philosophy made their way unobserved even among them, and the struggle with the universal sovereignty of Rome caused their ancient ideal, the kingdom of God, the universal sovereignty of the only true God, to awake with new power. Out of the mutual co-operation of these factors, the union of Israelite piety with Persian morality, Greek humanism, and a universalism vying with that of Rome—in other words, out of the alliance of the Semitic with the Indo-Germanic mind—arose the mighty universal religion which reconciles them both, and has nowhere found so many adherents and reached so high a development as among the Indo-Germanic nations of Europe.

On the debts of Judaism to Pârsism, see Kuenen's *Religion of Israel*, vol. iii. pp. 1–44. A. Kohut, "Ueber die jüdische Angelologie und Dämonologie in ihrer Abhängigkeit vom Parsismus," in *Abhandl. für die Kunde des Morgenl.*, iv. 3. Id., "Was hat die Talmüd. Eschatologie aus dem Parsismus aufgenommen?" in the *Zeitschr. der Deutsch. Morgenl. Gesellsch.*, xxi. vi. pp. 552–591.

D. *Islâm.*

Literature. — Translations of the *Qorân*, by WAHL, Halle, 1848; SALE, London, 1836; KASIMIRSKI, with introduction by PAUTHIER, Paris, 1840; ULLMANN, Crefeld, 1840; RODWELL, London, 2d ed. (chronologically arranged, but very hypothetical). Some of these translations reproduced in Dutch by S. KEYZER, Haarlem, 1860.

Cf. TH. NÖLDEKE, *Geschichte des Qorâns*, Göttingen, 1860. G. K. NIEMANN, *De Korân*, Rotterdam, 1864. G. WEIL, *Muhamed der Prophet, sein Leben und seine Lehre*, 1843, and *Gesch. der Islam. Völker von Mohammed bis zur Zeit des Sultans Selim*, Stuttgart, 1866. Sir W. MUIR, *The Life of Mahomet and History of Islam*, 4 vols., London, 1858–61. A. SPRENGER, *Das Leben und die Lehre des Mohammad*, 3 vols., Berlin, 1861–65. R. DOZY, *Het Islamisme*, Haarlem, 1863, and *De Israëliten te Mekka van Davids tijd tot in de 5e eeuw onzer tijdrekening*, ibid., 1864.

G. K. NIEMANN, *Inleiding tot de kennis van den Islam*, Rotterdam, 1861. A. VON KREMER, *Geschichte der herrschenden Ideen des Islams*, Leipzig, 1868; *Culturgeschichtliche Streifzüge auf dem Gebiete des Islams*, ibid., 1873; and *Culturgeschichte des Orients unter den Chalifen*, 2 vols. Vienna, 1875–77. On Islam in India, GARCIN DE TASSY, *L'Islamisme d'après le Coran*, &c., Paris, 1874.

58. The purely Semitic universal religion is Islamism, which first arose in Arabia six hundred years after Christ. Some tribes had already abandoned their ancestral religion for Christianity in its Jewish or Ebionitish form, and the Jews also had made a number of converts. But neither the one nor the other religion had any great attraction for the Arabs; the one was too exclusively national, the other too dogmatic. Yet they imperceptibly brought about a modification of the religious conceptions, at least of the more advanced. There were poets before Mohammed who already displayed a deep conviction of the unity of God, and of man's responsibility towards him. A definite sect, even, had been formed, the Hanyfites, who rejected both Judaism and Christianity, and preached a very simple practical monotheistic doc-

trine, which they probably already designated Islâm. The ancient Fetishism was still kept up simply by habit, and by the personal interest of tribes or families, but few retained any belief in their idols. Even for those who still remained faithful to the national gods, Allâh was the Sheikh of the spirits (*Jinn*), and these were his daughters; nay, the worship of the fetishes was even justified by the assertion that they were invoked only as mediators with Allâh. Meanwhile the chief god possessed neither temples nor priests; of the sacrifices he received the worst part, and only in extraordinary circumstances did men pass by the gods who stood nearer to man, in order to seek a refuge with him. The seers (*'Arrâf*) and the soothsaying priests (*Kâhin*) had lost a great deal of their credit, religion was in deep decline, and a number of phenomena indicated that the need of a better was awakened.

Judaism and Christianity had given currency to the doctrines of one God, and of retribution, as well as to the ideas of a revelation and the moral government of the world.

The Hanyfites are commonly regarded as a sect which arose under the influence of the above-named religions. The name *hanyf*, "heretic," "unbeliever," may in that case have been given to them by Christians and Jews, because their belief was freer and also mingled with heathen errors. This is the view of Sprenger, i. 67. Dozy, in the *Israëliten te Mekka*, has defended the opinion that the Hanyfites were a remnant of the Israelites, who first made their way to Arabia in the time of David, and subsequently after the destruction of Jerusalem by Nebukadresar. Their doctrine, which they called *Dîn*

Ibrahîm, would in that case be, not "the belief of Abraham," but "the belief of the Hebrews," and the so-called heathen traditions and usages at Mekka which Mohammed adopted, would be originally derived from the Israelites.

Islâm (nom. verb.) signifies "submission," "surrender" to God. The professors of the doctrine took the name of *Moslim* (partic.), "the believer," "one who is blindly obedient to all God's commands" (Sprenger, i. 69; Dozy, *Islamisme*, 26).

Jinn, derived by Sprenger, i. 221, from a root meaning "to cover," "to veil," is erroneously explained by him as the "darkening of the mind." If the derivation is correct, the word must have been applied to the spirits, as the hidden and invisible, or to the fetishes, as the outward abodes of the spirits.

59. To constitute Hanyfism into a religion, a fixed doctrine, an organised worship, and a divine sanction were needed. These were provided by Mohammed. Born at Mekka in the year 571 A.D., of a family of distinction though of no great power, he was left an orphan at an early age, and was adopted by relatives. For a long time he was obliged to seek his maintenance in a lowly calling, till he became the third husband of a rich widow, Khadîjah, to whom he continued most closely attached till her death. It was not till he had reached the age of forty years that visions and ecstasies, the result of a sickly system and protracted religious meditations in gloomy solitude, brought him to the conviction that he was either insane or a messenger of God. The latter thought gained the victory. He felt himself called by God himself to be the prophet of the strictest monotheism, and he hesitated

not to obey the call. At first he found little belief outside the circle of his own family. Yet he had a powerful support in his wife, and in some friends of position. Among these last the foremost place is due to the intelligent and discerning Abu-bekr, and the courageous and elastic Omar, two men without whom Islam could never have triumphed. At Mekka, the preaching of Mohammed, whatever were the temporal or the eternal penalties with which he threatened the unbelievers, produced little other effect than ridicule and insult against himself and the persecution of his unprotected adherents. Twice were his followers obliged to retreat to Abyssinia, and when he recalled an utterance in favour of the ancient idolatry which had been extorted from him, the exasperation against him reached its height. He did not therefore hesitate long to comply with the invitation of the most vehement enemies of the people of Mekka, the inhabitants of Medina, who swore fidelity to him, and he fled thither with a number of his friends. This flight (the Hijra, 622–623 A.D.), is regarded by the Moslims as the first triumph of their faith, and is the starting-point of their chronology.

60. The favourable circumstances which surrounded Mohammed at Medina operated unfavourably upon his character. Beneath opposition and persecution he had displayed the courage of his conviction, but when he had once gained the mastery, the Prophet became an arbitrary tyrant, who gave the rein freely to all his passions. His vengefulness was felt by the Jews, who would not enrol themselves among his followers, and by those who had the misfortune to injure him. After the death of Khadîjah he began to keep a harem, to which he went on adding new wives, among them even the lawful wife of his adopted son. The scandal which such acts caused even among the faithful, was allayed by revelations received just as they were required, which can hardly be ascribed simply to self-deception, and must have been produced with intentional deceit. At Medina Mohammed instituted public worship, but he appears never to have lost sight of his great object, to make Mekka, already the centre of the national religion, the centre of his own religion. He preached the holy war, which was, however, inspired quite as much by desire of revenge and plunder, as by policy and fanaticism. After fighting against the Mekkans with varying success, he demanded permission to take part with his followers in the pilgrimage to the Ka'ba, and his request was granted under certain conditions. Not satisfied, however, with this, he violates the armistice, advances in the year 630 with a very considerable army against his native city, obtains possession of it by treachery, destroys the idols in the Ka'ba, forces the worship there practised into conformity with his own doctrine, and thus transforms the city which had rejected him into the chief seat, and its ancient temple into the principal sanctuary, of the true faith. All the Arab tribes now submitted, at any rate outwardly and simply out of fear, to Islâm, although the general rising after the death of the Prophet proves how superficial was their conversion. The idea of even universal dominion began to be entertained. Shortly after the pilgrimage to Mekka, Mohammed had already sent letters to different princes, even to the Roman emperor and the Persian king, demanding their submission; soon he despatched small armies beyond the boundaries, sometimes with considerable success, and he planned more and more distant expeditions. But the end approached with swift strides, and he felt that his task was finished. After a few days' illness, he collected all his strength to address the faithful in the Mosque once more, returned home exhausted, and died the same day, June 8th, 632, on the breast of his favourite wife, Ayesha, daughter of Abubekr, amid pious aspirations and in the firm hope of immortality.

61. The five pillars of Islâm, of which the foundations were laid in the teaching of Mohammed himself, are as follows: (1) the acceptance of the two great dogmas; (2) prayer, regarded rather as an outward religious action than as an impulse of the heart, all its forms therefore being regulated with precision; (3) almsgiving; (4) fasting, kept strictly in the month of Ramadhân from sunrise to sunset; (5) the pilgrimage to Mekka, which every free adult was bound to perform once in his life. The first of the two great dogmas is the doctrine of the unity of God, of whose existence the Prophet continually adduced proofs, but of whose nature he never attempted, or was not in a position, to form a pure conception. The Qorân is marked by a strong anthropomorphism, and well-attested traditions ascribe to Mohammed the assertion that he had seen the deity in human form. God is almighty and all-knowing, but terrible in his wrath: he rewards and punishes arbitra-

rily; he hardens the hearts of those whom he destines to destruction; and every one, therefore, must tremble before the fires of his hell. He requires men to surrender themselves to him with servile submission, yet not even then are they always sure of his grace. Such a representation of the deity naturally leads to the doctrine of unconditional predestination, and this was, accordingly, also taught by Mohammed; but he was too impulsive, and too little of a thinker, not to be untrue to it sometimes. Moreover, the strictness of his monotheism did not prevent him from admitting the *jinns* or spirits into his system; but he transformed them, in imitation of the Jews, into good and evil spirits, angels and devils, the latter of whom, however, were, in his view, capable of conversion.

Mohammed was very zealous in prayer and fasting, and spent whole nights in prayer with his disciples. Great value was ascribed to the invocation of the name of God (*dzikr*), not only mentally but aloud. All the ceremonies to be observed in connection with prayer, the lustrations, gestures, and genuflections, were arranged by the Prophet himself. Much value attached to their public performance. This duty was observed by 'Omar even in the days of the persecution. Sprenger, i. pp. 318, *sqq.*, 324, *sqq.;* comp. ii. p. 132.

The god of Mohammed stands no higher than the common Semitic ideal of morality. He is an arbitrary, vengeful, bloodthirsty tyrant, whose sombre traits are only rarely relieved by one of the brighter touches by which the Jewish prophets succeeded in throwing a kindly glow over the image of their Yahveh. Mohammed did not shrink from speaking even of Allâh's cunning. In the Qorân, *sur.* 8, 30, he is called the craftiest of the forgers of devices, who, by his own wiles, puts to shame those of unbelievers.

For the chief of the evil spirits, Mohammed even preserved the Hebrew name Satan, as well as the Christian name Iblîs (*Diabolos*).

62. With this gloomy conception of deity corresponds the view taken by Islâm of the world. The Qorân gives very frequent utterance to the idea that our earthly life has little value, and is but a passing game, while old traditions ascribe to Mohammed sayings in which the world is compared with all kinds of worthless objects. The door was thus opened for the severe asceticism in which the Moslims were soon to rival Christians and Buddhists. The misery of this world was only surpassed by the unspeakable pains of hell, which were depicted with the blackest colours. But with joyous expectation men might look to heaven, where in beautiful gardens, clothed with splendid garments, and surrounded by black-eyed girls, the blessed would drink the precious unintoxicating wine of paradise. The union of gloomy contempt for the world with luxurious sensuality is a characteristic of all Semitic religions, to which only Mosaic prophetism offers a favourable exception.

According to tradition, Mohammed compared the world to a sheep cast away by its owner, nay, even to a dung-heap with rotting bones. For unbelievers only is it a paradise.

While his doctrine looked for joy to the future only, the Prophet, with questionable consistency, contrived to secure here on earth a foretaste of the sensual bliss of heaven, a proceeding in which many believers have zealously imitated him.

63. Besides his faith in the unity of God, the Moslim must believe in the divine mission of Mohammed. This is the second main dogma. God has made known his will by thousands of prophets, one after another, of whom Adam, Noah, Abraham, Moses, and Jesus are the most eminent, while Mohammed is the last and greatest. God revealed himself in different ways; to Mohammed, however, for the most part through the angel Gabriel. The violent attacks of his chronic disease were regarded by him as divine inspirations, but not till his return to consciousness did he give utterance to any words. At first he undoubtedly believed with complete sincerity in the reality of these relations; afterwards, however, in the days of his power, they often came just at the right moment to justify him, to remove some scandal, or enable him to attain some definite end. Frequently they conflicted with each other, and the later were employed to modify or revoke the earlier. The conception was entirely mechanical. But they were always blindly believed and obeyed by his followers. Recorded in part during his life, and in part preserved by memory, they were not collected until after his death. This collection, fixed once for all, bears the name of Qorân, and is regarded by the orthodox as the uncreated word of God, though they also attach great authority to tradition (Sonna).

The modes of revelation also included dreams, such as that of Mohammed's journey to Jerusalem by night, and of his ascension to heaven. The symptoms of his disease have led many to regard it as epilepsy, but Sprenger considers it to have been *hysteria muscularis.* The angel Gabriel is a product of his imagination, not an unknown impostor, as Weil supposes. The form in which the Prophet himself cast his revelations was a rhymed prose, without any poetic value, but not free from rhetorical bombast.

When his numerous harem and his marriage with the wife of his adopted son gave general offence, he immediately provided divine revelations to justify himself. When severe vigils, enjoined by God, exhausted him too seriously, came a new command, kept secret all that while by God, to mitigate the old order; and when Mohammed, after having refrained from contending against the idols, began to oppose them with great energy, it was said that God had not desired him to do so until then.

The revelations were called *Qorân* (to "read," to "explain"), or *Sûra* ("line of a book," "chapter"). After they were collected, the first name became the title of the whole, while the second was used to designate particular revelations. Both words are of Hebrew origin. The first collection was made by Mohammed's secretary, Zaid ibn Thâbit, by order of Abu-bekr and 'Omar, and for their use. The second proceeded afterwards from the same hand, in conjunction with some others. All the texts not inserted in it were then destroyed.

64. The religion founded by Mohammed is exclusively Semitic, for in doctrine and organisation it is purely theocratic. God is the sole, absolute, and arbitrary sovereign, standing in an attitude of hostility against the world, revealing himself mechanically by his prophets, and especially by the last of them, to whose words and commands all must blindly submit. Mohammed himself, also, was both in his virtues and his vices a genuine Semite. His teaching contained nothing original; the whole of his preaching had been already put forth before him, and was adopted by him from Judaism, from Eastern Christianity, and from Hanyfism, and at first he even designated himself a Hanyf. Even the idea of his prophetic calling he borrowed from the Jews. His visions were the result of his sickly condition. His preaching was not, however, merely an imitation of others, but the result of the overpowering impression which the religion of the Jews and their spiritual kindred made upon his mind, and which impelled him to oppose the worship of idols, and proclaim monotheism. He believed in his calling, accepted it from conviction, and on account of it for a long time courageously bore ridicule and abuse.

Before Mohammed, his older contemporary Zaid ibn 'Amr, a Hanyf, had vigorously opposed the idolatry of the Mekkans. Mohammed was acquainted with him, and was certainly much indebted to him. See Dozy, *Isl.*, p. 14; Sprenger, i. p. 119, *sqq.* Another view is taken by Nöldeke, *Gesch. des Qor.*, p. 14. The influence also of the Christians upon the Prophet must have been considerable (Sprenger, ii. p. 180, *sqq.*) Waraka, the nephew of Khadîjah, was a Christian, and was even canonised by Mohammed (Sprenger, i. p. 124, *sqq.*)

65. The history of the subsequent development of Islâmism lies beyond our compass. It must, however, be observed that the death of the Prophet was followed immediately by a great defection through the whole of Arabia, which was only suppressed by violence, and that

the mastery soon came into the hands of the party which had the most vehemently opposed Mohammed during his lifetime. In its doctrines, especially in its conception of God, and above all in its moral value, Islâm is far inferior not only to Christianity, but also to Mosaism and to Judaism. But over the degraded forms of these religions, which prevailed in Arabia and other Eastern countries, it deserves the preference. The elements which qualified it, in distinction from Judaism, to become a universal religion, lay, first of all, in its freedom from the bonds of a particular nationality, and next, in the ease with which it could be summed up in two simple doctrines. What Buddhism possessed in the doctrine of *Nirvâṇa*, and Christianity in the preaching of love, Islâm found in the formula—"There is no God but God, and Mohammed is his prophet." Its triumph in Arabia was due to political considerations, and to the absence of anything better to occupy the field. The way for its diffusion beyond was paved by arms, and the pecuniary and civil privileges conferred on believers among vanquished peoples, secured for it a multitude of adherents. True and zealous followers it found only among nations of imperfect development, such as the superficial Christians of Egypt, North Africa, and Spain, among the Berbers, Negroes, Malays, and Turks. In Persia and India it only conquered by force. The Persians were always regarded as heretics, and the Mohammedan are, for the most part, distinguished from the Brahmanical Hindus only by a few forms. Founded among a people which developed late, it is the youngest and also the lowest of the universal religions. Only for a short time, under the stimulus of favouring circumstances, and in conflict with its own principles, did it call forth a higher civilisation. When carried out with due strictness it brings all civilisation to nothing.

> Monotheism in itself, when the one God does not combine everything that is divine, and the conception of deity is one-sided and limited, by no means possesses the great value commonly ascribed to it.
>
> As a universal religion, Islâm did not grow out of the Arabian polydæmonism, but, like Christianity and Buddhism, out of a nomistic religion.

CHAPTER IV.

RELIGION AMONG THE INDO-GERMANS, EXCLUDING THE GREEKS AND ROMANS.

I.

THE ANCIENT INDO-GERMAN RELIGION AND THE ARYAN RELIGION PROPER.

Literature.—Lieut.-Col. VANS KENNEDY, *Researches into the Nature and Affinity of Ancient Hindu Mythology*, London, 1831. R. ROTH, "Die höchsten Götter der Arischen Völker," in *Zeitschr. der Deutsch. Morgenländ. Gesellsch.*, vi., 1852, p. 67, *sqq.* A. PICTET, *Les Origines Indo-Européennes, ou les Aryas Primitifs*, 2 vols., Paris, 1859–63, now antiquated in some parts. M. MÜLLER, *Lectures on the Science of Language*, 2 vols., especially lects. viii.–xii. of the second vol., London, 6th ed., 1873. G. W. COX, *The Mythology of the Aryan Nations*, 2 vols., London, 1870. A. DE GUBERNATIS, *Zoological Mythology, or the Legends of Animals*, 2 vols., London, 1872. A. KUHN, *Die Herabkunft des Feuers und des Götter-tranks*, Berlin, 1859. L. MYRIANTHEUS, *Die Açvins oder die Arischen Dioskuren*, Munich, 1876. G. SCHOEBEL, *Recherches sur la Religion première de la Race Indo-Iranienne*, Paris, 1872; and K. M. BANERJEA, *The Aryan Witness, or the Testimony of Aryan Scriptures in corroboration of . . . Christian Doctrine*, Calcutta, 1875, both written under the influence of a theological system, and largely hypothetical.

P. Asmus, *Die Indo-Germanische Religion in den Hauptpunkten ihrer Entwickelung*, vol. i. Halle, 1875, vol. ii. (part 1st), 1877.

66. Comparative mythology has proved that all Indo-Germans, or Aryans in the broadest sense, including the Indians, Persians, Wends or Letto-Slavs, Germans, Greeks, Romans, and Kelts, once possessed not only the same language, but also the same religion. This religion cannot have differed much in character from the Indo-Germanic religions known to us from historic times. It is certain that they named their gods "the heavenly," or the "shining ones," (*deva, deus, tîvar*), a name which was preserved among the Indians, Romans, Scandinavians, and Letto-Slavs, and probably also among the Greeks (θεός), being replaced among the remaining races by other designations, and employed by the Persians in an unfavourable sense. Their principal god, or, at any rate, the object of their highest worship, was the heaven-father (*Dyaus-pitar, Ζεὺς πατήρ, Jupiter*). Among the Greeks and Romans he was maintained in his supremacy; among the Indians he was, to some extent, supplanted by other deities, though even among them he always remained the father of the highest gods; but among the Germans (*Zio, Tyr*) he was entirely changed in character. By his side was then worshipped another heaven god (*Varuṉa, Ouranos*), perhaps a deity of the nightly sky, and probably of higher rank, of whom the Greeks retained only a faint recollection, though the Indians continued at first to stand in great awe of him. In the tempests and thunderstorms they saw, as the correspondence of myths proves, the contest of the gods of light against the powers of darkness, and they already

recognised and worshipped a fire-god, the friend of men, who stole fire from heaven. A female deity was regarded as the mediator or messenger between men and gods (*Ila, Iḍa, Ira*), or between gods and men (*Iris*). The sun-god (*Sûrya, Hvarĕ,* Ἥλιος, *Sol*) likewise, and the dawn-goddess (*Ushas,* Ἠώς, *Aurora*), were probably objects of adoration. We are not at liberty, therefore, to ascribe to them a kind of monotheism or henotheism at so early a period. It is even very doubtful whether their religion may be rightly called polytheism, or whether it was really more than a very advanced polydæmonism. The stage of development which they had reached, can in any case only be matter for conjecture, and does not admit of exact determination.

I keep the ugly but established designation "Indo-Germans," to distinguish the race from the Aryans proper, who were the ancestors of the Indians and Persians. The name Indo-Europeans is to be rejected on every account. The name Aryans may also be applied to the whole race, and the Indo-Persians may then be called East-Aryans. The name Indo-Germans indicates the two peoples between whom all the others belonging to the race are scattered.

The connection of the Greek θεός, also, with *deva*, is disputed by G. Buhler in *Orient und Occident*, i. p. 508, *sqq.*, by G. Curtius, and others.

Varuṇa signifies "the coverer," or the "surrounder." As he becomes later on the god of the ocean, he may originally have been the special ruler of the heaven-ocean, like Hea in Mesopotamia.

On the theft of fire and the agreement of *Pramâtha* and *Prometheus*, of the *Bhṛgu's* with the *Phlegians* (lightnings), and of *Bhuranyu* with *Phoroneus*, see the work of Kuhn cited above.

The opinion that the Indo-Germanic races began with monotheism or henotheism, is defended by Max Müller, *Introduction to the Science of Religion*, London, 1873, p. 170, *sqq.* See on the other side my essay in *De Gids*, 1871, No. 1, translated into German, *Max Müller und Fr. Schultze über ein Problem der Religions-Wissenschaft*, Leipzig, 1871.

67. At a very early date the Indo-Germans fell apart into a number of nations, which, one after another, quitted their common home, and settled, some in Asia, and some in Europe. They were not at first separated into the nations which afterwards became independent, but formed groups like the Indians and Persians (to whom the Slavs or Wends remained attached the longest), the Teutons and Scandinavians, or the Greeks, Romans, and Kelts. Of this the agreement of their religions affords evidence, besides the indications of language and history. The Indians and Persians must have remained the longest united as one people, under the name of the Âryans. From the Aryan religion proceeded, on the one hand, the Vedic religion, the parent of Brâhmanism and Buddhism, and on the other,—though certainly not by immediate descent, —the Mazdeism of the Bactrians and Persians.

Ârya (from *ari*, "devoted," "faithfully attached") is explained by some scholars (Böhthlingk-Roth, *Wörterb.* sub voc., Grassmann, *Wörterb. zum Rig Veda*, sub voc.) as "faithful," "attached," "devoted," *les fidèles;* by others (Benfey, *Dict.* sub. voc., Bopp, *Gloss.*) as "honourable," "noble." It is a general national name of the same kind

as Teutons and Slavs, including within it the idea of the entire body of free men, and employed by a conquering nation to distinguish themselves from their neighbours.

68. The Aryan religion is known to us from mutual comparison of the Indian and Persian religions. The elements they possess in common must once have been the joint property of both. The Aryans, like the Indo-Germans, were polytheists. This is proved by a great number of names of deities and semi-deities, which remained in use among both Indians and Persians. Among them *Varuṉa*, *Mitra*, and *Aryaman*, occupied the highest rank, though in Mazdeism the first of these was replaced by Ahura Mazda. Varuṉa, the heaven-god, and Mitra, the light-god, were very severe, and were especially dreaded by liars and cheats. Aryaman, the companion and bosom friend, who presided over the contracting of marriage, probably a fertilising sun-god, was a more kindly being. With him was connected *Bhaga* (*Bagha*), the assigner of destinies, whose name became at an early date a general designation of the gods among the Persians and Slavs. Next to the Devas, who were afterwards degraded in Erân by the Zarathustrian reformation to the rank of evil spirits, the *ásuras* (*áhuras*), "the living ones," or "spirits," were worshipped as chief gods. The most striking characteristics of this period, however, seem to have been the great development of the worship of fire, combined with magic, and the introduction of the drink of immortality (*soma*, *haoma*) at sacrifices as well as into mythology. There is reason to believe that both usages were adopted from a non-Aryan race, since they were

familiar to the original inhabitants of Mesopotamia and Media, and do not occur in this form among the other Indo-Germanic races, though they also found points of attachment to similar genuinely Indo-Germanic myths.

The worship of fire and the ideas and customs connected with the drink of immortality, prevalent among Indians and Persians, differ entirely from the usages of kindred races, and exhibit much more agreement with those of the oldest inhabitants of Mesopotamia, and probably also of Media. *Soma* (*Haoma*) is a word belonging to the Aryan period, as it does not occur among the other Indo-Germans. I am only able to explain this phenomenon by the influence upon the Aryans of the peoples already named.

II.

RELIGION AMONG THE HINDUS.

General Works.—J. GILDEMEISTER, *Bibliothecæ Sanscritæ Specimen*, Bonn, 1847. TH. BENFEY, "Indien" in Ersch and Gruber's *Allg. Encyklopädie*, sect. ii. part xvii., Leipzig, 1840. On the Literature of India, A. WEBER, *Academische Vorlesungen über Indische Literaturgeschichte*, Berlin, 1852; Id., *Indische Skizzen*, Berlin, 1857; Id., *Indische Streifen*, vol. i. "Zerstreute kleinere Abhandlungen," vol. ii. "Kritisch-bibliographische Streifen," Berlin, 1868–69, Cf. his *Indische Studien, Zeitschr. für die Kunde des Indisch. Alterthums*, since 1849. M. MÜLLER, *A History of Ancient Sanskrit Literature so far as it Illustrates the Primitive Religion of the Brahmans*, London, 1859. MONIER WILLIAMS, *Indian Wisdom, or Examples of the Religious, Philosophical, and Ethical Doctrines of the Hindus*, London, 1875.

On the History of India.—CH. LASSEN, *Indische Alter-*

thumskunde, 4 vols., Bonn, 1847–61, 2d ed. of vol. i. 1866, and of vol. ii. 1874. J. TALBOYS WHEELER, *The History of India*, vols. i.–iii., London, 1867, &c. J. MUIR, *Original Sanskrit Texts on the Origin and History of the People of India, their Religion and Institutions*, vol. i., "Origin of Caste," 2d ed., London, 1868; vol. ii., "Origin of the Hindus," 2d ed., 1871; vol. iii., "The Vedas, Opinions on their Origin," &c., 2d ed., 1868; vol. iv. "Comparison of Vedic with later Representations of the principal Indian Deities," 2d ed., 1873; vol. v. "Cosmogony, Mythology, Religious Ideas, &c., in the Vedic Age," 1870. *Popular.*—MRS. MANNING, *Ancient and Mediæval India*, 2 vols., London, 1869.

On Religion.—H. T. COLEBROOKE, *Miscellaneous Essays*, 3 vols., London, 1837, 2d ed., with Life of the Author by his son, T. E. C., 3 vols., ibid., 1873. H. H. WILSON, *Essays on the Religion of the Hindus*, 2 vols., edited by R. Rost, London, 1862. P. WURM, *Gesch. der Indisch. Religion, in Umriss*, Basel, 1874. S. JOHNSON, *Oriental Religions and their Relation to Universal Religion*, i. "India," London and Boston, 1873. J. ROBSON, *Hinduism and its Relations to Christianity*, Edinburgh, 1874. Cf. also the journals,—*Journal of the Royal Asiatic Society* of London and of that of Calcutta, *Zeitschr. der Deutsch. Morgenländ. Gesellsch.*, Benfey's *Orient und Occident*, the *Rivista Orientale* of A. de Gubernatis, &c., and MAX DUNCKER'S *Geschichte des Alterthums*, vol. ii.

A. *The Vedic Religion.*

Literature.—Editions of the oldest Veda: F. ROSEN, *Rigveda-Sanhita*, lib. prim. Sanscr. et Lat., London, 1838. M. MÜLLER, *Rigveda Sanhitâ*, with the commentary of Sâyana, London, 1849, and foll., smaller edition in Pada and Sanhitâ text, 2 vols., London, 1873. TH. AUFRECHT,

Die Hymnen des Rigveda, in Roman character, 2 vols., Berlin, 1861, 2d ed., 1877. A. DE GUBERNATIS, *I primi Venti Inni del Ṛigveda, ripubbl., trad. e annot.*, Firenze, 1865.

Translations.—M. MÜLLER, *Rigveda Sanhita, translated and explained*, vol i., "Hymns to the Maruts," London, 1869 (no further volumes have appeared, but a complete translation is promised). K. GELDNER, A. KÄGI, and R. ROTH, *Siebenzig Lieder des RV. übersetzt*, Tübingen, 1875. A. LUDWIG, *Der Rigveda, zum ersten male vollständig ins Deutsche übersetzt mit Comment. und Einleitung*, vol. i., Prague, 1876. H. GRASSMANN (author of the *Wörterbuch zum Rigveda*,) *Rigveda übersetzt mit krit. und erläut. Anmerkk.*, vol. i., parts i.–iv., Leipzig, 1876–77. The translation of LANGLOIS cannot be trusted. That of WILSON only reproduces the commentary of Sâyana. H. T. COLEBROOKE, "On the Vedas or Sacred Writings of the Hindus," in *Asiatic Researches*, vol. viii., Calcutta, 1805, pp. 369–476, and in *Miscellaneous Essays* (see above). R. ROTH, *Zur Litteratur und Gesch. des Weda*, Stuttgart, 1846. E. BURNOUF, *Essai sur le Vêda*, Paris, 1863. N. L. WESTERGAARD, *Ueber den ältesten Zeitraum der Ind. Gesch., mit Rücksicht auf der Litteratur*, Breslau, 1862. F. NÈVE, *Essai sur le Mythe des Ribhavas*, Paris, 1857. A. DE GUBERNATIS, *La Vita ed i Mirac. del Dio Indra nel ṚV.*, Firenza, 1866. A. LUDWIG, *Die Philosoph. und Religiös. Anschauungen des Veda in ihrer Entwicklung*, Prague, 1875.

69. After the separation of the Eranian and Indian peoples, the Hindus established themselves in the land of the seven rivers, at the mouths of the Indus, whence their western neighbours called them *Hapta Hiñdu, Sapta Sindhâvas* (now the *Panjâb, Panchanada*, the five rivers).

There the old Aryan religion gave way before the independent development of the Vedic religion, so called because it is only known to us through the Veda *par excellence*, the Ṛigveda. It corresponds with the tolerably advanced civilisation which the Hindus had already attained. If in its doctrine of spirits and worship of ancestors, as well as in the childlike nature of some of its ideas, it still exhibits the survivals of an earlier animistic conception, it has on the whole outgrown its influence. The Devas, originally nothing more than the phenomena and powers of the shining heaven, conceived as persons, children of Dyaus, the heaven-god, and *Pṛithivî*, the earth-goddess, are no longer simple powers of nature, but to some extent, at least, beings endowed with moral qualities, raised above nature, creators and governors of the world. An idea of deity, which evinces great progress in thought, is applied to the chief gods, so that each in turn is honoured by his worshippers as the highest.

70. Among all these gods, however, Indra and Agni were the principal objects of praise. *Indra vṛitrahan*, the slayer of the foe, is the god who in the thunderstorm defeats the cloud-serpent Ahi, and thus makes the fertilising rain pour down upon the earth. In this conflict he is surrounded by the Maruts or storm-gods, led by Rudra; or Vâyu, the wind-god, stands by his side. He is also frequently united with Vishnu, the god of the solar disc. At a later period his two comrades, Rudra and Vishṇu, were destined entirely to overshadow him. Agni, as god of fire (*ignis*, Slav. *ogni*), is the soul and origin of the universe, the mediator between men and

gods, lord of spells and of prayer. If Indra was rather the god of princes and soldiers, Agni was the special god of the priests. The worship paid to Soma, the god of the drink of immortality, to whom even a whole book of the Ṛigveda is consecrated, was little inferior.

There are passages in the Veda which justify the conjecture that Indra and the Maruts were at first rivals, and were not united until later. See RV. i. 165.

Brahmaṇaspati is the lord of spells, and *Bṛihaspati* the lord of prayer. Both are surnames or forms of Agni. Another very ancient fire-god is the heavenly carpenter *Tvashṭṛi.*

Almost all the 114 hymns of the ninth *Maṇḍala* of the RV. are addressed to Soma.

71. That the sun-god should occupy a prominent place among the Devas or light-gods, was natural. He may still be traced in a number of gods and demigods. But the proper sun-god of the Vedic period appears in three forms, *Sûrya,* "the shining one," *Pûshan,* "he who makes all things grow," and *Savitṛi,* "the vivifying." He was also named briefly *Aditya,* as son of Aditi, originally, we may suppose, the goddess of the twilight. Aditi, raised to the rank of universal mother, is also regarded, however, as the mother of various other gods, and even of the highest. The chief of these Adityas is the old Aryan Varuṇa, who maintains during this period likewise his significance as the Asura *par excellence,* and whose dreadful anger the sinner endeavours to appease by fervid prayers and by sacrifices. Mitra also is still worshipped, but he seldom occurs alone, and he is generally united with Varuṇa. Besides these two, and Savitṛi, whom we have already named, the old Aryan deities Aryaman and Bagha, and the Vedic gods *Daksha*, "the power," and *Aṁsa*, "the sharer," were also reckoned among the Adityas, to whom Sûrya was sometimes added as the eighth. At a later period their number rose to twelve. Some gods, like the Asvins, the heavenly physicians, are so completely raised to the rank of rational beings, with human passions and emotions, that it is hard to say what were the natural phenomena with which they were once connected. The goddesses are still kept in the background, which is a proof of youthful and vigorous religious life. The dawn-goddess *Ushas*, to whom hymns of extreme beauty are dedicated, the river-goddess *Sarasvatî*, who was afterwards fused with *Vâch*, the goddess of language, and *Sraddhâ*, the personification of faith, deserve to be specially named. The more abstract divine figures, and the beginnings of a monotheistic or pantheistic creed, which are found in some of the hymns of the Ṛigveda, probably belong to a later period.

Sarasvatî, "the rich in water," by whom there sometimes stands a male *Sarasvat*, is probably an old Aryan water-goddess, a conjecture supported by the Baktrian *Haraqaiti* and the Persian *Harauvati* (*Arachotos*, *Arachosia*), and not the deified river-nymph, whether of the Indus, to which her name was perhaps first applied, or of the small river which also subsequently bore it. In the Ṛigveda she is also the goddess of the piety which utters itself in prayers and hymns.

72. It cannot be doubted that the ancient Aryan

people at this early date also had their own priests, who were very likely called, as was afterwards the case in Baktria, *atharvans*, or priests of fire. In the Ṛigveda they bear other names, especially that of *brahman*, which appears to have originally meant nothing more than a "singer of sacred songs," but soon, came to designate a religious functionary. Sometimes, though rarely, the word is used to designate a regular priestly order. The office even seems to have become hereditary; at any rate, the older hymns contain occasional references to a *brâhmaṇa* or Brahman's son, and in the later hymns these are more numerous. The Brahmans were regarded, though not universally, with high honour, and the poets especially might count on rich rewards. Their claims and pretensions rose higher and higher, but they did not yet form an exclusive caste, for kings and kings' sons are also designated as sacred singers, and performed priestly functions, though, like many of the nobles also, they generally had their house-priests (*purohita*).

Brahman, from the neuter *brahma*, a prayer or hymn, seems to have been in early times a synonym for *kavi*, *ṛishi*, and other similar words. On the derivation and original meaning of the word see M. Haug, *Ueber die Ursprüngl. Bedeutung des Wortes Brahma*, Münch., 1868, and *Brahma und die Brahmanen*, ibid., 1871, the conclusions of which, however, cannot all be accepted without further inquiry.

73. Morality and religion were already closely connected. The gods ruled over the moral as well as over the natural order. Some of the hymns, especially those

addressed to Varuṇa, are marked by a deep sense of guilt, and the mighty Indra must be approached in faith (*srat*). The doctrine of immortality also indicates the ethical character of the Vedic religion. The ideas of the Vedic Hindus about ancestors and their worship were exactly the same as those of savages, and their representations of future bliss were still very sensuous, but they looked for requital of their actions after death. The oldest songs, however, say but little of immortality. Of the doctrine of the transmigration of the soul, the entire Ṛigveda exhibits not a single trace.

B.—*Pre-Buddhistic Brâhmanism.*

Literature.—Editions of the later Vedas. TH. BENFEY, *Die Hymnen des Sâma-Veda* (with translation), Leipzig, 1848. A. WEBER, *The White Yajur-Veda*, Berlin, 1849, &c. R. ROTH and W. D. WHITNEY, *Atharva-Veda Sanhitâ*, 2 vols., Berlin, 1855. The *Aitareya Brâhmana* (of the Ṛigvẹda), edited by M. HAUG, 2 vols. (with translation), Bombay, 1863. Translations from the *Satapatha Brâhmana* in MUIR'S *Sanskrit Texts*, passim, and WEBER'S *Indische Streifen*, vol. i. *Gṛhyasûtrâni, Indische Hausregeln, Sanskr. und Deutsch*, von A. F. STENZLER, I. Asvalâyana, 2 vols., Leipzig, 1865. *Manava-dharmasastra; Lois de Manou, trad. par* A. LOISELEUR DESLONGCHAMPS, Paris, 1833. Cf. *Yâjnavalkyadharmaṣâstram, Yâjn.'s Gesetzbuch, Sanskr. und Deutsch von* A. F. STENZLER, Berlin and London, 1849. C. SCHOEBEL, *Étude sur le Rituel du Respect Social dans l'État Brahman*, Paris, 1870. H. KERN, *Indische Theorieën over de Standenverdeeling*, Amsterdam, 1871.

74. With the diffusion of the Hindu-Aryans over the region south-east of the Seven Rivers, and their settlement on the banks of the Ganges and Yamunâ, their religion enters upon a new era. The Vedic religion gives birth to Brâhmanism or the hierarchy of the Brâhmans. The fresh originality of the Vedic age, though not at first entirely extinct, for the most part disappears. A number of hymns, occurring chiefly in the later books of the Ṛigveda, were certainly not composed till the first portion of this period, and tolerably far down in it too; but they no longer breathe the same spirit as the earlier, and the chief concern was the collection, arrangement, and interpretation of the hymns handed down by tradition, of which the true meaning was but rarely grasped. It is not possible to determine with certainty in what century Brâhmanism arose. If, however, as is most probable, Buddhism was founded in the fourth and third centuries before our era, the growth of Brâhmanism cannot have begun much later than the eighth century B.C., and perhaps we ought, with some scholars, to carry it considerably further back. The history of Brâhmanism falls properly into three periods—the pre-Buddhistic; that of its conflict with Buddhism; and that which follows its victory over Buddhism; but the last two are too closely connected to admit of sharp distinction from each other. We have, therefore, to trace, first of all, the origin, establishment, and internal development of Brâhmanism, as a national and purely Aryan sect, in contrast with the non-Aryan religion and morals of the older occupants of the country; and next, its contest with Buddhism and other heresies, over which it triumphed, though not till after it had enlarged its own boundaries, adopted much that was not Aryan, and entirely transformed itself into a religious communion, the character of which was no longer exclusively national.

On the date of the foundation of Buddhism, see below, § 85.

75. The Brâhmanic religion is entirely under the control of what Europeans call the caste system. Between ranks and castes there is an essential difference. Caste is rank with sharp impassable boundaries, which admit no one who is not born within them. The four Indian castes appear as ranks, with different though corresponding names, in Baktria also, as well as in Europe in the middle ages, and wherever society stands at the same stage of development. Castes, at any rate with the same rigid separation, are found nowhere but in India. There they were originally four in number, three being Aryan, viz., that of the Brâhmans, *i.e.*, the learned; that of the Rajanyas or Kshattriyas, *i.e.*, the princes and warriors; and that of the Vaisyas, *i.e.*, the commonalty, the people (*vis*), and one being non-Aryan, viz., the Sûdras, *i.e.*, the natives, who served the Aryans, and especially the Brâhmans, as slaves. The general name which they bore enables us to conjecture how they arose. They were called *Varṇa*, which denotes both "kind" and "colour." This term at first simply indicated the difference between the whiter Aryans and the dark-coloured natives whom they subjugated, and with whom, as though belonging to a different kind, they would hold no intercourse. When settled ways and agriculture had replaced their wandering shepherd-life, the warriors began to keep themselves strictly apart from the working-class, and the learned in

the same way separated themselves from both warriors and workers; and although they were all counted members of the religious community, the idea of *varṇa* colour, or kind, was also transferred to them. Thus arose the doctrine, already expressed in a later hymn of the Ṛig-veda, that not only the two races, but also the four ranks, were of different origin, and had been separately created.

Differences of opinion exist about the antiquity of the castes. See the essays already referred to: Kern, *Ind. Theorieën over de Standenverdeeling*, and Haug, *Brahma und die Brahmanen*, and, on the other side, Muir's *Sanskrit Texts*, ii. p. 454, *sqq.* I adopt the view of those who regard the four ranks as ancient, at any rate as a natural division of society at a definite stage of its development, while they consider the castes proper as purely Indian.

The members of the three highest castes are all of them *dvijâ's* or twice-born, but not so the Sûdras.

The hymn of the Ṛik, in which the four castes proceed out of four parts of Purusha's body, is the well-known *Purusha-sûkta*, x. 90.

76. The same causes, combined with the circumstance that writing was unknown, or at any rate was not generally employed for literary purposes, contributed to give increasing influence to the Brâhmans. Subject at first to the princes and nobles, and dependent on them, they began by insinuating themselves into their favour, and representing it as a religious duty to show protection and liberality towards them. Meanwhile they endeavoured to make themselves indispensable to them, gradually acquired the sole right to conduct public worship, made themselves masters of instruction and of the most influ-

ential civil offices, and set themselves up as the exclusive guardians and interpreters of revelation (*ṣruti*) and tradition (*smṛiti*), in virtue of possessing a higher knowledge, which the mass of the people did not comprehend. They had frequently, however, to encounter grave resistance from the princes. Sometimes they were compelled to acknowledge the spiritual superiority of a *râjanya;* on some occasions they were unable even to withhold from him the dignity of Brâhman; generally, however, they contrived, either by assumption and arrogance, or by cunning, to attain their end.

On the introduction of the art of writing, see M. Müller, *Sanskrit Literature*, p. 500, *sqq.*, Westergaard, *Aeltest. Zeitraum*, &c., p. 30, *sqq.* Nearchus (325 B.C.) and Megasthenes (300 B.C.) both state that the Indians did not write their laws, but the latter speaks of inscriptions upon mile-stones, and the former mentions letters written on cotton. From this it is evident that writing, probably of Phœnician origin, was known in India before the third century B.C., but was applied only rarely, if at all, to literature. The oldest known inscriptions, those of Asoka, may be placed about 250 B.C.

Among the princes whose intellectual superiority is recognised by the Brâhmans, Janaka, the Prince of Videha, occupies the foremost place. As early as the *Ṣatapatha Brâhmana* (xi. 6, 2, 1), it is related how he reduced a party of four Brâhmans, among whom was the famous Yâjnavalkya, *ad terminos non loqui.* Another king, Ajâtaṣatru of Kâṣi, did something similar, and men shouted after him, as he himself complained, "Janaka! Janaka!" See these and other examples in Muir's *Sanskrit Texts*, i. p. 427, *sqq.*, and Westergaard, *op. cit.*, pp. 13-16.

77. The character of the religion of this period is revealed by what we may call its religious literature. By far the greater number of the works belonging to it were composed with a view to the sacrificial service. Together they constitute the Veda, the sacred knowledge, or the four Vedas. Of these, it was necessary that the Hymn-Veda (*Ṛig-Veda*) should be known by the reciting priest (*hotṛi*), the Chant-Veda (*Sâma-Veda*) by the singing priest (*udgâtṛi*), and the sacrificial-formula-Veda (*Yajur-Veda*) by the officiating priest (*adhvaryu*). The *Atharva-Veda* was not recognised until later, and was assigned to the presiding and supervising priest, who was, however, required to know much more than this. The Yajur-Veda was divided, after two rival schools, into the "White" and the "Black."

Each of these Vedas had its *Sañhitâ* or collection of hymns, of which only two, those of the Ṛik and of the Atharvan, deserve this name. That of the Sâma-Veda contains, with two exceptions, only Ṛik verses, arranged in the order in which they were sung at the sacrifice. Those of the two Yajur-Vedas (*Taittiriya-* and *Vâjasaneyi-Sañhitâ*) are simply a portion of, and selection from, the Brâhmaṇas of the Adhvaryu priests, drawn up for the purpose of giving them a Sanhitâ of their own, though they had no need of one. The two first collections contain some very ancient and remarkable remains from a previous period, but poems of the Brâhmanic age were not excluded from the Ṛig-Veda, and in the Atharva-Veda are very numerous.

Further, to each Veda belong different Brâhmaṇas, treatises of ritual and theology, afterwards supplanted by the *Âranyakas* ("forest treatises"), and the connected *Upanishads* ("confidential communications"), theological-philosophical treatises, prepared more especially for the use of the hermits. The Brâhmaṇas contain here and there occasional elevated thoughts, and not a few antique traditions of the highest importance, but they are in other respects marked by narrow formalism, childish mysticism, and superstitious talk about all kinds of trifles, such as may be expected where a pedantic and power-loving priesthood is invested with unlimited spiritual authority.

Finally, each Veda had its *sûtras* ("threads"), short compact guides for public and domestic sacrifices, and the knowledge of the laws.

All these books were handed down orally, and each school (*charaṇa*) had its own text (*ṣâkhâ*), both of Saṅhitâs and of Brâhmaṇas. Even when the art of writing was already known, it was regarded as a grave sin to write them down.

The preceding section deals only with the religious writings of this period. That it was not deficient (also) in other literary productions, such as epic narratives, poems, &c., is certain; but these have perished, or have been in part interwoven and remodelled in later works of this kind. The Ṛig-Veda also contains hymns of a non-religious character.

The schism in the school of the Yajur-Veda, among the Adhvaryus, is attributed, not without reason, to Yâjnavalkya, to whom, therefore, the white Yajush owes its origin. He or his school extracted the poetical quotations which occurred in the Brâhmaṇa, and collected them into a Saṅhitâ, whence some scholars (*e.g.*, Max Müller) explain the name "White Yajush" (*ṣukla*). This would then mean "the cleared," "the purified." Thereupon, the representatives of the old school, in order that they also might have a Sañhitâ, simply affixed this by no means appropriate title to the first portion of their Brâhmaṉa.

Of the existing Upanishads only a few belong to this period; the rest are of later date.

Following these three kinds of works (Vedas, Brâhmaṉas, and Sûtras), Max Müller has incorrectly divided this age into three sharply defined periods, and on this division has founded his history of ancient Sanskrit literature. Westergaard falls into another extreme, in actually placing the Sûtras before the Brâhmaṉas. It is certain that the composition of Sûtras and Upanishads continued when the Vedic Sañhitâs were already closed, and no new Brâhmaṉas were composed. Brâhmaṉas only satisfied the requirements of the time when a trifling theology was in the ascendant.

The dread of the reduction of the sacred Scripture to writing may have had its ground in the fear of seeing it fall into unqualified hands, and at the same time in deep reverence for the divine word, which would be thereby polluted.

78. In the doctrine of the gods Brâhmanism made but little change. This was the natural result of the recognition of the Vedas as a book of revelation, and of the prominence of sacrifice, in which the Vedic gods always occupied the highest place. The Brâhmans simply attempted to arrange the Vedic gods, whether by the three worlds, earth, air, and sky, or by the nature of the deities, so that, for instance, Indra was the king, Agni the priest,

or by some other standard. The Asuras, however, who had been in earlier times the chief of the gods, and in the beginning of this period were still placed along with the Devas, were lowered, perhaps in consequence of their resemblance to the gods of the old hostile occupants of the country, to the rank of evil spirits. The reverence for the Devas also perceptibly diminished as the Brâhmans placed themselves on their level, and the hermits especially, who did penance, regarded themselves as superior to them in power and dignity. The only exception was in favour of Rudra, the violent storm-god, whose worship increased considerably in this period, and served as one of the foundations of the later Ṣiva-worship; he had not yet, however, become the chief god. Men felt, however, the need of such a supreme god as the maker and ruler of the universe, and this need could only be imperfectly satisfied by the creations of the Vedic *Ṛishis.* Another plan, therefore, was adopted. At first, and this appears even in the later Vedic hymns, some of the surnames of the ancient gods, in particular of the fire-god Agni, were endowed with a separate existence, or such a god under one of these surnames (*Viṣvakarman*, "the maker of all things," *Brahmaṇaspati*, "the lord of spells, or of prayer," *Prajâpati*, "the lord of creatures") was regarded as the creator and lord of the world. From these speculation ascended to the *Brahma*, the magic power hidden in the sacred word and in prayer (and as such the special inheritance of the priests), and regarded this as the impersonal, self-existent (*svayambhû*), supreme cause of the universe. This brahma, though always neuter in the Brâhmaṇas, soon became, in a certain sense, personified;

and finally, as the male Brahmâ, was exalted to be the all-ruling personal deity, without ever becoming a true national god.

To the three worlds, earth, air, and sky, correspond the three chief gods Agni, Indra united with Vâyu or Vishnu, and Sûrya. Besides the name Viṣvakarman, &c., the name *Hiraṉyagarbha*, "the golden world-egg," was also used to designate the sun fire-god as creator. *Kaṣyapa*, also, in the later tradition a famous sage, must be regarded as a universal creator and sun-god of the same kind.

79. In spite of the supreme power of the Brâhmans, the right of the head of the family to offer the family sacrifices remained unimpaired. But at the public sacrifices, with the arrangements and symbolism of which we are still but imperfectly acquainted, the usages and ceremonies became more and more elaborate and involved, requiring a constant increase in the number of ministrants, all of whom were of necessity Brâhmans. The sacrificial ceremonial at the consecration of a king (*râja-suya*), the very common horse-sacrifice (*aṣvamedha*), the proper human sacrifice (*purushamedha*), and the general sacrifice (*sarvamedha*), were the most important. At these four sacrifices, human victims were really offered in ancient times, but as manners grew more gentle, this practice began to decline, and at an early date, though not with universal approval, fell into disuse. The idea was even expressed that all sacrifices of blood were unnecessary, though they still prevailed for a long while after this period.

At length men grew weary of pondering on the meaning of sacrificial actions and quarrelling over points of theology; and while some, with more practical aims, and contented, therefore, with short Sutras, neglected the study of the Brâhmaṇas, others sought in the Âranyakas and the oldest Upanishads satisfaction for their craving for mystic contemplation and philosophical reflection, and occupied themselves by preference with the questions of the origin of the universe, the nature of the deity and of the soul, the relation of spirit and matter, and other problems of the same kind. These were the beginnings from which Hindu philosophy was afterwards developed.

The commutation of the old human sacrifice by a substitute is certainly alluded to in the legend of Ṣunaḥṣepa, quoted from the *Aitareya Brâhmaṇa* by M. Müller, *Sanskr. Literature*, Append., p. 573, *sqq.*, cf. pp. 408–416. It has some correspondence with that of Abraham and Isaac. The superfluous nature of all sacrifices of blood is taught in the *Aitar. Brâhm.*, vi. 8, see M. Müller, *op. cit.*, p. 420, and in the *Ṣatap. Brâhm.* 1, 2, 3, 6, cf. Weber, *Ind. Streifen*, i. p. 55, in an important essay which deserves to be consulted on the subject.

80. The moral and social ideal of the Brâhmans is known to us from the so-called lawbook of Manu, the main features of which are pre-Buddhistic. Their moral teaching stands relatively very high, though it has not risen above eudaemonism. With much that is genuinely humane, it contains much that is arbitrary and unnatural, and resembles all the laws of antiquity in placing moral purity on a line with the prescriptions of sacerdotalism and magic.

Purified by various ceremonies from the stains of birth, the Arya, invested with the consecrated cord and girdle, enters as a disciple of the Brâhmans on the first stage of his training, and after completing his course, he celebrates, by the offering of his first sacrifice, the feast of his new birth. He then becomes a householder (*griha-pati*), and after having discharged his duties in this capacity, he hands over to his son, who has in the meantime himself attained the same position, the care of all belonging to him, and retires into the forest to pass his days undisturbed in religious works and silent meditations. The highest ideal that a man can reach on earth is to become a *yati* (self-conqueror) or *sannyâsi* (self-renouncer). The latter offers no more sacrifices, he is raised above the things of the world and of sense, and devotes himself exclusively to the contemplative life. Such is the way to final deliverance (*moksha*) from the bonds of sensual existence.

The majority of men, however, do not as yet attain this goal. The wicked and the impious are condemned to hell, and there suffer dreadful torments. Those who have faithfully discharged their religious duties are rewarded with heaven, and become *Devas.* Every one, however, who has not yet obtained deliverance must be born again on earth, in the shape of a plant, an animal, or a man of lower or higher rank, in proportion to the number of his sins. This process continues until he has reached the highest stage of self-abandonment and contemplation (*tapas*), when, freed from everything material, he sinks away into the soul of the universe and is united with it. This dogma, improperly called that of the transmigration of the soul, is unknown to the oldest Vedic books, but it was current before Buddhism, as it is the foundation of the Buddhist doctrine of deliverance.

On the age of the *Manavadharmaṣâstra* there is great difference of opinion. Max Müller, *Sanskrit Literature*, p. 62, *sqq.*, combats the view of Sir W. Jones, who thought that the law-book could not have been drawn up later than 800 B.C. A. Barth, *Rev. Critique*, 1875, No. 48, considers even 500 B.C., as proposed by Monier Williams and others, too early. That those passages which refer to a much later time are interpolations, is conceded by all. The main contents of the work may be safely brought down towards the close of the pre-Buddhist period.

For our purpose it is to a certain extent unimportant whether it was ever actually applied in its entirety as a law. It is sufficient that it exhibits to us the ideal of the Brâhmans.

81. The social ideal of the Brâhmans is the unlimited power of the hierarchy and the strict separation of castes. At the end of this period, owing to mixed marriages and other causes, the old castes were increased by a number of half-pure and impure castes. Various useful callings were thus branded as sinful, and men were prevented from withdrawing even from shameful occupations to which birth condemned them. The highest claims were made by the law-book on the Brâhmans, but they also received from it the most extravagant privileges, and it provided that the unlimited authority of the kings should be placed at their service. Woman was kept in complete dependence, the Ṣudra was despised, and those who stood outside the community (*Chândâlas, Svapâkas*) were doomed to a life of the greatest misery, and were esteemed no higher than sacrificial animals. Such a position could not be long endured, and this serves to explain not only the rise of Buddhism, but also its rapid diffusion, and the radical revolution which it brought about.

C. *The Conflict of Brâhmanism with Buddhism.*

Literature.—Among editions of Pali texts, the following are the most important: the *Mahâwansa*, edited by Hon. G. TURNOUR, Colombo, 1837. *Dhamma-pada*, ed. by V. FAUSBÖLL, Copenhagen, 1855. The *Upasampadā-Kammavâcha* and *Pâtimokkha*, by J. F. DICKSON in the *Journ. Roy. As. Soc.*, 1873 and 1875. *Khuddaka-Pâṭha*, ibid., 1869, by R. C. CHILDERS. The *Jâtaka Commentary*, by FAUSBÖLL, vol. i., pt. i., London, 1875. *Sept Suttas Palis*, ed. by GRIMBLOT, with translations by BURNOUF and GOGERLY, Paris, 1876. *Mahâ Parinibbâna Sutta*, by CHILDERS, *Journ. Roy. As. Soc.*, 1874 and 1876.

E. BURNOUF, *Introduction à l'Histoire du Buddhisme Indien* (1844), 2d ed., Paris, 1876. Id., *Le Lotus de la Bonne Loi* (*trad. du Saddharma Puṇḍarîka*), Paris, 1852. C. F. KÖPPEN, *Die Religion des Buddha und ihre Entstehung*, Berlin, 1857. Id., *Die Lamaische Hierarchie und Kirche*, ibid., 1859. BARTHÉLEMY SAINT HILAIRE, *Le Bouddha et sa Religion*, 2d ed., Paris, 1862. W. WASSILJEW, *Der Buddhismus, Seine Dogmen, Gesch. und Literatur*, 1860 (translated into French by La Comme, Paris, 1865). A. SCHIEFNER, *Târanâtha's Geschichte des Buddhismus in Indien, aus dem Tibet.*, St. Petersburg, 1869. R. SPENCE HARDY, *A Manual of Buddhism in its Modern Development, translated from Singhalese MSS.*, London, 1860. Id., *Eastern Monachism, compiled from Singhalese MSS.*, London, 1860. Id., *The Legends and Theories of the Buddhists compared with History and Science*, London, 1866. *Histoire du*

Bouddha Sakya Mouni, trad. du Tibétain par PH. ED. FOUCAUX, Paris, 1868. *Lalita Vistara, Erzälung von dem Leben und der Lere des Çâkya Simha, übersetzt von* S. LEFMANN, part i., Berlin, 1874. *Foĕ kouĕ ki, ou Relation des Royaumes Bouddhiques par Chў Fă Hian, trad. par* A. RÉMUSAT, Paris, 1836. STANISL. JULIEN, *Voyages des Pêlerins Bouddhistes,* vol. i.; "Vie de Hiouen Thsang," vols. ii. and iii.; "Mémoires sur les Contrées Occidentales, par Hiouen Thsang," Paris, 1853–58. L. FEER, *Études Bouddhiques,* 1re Série, Paris, 1870. Id., *Études Bouddh. L'Ami de la Vertu et l'Amitié de la Vertu,* Paris, 1873. H. KERN, *Over de jaartelling der zuidelijke Buddhisten en de Gedenkstukken van Açoka den Buddhist,* Amsterdam, 1873. É. SÉNART, *Essai sur la Légende du Buddha, son Caractère et ses Origines,* Paris, 1875. Popular, C. D. B. MILLS, *The Indian Saint, or Buddha and Buddhism,* Northampton, Massachusetts, 1876. T. W. RHYS DAVIDS, *Buddhism, a Sketch of the Life and Teachings of Gautama Buddha,* London, 1877.

On the question of Nirvâṇa see J. F. OBRY, *Du Nirvâṇa Bouddhique,* Paris, 1863; R. C. CHILDERS, *Dictionary of the Pali Language,* s. voc. *Nibbânam,* and the authorities cited by these writers; and T. W. RHYS DAVIDS, *Contemporary Review,* January 1877, on "The Buddhist Doctrine of Nirvâṇa," &c.

On the Jainas: J. STEVENSON, *The Kalpa Sûtra and Nana Tatva, translated from the Mâgadhi,* London, 1848. A. WEBER, "Ein Fragment des Bhagavatî," *Akad. der Wissensch.,* Berlin, 26th October 1865, and 12th July and 25th October 1866. S. J. WARREN, *Over de Godsdienstige en Wijsgeerige Begrippen der Jaina's,* Zwolle, 1875.

82. Buddhism, which was to prove so dangerous an enemy to Brâhmanism, seems not to be much older than the fourth century before our era. Its founder, who was called Siddhârta, according to tradition, though commonly named the Buddha or "enlightened," the "sage" or the "lion" "of the tribe of Ṣakya" (Ṣâkya-muni, Ṣâkya Ṣim̃ha), and also designated by many other titles of honour, lived and worked probably in the second half of the fifth century B.C., but the legends which have surrounded his career have completely hidden it from our view. The chief features of this legendary history are as follows:—In order to deliver the world from the misery beneath which it sighs, the sage descends from heaven, where he occupies the highest rank among the gods, to earth. Here he was miraculously conceived in the womb of Mâyâ ("illusion"), the wife of the Ṣâkya king Ṣuddhodhana of Kapilavastu, in Ayodhyâ (Oude), and there he was born in an equally extraordinary manner. Educated as a prince, and excelling in knowledge and ability of every kind, he early betrays an inclination to a contemplative life, which is strenuously resisted by his father, who supposes that he has overcome it by inducing his son to marry. He contrives, however, to flee from the luxurious court, and to reach Râjagṛiha, the capital of Magadha. There he becomes a disciple of the most famous Brâhmans, devotes himself to the severest mortifications, triumphs over the repeated temptations of the god of love and death, Mâra, but remains inwardly dissatisfied. He then abandons asceticism, and endeavours by means of calm and intent contemplation to penetrate to the deepest insight (*bodhi*), and thus to gain deliverance from the miseries of existence. At Gâya, a little village in Magadha, under the shadow of the sacred fig-tree (bodhi-tree), seated on the throne of knowledge (*bodhi-manda*), he actually attains the dignity of Buddha. Upon this he begins to preach, first at Benares (*Vâranâṣi*) and subsequently all through India; multitudes without number, including not a few princes and Brâhmans, and the Buddha's own family, are converted, and even women are admitted to discipleship. After triumphing over every obstacle, he is doomed to witness, by the desolation of his native city, the ruin of his whole race, and at last, at the age of eighty years, he dies, or rather enters into Nirvâṇa. No fire can burn his corpse, but it is consumed at last by the glow of his own piety, and his bones are collected out of the ashes by his disciples as precious relics, and deposited in eight Stupas.

The dates assigned to Buddha's death vary widely. That of the Southern church has been most generally accepted, according to which the attainment of Nirvâṇa falls in 543 B.C. Westergaard, *Buddha's Todesjahr*, p. 95, *sqq.*, places it 368–370, with which result A. Weber, *Indische Streifen*, ii. 216, agrees. Kern, *Jaartelling der Zuid. Buddh.*, p. 1, *sqq.*, assigns Buddha's entrance into Nirvâṇa to 388 B.C., and T. W. Rhys Davids, *Academy*, 25th April 1874, fixes it about 410.

Sénart, *Essai sur la Légende du Buddha*, endeavours to prove that the whole story of the Buddha is a legend, composed of the ordinary elements of a solar myth, and that we are no longer in a position to extract from it the kernel of historic truth. He is, no doubt, right to a certain extent; further investigation must determine whether his conclusion is not too decidedly negative. He does not, however, like Wilson, deny the existence of the Buddha. The narratives of birth and childhood, independently of their supernatural character, are doubtful in the highest degree. Mâyâ is a purely mythical being, and Kapilavastu an altogether unknown city, while its name suggests that of Kapila, the reputed founder of the Sânkhya philosophy, which has so many points of agreement with the later Buddhist teaching. The other places named in the legend are familiar enough, Râjagṛiha, at that time a resort of sages and hermits, Vâranâṣi (Benares), which continues the holy city to this day, and Gâya (Buddhagâya), where the bodhi-tree beneath which Buddha sat is still pointed out. This is, however, no guarantee for the historical character of the stories connected with these places.

83. Whether the Buddha was really the son of a king or not, it may be regarded as certain that he did not belong to the caste of the Brâhmans. There is equally little reason for doubting that he sought for peace first of all among the Brâhmans, then in solitary penance,—yet in both instances in vain,—and attained it only by that contemplation absorbing the soul, which became the characteristic of his followers. His wandering life in the garb of a mendicant, his preaching that all who followed him in this might be delivered from sickness, pain, old age, and death, and should strive after *Nirvâṉa* as the highest goal, the great impression which this doctrine made on men of all classes, if not through the whole of India, yet according to the oldest tradition, in particular districts, the opposition which he encountered from many, the loyal devotion of his disciple Ânanda, the few details related of his death—all this cannot belong to the realm of fiction. And this suffices to show us in the Buddha a

man, who, whatever may have been the value of his philosophy of life, out of genuine conviction and pity for his fellowmen, chose a life of self-denial and renunciation to realise a great idea and promote the universal salvation.

> Even though we should be obliged to concede that the whole course of Buddha's life is borrowed from the well-known myth of the sun-god, and that the majority of the details of his legend find their explanation in this myth, it will still be impossible to derive the traits we have enumerated from this source.

84. Buddhism, though it is a reaction against the Brâhmanic hierarchy, is, in fact, an outgrowth of Brâhmanism. It rests upon the so-called dogma of the transmigration of the soul, and the Buddhist, like the Brâhman, seeks for deliverance from the endless succession of re-births. But it pronounces the Brâhmanic penances and abstinence inadequate to accomplish this, and aims at attaining, not union with the universal spirit, but Nirvâṇa, non-existence. Without denying the existence of the devas, at any rate at first, it places each Buddha, as the Brâhmans ranked every ascetic, above them, but it goes a step further, and makes even the supreme Brahmâ subordinate to a perfect saint. It differed from Brâhmanism, as primitive Christianity differed from the Jewish hierarchy, by rejecting outward works or theological knowledge as marks of holiness, and seeking it in gentleness, in purity of heart and life, in mercy and self-denying love for a neighbour. Above all, it is distinguished by its relation to castes. The Buddha comes neither to oppose them, nor to level everything. On the other hand, he adopts the doctrine that men are born in lower or higher castes, determined by their sins or good works in a former existence, but he teaches, at the same time that, by a life of purity and love, by becoming a spiritual man, every one may attain at once the highest salvation. Caste makes no difference to him; he looks for the man, even in the Châṇḍâla; the miseries of existence beset all alike, and his law is a law of grace for all. The Buddhist teaching is, therefore, quite popular in its character, its instrument is preaching rather than instruction, it is not esoteric like the Brâhmanic, or intended only for individuals. And while the piety of the Brâhman aimed at selfishly securing his own redemption, the Buddhist cannot attain salvation without regard to the well-being of all his fellow creatures. The ideal of the first is a hermit striving to save himself, the ideal of the second a monk, enrolled in a brotherhood, striving to save others. Buddhism, in fact, rejected the authority of the Veda, the whole dogmatic system of the Brâhmans, their worship, penance, and hierarchy, and simply substituted for them a higher moral teaching. It was a purely ethical revolution; but it would certainly have succumbed beneath this one-sided tendency, had it not in the course of time taken up into itself, under another shape, much of what it had first opposed.

There are two degrees of Nirvâṉa, one consisting of the complete sanctification by which a man became an Arhat, or "venerable person," and the other being the annihilation of all existence, for which the Arhat strives, and which he cannot attain until death. The first of these is called in Pâli *savupâdisesanibbânam̃,—i.e.*, "the annihilation of everything except the five *khandhas* (*skandhas*) or qualities of being;" sometimes also *kilesanibbânam̃*, the "extinction of passion." The second is described as *anupâdisesanibbânam̃* or *khandanibbânam̃*, "extinction of being." Thus Childers correctly, *loco cit.*

The sketch which we have presented of the relation of the Buddha to the caste-system, is, of course, founded on the picture of him drawn by his followers. It is possible that this conception belonged to him originally, but it may also have been an inference from his teaching.

Primitive Buddhism ignored religion. It was only when in opposition to its first principles, it had made its founder its god, and had thus really become a religion, that the way was open for its general acceptance.

85. The real history of Buddhism does not begin till the middle of the third century before our era. Of the first century of its existence we know nothing with certainty. It appears to have developed silently but steadily. Monasteries were founded, and sects were formed. If it had been the original idea of the Master to turn all men into clergy, that is, into mendicant monks, practical reasons, of course, soon rendered it necessary to admit lay brothers and sisters by their side, who were bound only to fulfil the moral law. The foundations of the discipline (*vinaya*) and of the law or belief (*dharma*) were laid; even metaphysical problems (*abhidharma*) were already to some extent discussed. But in the middle of the third century B.C., a great change took place. The expedition of Alexander the Great had brought the Hindus into contact with the Greeks. His rival Chandragupta, following his example, founded a mightier empire than India had ever known before, and, perhaps, favoured Buddhism. Further advance was made by his grandson Aṣoka, who even became a convert to the new faith, and raised it to the position of the state religion. His numerous inscriptions show us that the Buddhism of this period was still exceedingly simple, and they prove that it had not yet assumed an attitude of hostility towards the Brâhmans. The royal protection naturally brought a multitude of converts, especially Brâhmans and hermits, who were admitted into the monasteries without instruction in the law and without ordination. The heresy, the laxity of discipline, and the neglect of ordinances, which resulted from these circumstances, rendeed a tribunal for the trial of heretics indispensable, and a council desirable. A council was therefore held under the presidency of Maudgaliputra (Moggaliputto), which, after fixing the canon, resolved on a vigorous effort to spread the true doctrine. Missionaries were now despatched to all parts of the peninsula, and even to Kashmîr and Gandhara, west of the Indus. Mahendra, the king's own son, went to Ceylon, and there founded the Southern Buddhist church, which was destined to remain so much purer than the Northern, and was at a later date to carry Buddhism to Burma and Siam. While the dynasty of Chandragupta was on the throne (till 178 B.C.), Buddhism enjoyed golden days in India. But under King Pushpamitra, the founder of a new dynasty, a violent persecution was commenced, at the instigation of the Brâhmans, against the followers of Ṣâkya-muni, so that it became necessary to hold the next council—which followed within two hundred years, and at which the hierarchic and contemplative school of the Great Passage (*Mahâyana*) was recognised as orthodox—in Kashmîr, under the protection of the non-Hindu king Kanishka. The period of conflict now began.

According to the Buddhist reckoning the council which met under Aṣoka was the third. The second, said to have been held a hundred years earlier under a certain king Kâlâṣoka, is as little historic as that prince himself. The convocation of the first council, also, by Ajâtaṣatru near Râjagṛiha, is open to serious doubts.

Vinaya, Dharma, and Abhidharma, together constitute the Tripiṭaka (*Tipiṭakam̃*), "the three Baskets," the complete Holy Scriptures. The rise of metaphysical discussion before the time of Aṣoka is proved by the fact that in one of his inscriptions he cites an Abhidharma of Châriputta.

The dynasty of Chandragupta was called the Maurya, and that of Pushpamitra, the Sunga.

86. The struggle lasted long, and the Brâhmans and the Buddhists gained by turns the upper hand. Till the fourth century A.D., the latter seem to have been in the majority. But in the two following centuries, they rapidly declined. In many places still occupied, at the time of the Chinese traveller Fa Hian (400 A.D.) by Buddhist temples, towers, and monasteries, his fellow-countryman Hiouen Thsang, in the first half of the seventh century, found nothing but ruins, or Brâhmanic sanctuaries. Under the protection of the powerful King Ṣîlâditya, about this period, Buddhism revived once more for a time, and a great council, even, was held at which the Chinese pilgrim played a distinguished part. Not long after-

wards it encountered a violent opponent in the celebrated teacher of the Mîmânsâ school, Kumârila-Bhaṭṭa, and later still in the great enemy of all heresies, the orthodox Ṣankarâcharya, who was born in 788 A.D. It is commonly supposed that the Buddhists were the victims in India of bloody persecutions and were exterminated with violence, but of this supposed fact no satisfactory proofs are forthcoming. On the contrary, Buddhism appears to have pined away slowly. It continued to exist for some centuries in some of the remoter districts. In Kashmîr it held its ground at all events till 1102, and in the modern Bengal certainly down to 1036, while it has continued in Nepâl till the present day. The majority of believers who remained faithful fled to foreign lands, amongst others to Java, and spread their faith there. Others passed into the sect of the Jainas which was not exposed to persecution.

87. The sect of the Jainas derived its name from its veneration of *Jinas* or eminent ascetics, who had conquered all the desires of sense, and thus raised themselves above the gods, Mahâvîra being the most celebrated among them. It is very closely related to Buddhism, and in Sanskrit literature is hardly to be distinguished from it. While some scholars regard it as a Buddhist sect, others believe it to have been founded before Buddhism; it is at any rate certain that it existed in the sixth century of our era. Its sacred books, the most important of which, called the Kalpa-Sûtra, was written in the same century, are composed in a dialect belonging to the district in which Buddhism took its rise (the

Ardhamâgadhî). Its origin lies hidden in obscurity, but it is not improbable that it proceeded from a compromise between Buddhism and Brâhmanism in the first centuries after Christ.

The Jainas are divided into two bodies, those dressed in white robes (*Ṣvetâmbara*) and the naked (*Digambara*, literally "persons robed in air"), the latter of whom, however, only lay aside their dress at meals. Like the Buddhists, they look to Nirvâṉa as their goal, they treat the devas as inferior beings liable to rebirth, they divide themselves into clergy and laymen, they reduce their law to a few leading commands, they impose confession on the believer as the preliminary to obtaining priestly absolution, and every year they keep a solemn fast (*paryû-shaṉa*). They have, however, a great aversion to the Buddhist worship of relics. In their worship of the greater number of the Hindu gods, especially of the three principal deities of this era and of Ganeṣa, in their maintenance of a certain division of castes, and even in their application of the name Brâhmans to their priests in Western India, they were not essentially different from the Buddhists, for much the same usages prevailed among them also. The doctrines set forth in their holy Scriptures differ in many respects from both the Brâhmanic and the Buddhist systems. The toleration extended to them by the Brâhmans even though they were regarded as heretics, led large numbers of Buddhists to take refuge in their community in the days of the persecution.

Jina, "the conquering," is also one of the commonest surnames of the Buddha. According to the Jainas, Gautama (Buddha) was a disciple of their great saint,

Mahâvîra. They are mentioned in 587 A.D. by Varâhamihira.

The clergy or monks are called *Sâdhus* or *Yatis*, the laymen *Srâvakas*, "hearers." The five (or ten) chief commandments of the Jainas and those of the Buddhists exhibit very close agreement. Their great fast, or period of silent meditation, in the rainy season, Paryushâna or Pajjûsan, does not differ much from the Buddhist *vassa* (*varsha*) or rainy season, in which the followers of Buddha also were accustomed to abstain from travelling, and to stay in some remote spot absorbed in contemplation.

D. *The Changes in Brâhmanism under the Influence of its Conflict with Buddhism.*

Literature.—For a list of editions and translations of the *Râmâyaṇa* and *Mahâbhârata* up to 1847, see GILDEMEISTER'S *Bibliothec. Sanscr. Specimen*, pp. 29–53. Since that date, the edition by GORRESIO has been finished, and a complete translation of both epics by HIPP. FAUCHE has appeared. The Râmâyana has also been translated by GRIFFITHS.

Portions of the poems have been translated by THÉOD. PAVIE, and subsequently by PH. ED. FOUCAUX, *Le Mahâbhârata, onze episodes*, Paris, 1862. Of the *Bhagavad-Gîtâ*, the most recent translations are those by ÉM. BURNOUF (Nancy and Paris, 1861), and F. LORINSER, *Die Bhag.-Gita, übersetzt und erläutert*, Breslau, 1869. The latter work has been severely criticised by K. T. TELANG, *Bhagavad-Gîtâ, translated, with Notes and an Introductory Essay*, Bombay, 1875. Cf. A. DE GUBERNATIS, *Studie sull' Epopea Indiana*, Firenze (no date).

For the Purâṇas, see GILDEMEISTER, *op. cit.*, pp. 54–60. The most important translations are those of the *Bhâgavata-Purâṇa*, by EUG. BURNOUF, Paris, 1840, and following years, and of the *Vishnu-Purâna*, by H. H. WILSON, London, 1840, re-edited in the complete collection of Wilson's works by Dr. Fitzedward Hall, 4 vols., London, Trübner & Co., 1865 and foll.

88. The Brâhmans perceived that it was not enough simply to exterminate their dangerous rival, they must also endeavour to provide for the wants which Buddhism had satisfied. To give up their doctrinal system and their hierarchy, to make their esoteric teaching the common property of all, to let go the authority of the Veda—this was impossible for them, without destroying their order. But it was possible for them to modify that system, to supply a new basis for their hierarchy, to combine their own doctrine with the prevailing popular belief, and by setting the claims of orthodoxy very low, to gain allies out of various sects. These methods were applied by them in the days of the ascendency of Buddhism with such success that its power declined more and more, and persecution and violence seem to have been superfluous, if they were practised at all.

89. The first thing needed for this purpose was a popular conception of deity. Neither the somewhat abstract gods of the latest Ṛik-hymns, nor their own Brahmâ (masc.), and least of all the impersonal—or at any rate neuter—Bráhma, could fulfil this requisite, for not one of them had become a god of the people. Such a deity they found in Vishnu, the worship of whom seems to have increased considerably in the last four centuries B.C. In the old-Vedic time Vishnu was a god of subordinate importance, generally connected with Indra,

and seldom celebrated by himself. He was a sun-god, who traversed the whole world in three steps, but he was thrown almost entirely into the shade by Sûrya and Sâvitṛi. He did not rise much higher in the Brâhmaṇa period, at least among the Brâhmans and Kshattriyas. Now, however, he is ranked among the twelve Âdityas, and is soon elevated to be the supreme god. In this capacity the names and forms of Prajâpati, Brahmâ, and other creative deities, are transferred to him. By the infinite world-serpent (*ṣesha* or *ananta*) he is drawn over the waves of the primeval ocean, or by the sun-bird *Garuḍa* through the sky, or he appears in human form with four hands, three of which carry a shell, a dart, and a club. In his heaven, Vaikuṇṭha, his consort Lakshmî or Ṣrî, the goddess of love and beauty, of fruitfulness and marriage, dwells by his side ; to her the cow was dedicated, and her symbol was the lotus flower.

The slight estimation in which Vishṇu was held by the Brâhmans, even as late as the end of the Brâhmanic period, may be inferred from the fact that in the laws of Manu he stands no higher than in the Veda, and that Yâska, 400 B.C., still places him in the second rank. It has even been conjectured (Muir, *Sanskrit Texts*, iv. p. 165, *sqq.*, and *passim;* Lassen, *Ind. Alterth.*, i. p. 488, *sqq.*, 2d ed., i. p. 586, *sqq.*), that in the oldest versions of the epics, which were certainly especially current among the Kshattriyas and reflected their belief, he had not as yet attained the eminent place assigned to him in the later redactions of the poems.

Garuḍa or Garutmat, who appears already in the Ṛig-veda as a divine sun-bird, and is also enumerated in the oldest Buddhist Sûtras among the lesser gods, was formerly connected with Indra. How he was transferred from the cultus of this deity to that of Vishṉu, is related in the *Mahâbhâr.* 5, 104, vs. 3674, *sqq.*

90. Of the Vishnu worship the doctrine of the *avatâras* or incarnations (literally, " descents "), is characteristic. Just as the Buddha becomes man whenever the world needs to be redeemed from misery, Vishṉu also, if danger threatens the devas or their worshippers, assumes one form or another to bring them deliverance. The number of these avatâras was not at first strictly defined, and kept mounting higher and higher. Among the oldest of them is the " dwarf-incarnation " (*vâmanâvatâra*) borrowed from Vishṉu's own sun-myth: then he appears as the fish who saves Manu at the deluge (*matsyâvatâra*), as the tortoise who, at the churning of the heavenly ocean (*i.e.*, at the creation), supports the earth (*kûrmâvatâra*), and as the boar which restores it to equilibrium when it has sunk into the under world (*varâhâvatâra*),—three sun-myths which were first applied to Brahmâ as creator, and were transferred from him to Vishṉu. With the last of these myths is connected that of the " man-lion " (*nṛsiṁhâvatâra*), under which shape Vishṉu freed the world from the sway of a demon-king. Besides this the doctrine of the avatâras afforded an opportunity of identifying him with favourite heroes of tradition, who were probably once deities. Such were Râmachandra, who, like Buddhism, extended his conquests to Ceylon; Paraṣurâma, the " axe-Râma," an ancient deity of fire and lightning, whom the Brâhmans raised to be their hero as the slayer of all the Kshattriyas; and Kṛishṉa the hidden sun-god of the night, always connected in the

Epos with the light Arjuna, the visible sun-god, and whose myth forms a counterpart of the legend of Buddha, though they are as far apart as the poles in character. In later times Vishṇu was also connected with several other divine beings.

The myth of Vishṇu as a dwarf is to be found as early as the *Ṣatapatha Brâhmaṇa* (see Muir, *Sanskrit Texts*, iv. p. 122, *sqq.*) It is noteworthy that in this version Vishṇu does not assume the form of a dwarf, but actually is a dwarf. The only use there made of the myth by the Brâhmans is to attach to it their theory of sacrifice. It is highly instructive to compare their representation with the much more original story in the *Râmâyaṇa* (i. 32, 2, *sqq.*), and with the form in the *Bhâgav. Purâṇa* (viii. 15, 1, *sqq.*), which has been in many respects modified, where Vishṇu only needs two steps to traverse earth and heaven, and the Asura prince Bali, whom he dethrones, is placed in a very favourable light.

Some of the avatâras appear to have been borrowed from the mythology of non-Hindu inhabitants of India. Lassen, *Ind. Alterth.*, iv. p. 583, conjectured that this was the case with the dwarf. The man-lion also appears to me to belong to a system different from the Hindu. The boar is also a form of the sun-god in the Zend-Avesta. Râma-chandra, like Kṛishṇa, is a god of night; his name connects him both with the night (*râma*, "night," "rest," "dark,") and with the moon (*chandra*). His spouse is Sîtâ, "the furrow," the ploughed earth, which, according to a representation common in antiquity, was fertilised by the moon and by the dew descending from it, or the night wind sent by it (in the Zend-Avesta, Râman is the genius of the air [*Vayu*, the Sanskr. Vâyu], who gives taste to food). That *Paraṣu-Râma* is a god of the solar fire admits of no doubt. He springs from the Brâhman race of the Bhṛigus (lightning), his father's name is Jamadagni, "the burning fire." Like all gods of solar fire he is the nightly or hidden one, and accordingly he slays Arjuna, the bright god of day. Out of this the myth of the Kshattriya-slayer developed itself spontaneously. In the myth of Kṛishṇa, on the other hand, the two sun-gods are friendly, the old pair of deities Vishṇu and Indra in a new shape.

91. In the cultus of Kṛishṇa the worship of Vishṇu reaches its climax. Traces of Kṛishṇa-worship indeed make their appearance at an early date; but not till he was regarded as an avatâra of Vishṇu, especially in the form of Nârâyaṇa, who had previously been identified with Brahmâ, did it spread through the whole land. In the Epos he is represented as a demi-god, who distinguished himself by his heroic deeds, his higher knowledge, and his miraculous power, while later on he took the rank of the highest god. The Brâhmanic theosophists make him a disciple of the Brâhmans, who devotes himself to mystic meditations, and thus in the Bhagavad-Gîtâ he appears as the preacher of an ethical-pantheistic doctrine, and proclaims himself as the Supreme Being and the Redeemer. At a later date, viz., in the Gîtâ-govinda, special prominence was given to the legends of his miraculous birth, his intercourse with the shepherds, and his luxurious life with the shepherdesses, the remembrance of which was celebrated by special religious festivals.

When Buddhism had ceased to be dangerous to the Brâhmans, the Buddha himself was included among the atavâras of Vishṇu, and the sect of the Bauddha-

Vaishṉavas arose, which attempted to fuse the two systems together.

At the end of this age (Kaliyuga) Vishṉu is to appear as Kalkin, to root out all wickedness.

In all his incarnations Vishṉu is a god of salvation and beneficence, and as a human being he is in no way inferior to the Buddha in gentleness, humanity, and self-denial, of which the Brâhmans had many striking examples to present. To this Paraṣurâma forms the only exception, but it is probable that the Brâhmans did not connect this form with him till they felt themselves strong enough to re-establish their authority again, if need be, by force.

If the Indian Herakles, of whom Megasthenes speaks, is really Kṛishṉa, as Lassen affirms (*Ind. Alterth.*, i. p. 647), the worship of Kṛishṉa must have become tolerably general by 300 B.C. But the identification leaves much to be desired. The name occurs in an inscription dating probably from the beginning of our era (Bayley, *Journ. As. Soc. Bengal*, 1854, cf. Weber, *Zeitschr. der Deutsch. Morgenl. Gesellsch.*, ix. p. 631). The figure and the myth of Kṛishṉa are certainly of great antiquity, though it was not till later times that his cultus spread over the whole of India.

Nara and Nârâyaṉa also are ancient gods. Their names signify "man" and "son of man" (Böhtlingk and Roth, *Wörterb.* Bopp explains Nârâyaṉa otherwise, "he who goes through the waters"), and are doubtless connected with Nereus and the Nereids. They correspond with Arjuna and Kṛishṉa, Indra and Vishṉu. In the Brâhmanic period, even as late as in the laws of Manu, Nârâyaṉa is a surname of Brahmâ.

The legends of the Gîtâ-govinda are not of more recent growth than the stories about Kṛishṇa in the epics, though they were not adopted into the Brâhmanic system until later. They belong, on the contrary, to the oldest myths of the Aryan race. The representation of the god as a disciple of the Brâhmans, which we meet with in the Chandogya-Upanishad, is, however, much more modern.

In the teachings of the Bhagavat-Gîtâ, Lorinser believes he can detect citations from the New Testament, and the stories of Kṛishṇa's birth and childhood appear to Weber to exhibit traces of Christian influence. They are, in my judgment, very doubtful. The works of Lorinser and Telang have been cited above. Comp. A. Weber, "Ueber die Kṛishnajaumâshtamî" (Kṛishṇa's Geburtsfest) in *Abhandll. der Königl. Akademie der Wissensch. in Berlin*, 1867. The views of Lorinser and Weber are shared by F. Nève, *Des Éléments Étrangers du Mythe et du Culte de Krichna*, Paris, 1876. On the whole question see C. P. Tiele, "Christus en Kṛishṇa," in the *Theolog. Tijdschr.*, 1877, No. 1. p. 63, *sqq.* Senart is of opinion that the Kṛishṇa-myth served as the type for the legend of Buddha. Even if that is correct, it still remains true that the Brâhmans took up the old popular representations which had been first adopted by the Buddhists, modified their form, and then employed them again as weapons against their opponents.

The significance of the future Buddha, Kalkin, whose name if translated would mean "contagion," "falsehood," is still very enigmatical.

92. At the same time with Vishṇu, perhaps even before him, Rudra also, whose worship had made such advances in the previous period (see § 78), was raised, under his euphemistic name of Ṣiva, to the position of

supreme deity (*Mahâdeva*). His character is not to be reproduced in a single word. As Rudra his nature is violent and dreadful; he lives in the wilderness on the loftiest mountains; in asceticism, and, therefore, in power, he surpasses all other beings. But at the same time he is a god of fruitfulness, and thence the creator; and he is from this time, therefore, generally worshipped under the symbol of the power of propagation, the *lingam*. It is not without reason that it has been supposed that this symbol is not of Aryan origin, and that the Ṣiva of this period has arisen out of the fusion of Agni-Rudra with a native deity. Certainly both the representation of his person and the character of his cultus are thoroughly unbrâhmanic, various foreign elements, such as the worship of serpents and spirits (*bhutas*) being connected with his worship. He was particularly popular in the mountain districts of the north and in the Dekhan, and the Brâhmans saw in Ṣivaism a welcome ally against Buddhism.

The consort of Ṣiva, who combines in her person the same conflicting characteristics, who is marked out by her self-renouncing piety (*tapas*) as an ancient fire-goddess, and by her relation to Sarasvatî, the goddess of the waters and of knowledge, as a goddess of mountains and streams, was invoked alike under the ancient names Ambikâ and Umâ, the "mother" and the "protectress," as well as by the titles Kâlî, the "black one," and Durgâ, the "terrible." As Kâlî-Durgâ she is the goddess of death, horrible in shape, and worshipped with bloody sacrifices. In the pantheon and in the cultus she takes a much more prominent place than all the other goddesses, whose qualities and names were transferred to her; and she was even connected with Kṛishṉa and as Devîmâhâtmya ("the majesty of the goddess") with Vishṉu.

Ṣiva means "the gracious," one of the euphemisms by which it was endeavoured to appease dreaded deities, in sound somewhat resembling his characteristic name, Ṣarva, the "destroyer," the "wrathful." The epics relate how the supreme gods, Vishṉu and Kṛishṉa on the one side, and Mahâdeva on the other, vied with each other in their compliments. All these passages in which they reciprocally glorify each other are, of course, interpolations. But the worship of Mahâdeva as the supreme god must be the oldest. Passages, however, are not wanting which show that his cultus was not introduced till after the first period of Brâhmanism, and then not without resistance. The Lingam is certainly not a symbol of ancient Brâhmanism, and Ṣiṣnadevas (phallus-gods) are opposed in the Vedas and excluded from pure sacrifices. He was regarded both as destroyer and creator, inasmuch as he was both storm-god and fire-god, and his union with Agni may have served as the point of attachment for the Brâhmans. I conjecture that Ṣiva or Ṣarva was not original, but was derived from his consort Durgâ, whose attributes were transferred to Agni-Rudra, when she was united with him. It is in this sense that we designate him a native deity, which cannot be absolutely proved, and is still doubted by many scholars, but is sufficiently clear from the non-Aryan character of his cultus.

In the case of his spouse we must distinguish with the same care between the mountain goddess Pârvatî or Haimavatî, the ancient mother-goddess Umâ or Ambikâ, and Kâlî, Karâlî or Durgâ, who is certainly not of Aryan origin. In the last who, properly speaking, has no consort, we may recognise the goddess of death and of the under-world, who is found both among the oldest inhabitants of Central Asia and among the Malays. As the spouse of Mahâdeva she is, however, the goddess *par excellence* (*Devî*), and all the goddesses, therefore, and not only Sarasvatî (who was connected with Pârvatî) and Nirṛiti (the goddess of evil, resembling Durga in character), but even Mâyâ, Ṣrî (spouse of Vishṉu), Sâvitṛî, and others, might be identified with her.

93. Among the gods adopted during this period into the Brâhmanic system, Gaṉeṣa, the god of arts and wisdom, occupies the principal place. The greatest difficulty was to find room in the same system for all the three chief gods whose worshippers were for the most part hostile to each other. The endeavours to fill up the gulf between the rivals may be speedily traced in different mythic narratives of their reconciliation. The first expedient was simply to place the three side by side, and ascribe the same rights to each of them. Generally, however, two of them had to submit to be subordinated to the third. Or Vishṉu and Ṣiva were united into one person, *Hari-harau*, who was then united with Brahmâ and regarded as the chief god. Last of all arose the doctrine of the *Trimûrti*, according to which the three gods were represented as so many forms or revelations of one supreme deity in his threefold activity as creator, sustainer, and destroyer. Among the people, however, this doctrine made little way. Moreover, it appears not only to have arisen in the South of India, but to have been confined exclusively to that portion of the Peninsula.

Besides the worship of Gaṉeṣa, practised by his particular sect, the *Gâṉapatyas*, we meet in this period with that of *Skanda Kârtikeya*, the god of war, and of *Kâma*, the god of love.

The union of Hari (*i.e.*, Vishnu) and Hara (Ṣiva) had its counterpart in the fusion of the male and female deity also into one under the name *Ardhanarî*. All this indicates a strong tendency to monotheism.

The first appearance of the Trimurtî is in the 14th century A.D., but the idea that the supreme being exercises by turns one of the three functions already specified, is of great antiquity. The application of this conception to Brahmâ, Vishnu, and Ṣiva, is entirely arbitrary, the two latter, for example, being creators no less than the first.

94. It is characteristic of this period that it gave rise to a new sacred literature, totally different in character from the Brâhmanic. But the Brâhmans perceived very clearly that the rich literature of the Buddhists, if its influence was to be rendered harmless, needed something to counterbalance it. With this view, the eighteen Purânas which still exist, and a similar number of Upapurânas, were composed: by the members of the sects they were placed on the same footing as the Vedas, and regarded as of great antiquity; none of them, however, were written till after the eighth century A.D., and the majority even are much later. Their object is nothing less than to give a history of the universe since its origin, and they are concerned not only with theology, but with all departments of knowledge.

At the same time, the two great epics, the Mahâbhârata and the Râmâyana, in which the ancient gods, already completely transformed into heroes, lived and moved as human beings on the earth,—or rather, in which the old myths were blended with some great historic events into an epic narrative,—were modified and interpolated by the worshippers of Vishṉu and Ṣiva, to make them the vehicles of their particular theology.

Purâṉa signifies "ancient tradition;" the *Upapurâṉas* are the By-Purâṉas, and are of less importance. Both perhaps contain some elements of older Purâṉas now lost, but they differ totally in spirit and contents from the character of these works, as we infer it by description. Following the number of the great gods, they are divided into three groups of six; but the six, which are devoted to the glorification of Brahmâ, while they contain a number of legends about him, chiefly insist on the worship of Ṣiva, and especially of Vishṉu.

In the older parts of the epic poems, the principal heroes and heroines are only compared with the chief gods and goddesses. In passages subsequently inserted they are elevated into their *avatâras.* Ever and anon the opportunity is seized to thrust in a panegyric on Vishṉu or Ṣiva, or to furnish a proof of their supreme power. It is often very easy to separate these additions from the original text, which must have been in existence before the year 300 B.C. It was a master-stroke of the Brâhmans to make these epics, which seem to have been originally the peculiar literature of the Kshattriyas, available for their purpose.

95. Meanwhile, the Brâhmans surrendered nothing of their claims and privileges. To prevent the people from escaping from their control, they lowered themselves to them, but they were always careful to make it appear what deep reverence was ever paid, even by the highest gods, to a member of their caste. They likewise remained faithful to their over-estimate of knowledge

(*jnâna*) as a means of deliverance. They therefore opposed the doctrine of Ṣâṇḍilya, which substituted piety (*bhakti*) and love to God for knowledge, and vigorously maintained the authority and infallibility of the Veda, which they now even declared to be eternal and uncreated. Practically, however, they made concessions upon this point, and regarded as orthodox every school or sect which acknowledged the authority of the Veda, even though it denied its eternity.

The dispute about the eternity of the Veda is highly instructive, especially when the Brâhmanic doctrine of revelation is compared with the teachings of Christian and Mohammedan theologians on the inspiration of the Bible and the Qorân. In subtlety and absurdity it far transcends anything which either of the latter have ever devised.

It was simply the recognition of the authority of the Veda that secured even for the Nyâya and the atheistic Sânkhya philosophy the credit of orthodoxy by the side of the orthodox Vedânta.

96. Of the six so-called philosophical systems, only three properly answer to this description. The *Vedânta*, the "end of the Veda," is purely pantheistic and monistic, and is connected (as *Uttara-mîmâṁsâ*, "later consideration") with the proper or older Mîmâṁsâ (*Pûrva-mîmâṁsâ*), a more ritualistic system. The *Nyâya* ("rule," "maxim") is occupied with the method of philosophical inquiry, and the *Vaiṣeshika* (from *viṣesha*, "difference," "attribute") which is connected with it, applies the method to nature. Analytical in their principles, they are diametrically opposed to the synthetic *Sânkhya*

("reasoning," "synthesis") a dualistic and atheistic system, which exercised very great influence not only upon thought but also on religion. The practical side of this system is represented by the Yoga philosophy, which is distinguished from the Sânkhya by its decided theism, and undertakes to show how, by concentrating the mind in profound reflection, it is possible to attain union with the divine principle, while its professors surpass in self-torture all the ascetics of the world. The so-called founders of these schools are for the most part mythical persons. Beneath the systems which bear their name, we may discern clearly the animistic view of the universe. In the doctrine of the independent existence of the soul, and the inferences to be drawn from it, they all agree.

The Vedânta, the Sânkhya, and the Nyâya, are the only schools that possess any of the characteristics of philosophical systems, and even they only deserve this designation in a limited sense, as the object of them all is not the search for truth, but the redemption of men.

The Pûrva-mîmâṁsâ is founded on the Brâhmanas, but the Vedânta, on the other hand, on the Upanishads, which suffices to indicate their respective characters. On this system, and on Ṣankara, the famous champion of orthodoxy, see A. Bruining, *Bijdrage tot de Kennis van den Vedânta*, Leiden, 1871.

The animistic character of these systems appears in the fundamental conceptions which they all possess in common. As the union of body and soul (which, like the substance of the universe, is eternal) is the cause of all misery, deliverance consists in the complete separation of the soul from the body, and it is to this goal that the different systems are intended to lead.

The reputed founders of the Vaiseshikas, Sânkhya, and Vedânta schools are certainly mythic beings,—Kanada (the "atom-eater"), Kapila (the "yellow"), and Vyâsa ("extension," "separation"); probably also Gotama, the supposed founder of the Nyâya, is of the same order. Jaimini, the founder of the Pûrva-mîmâñsâ, may very well be regarded as a historical personage, and Patanjali, the father of the Yoga, is certainly so.

97. As soon as Buddhism was overcome and driven out, the sects which had only been united by the presence of danger, burst through this artificial union, and were again separated. Vishnu was once more worshipped by the Vaishnavas, Ṣiva by the Ṣaivas, as the supreme deity, and each body split into a number of smaller communities, to which new ones were perpetually being added. The most famous of the later Vaishnava sects are those founded in the twelfth century by Râmanuja in Southern India, and sometime afterwards by Râmânanda. The first of these is distinguished by great strictness, and the avoidance of all profane persons; while to this the second is in many respects diametrically opposed, though its founder Râmânanda was originally one of the followers of Râmanuja. Expelled because he had eaten with unconsecrated persons, he abstained from imposing on the disciples whom he gathered round him, any commands of ceremonial purity, and even taught that the clergy ought to reject all forms of worship. From a disciple of Râmânanda came, further, the sect of the Kâbîrpanthi, from whose writings the famous Nânak Shâh, the founder of the religious community of the Sikhs (*Ṣishya*), derived a large portion of his doctrine.

The Kâbîrpanthi hardly belong to Vishnuism any longer, though they are counted among its adherents, but they have adopted many elements of Mohammedanism, and are zealous Monotheists. Like the followers of Râmânanda, they employ the vernacular. The repugnance to animal sacrifices is shared by all these communities, and they are all alike open to members of every caste.

The Ṣaiva sects are composed chiefly of clergy or monks, living in solitude, or united in fraternities. Ṣiva is their god, as the protector and the example of self-denying penitents. They have now, however, for the most part degenerated into mere jugglers, and no longer enjoy much respect.

The doctrine of the followers of Râmanuja accords, in many respects, with the Vedânta. Vishnu is in their view the same as Brahmâ. The adherents of Râmânanda worship Vishnu as Râma or Sîtâ-Râma. Kâbîr is certainly a fictitious name for the unknown founder of the community of the Kâbîrpanthi. Much as the author of their sacred books may have derived from the teachings of the Mohammedans, he was certainly far better acquainted with the Hindu writings than with the Islâmitic, and he must, therefore, have been a Hindu. A complete translation of the *Adi Granth*, the sacred book of the Sikhs, has been recently published by Dr. E. Trumpp, London, 1877. Comp. also his Festrede, *Nânak, der Stifter der Sikh-Religion*, Munich, 1876.

98. The deep decay of Brâhmanism is evinced by the rise and spread of the Ṣâkta-sects, who worship the personified power of the three great gods as female beings.

Though these bodies have some points of affinity with the other sects, they constitute really a return to representations and usages belonging to a lower stage of religious development. They are divided into two groups, those of the right hand (*Dakshiṉâchâri*), and those of the left hand (*Vâmâchâri*), of whom the first follow a stricter ritual, while the second are characterised by magic ceremonies and disgusting licentiousness. Sometimes, however, they merge in each other. The rise and spread of these sects affords an example of the revival of ancient elements as soon as the bonds of the hierarchy are weakened, and the chain of purified tradition is broken.

Meanwhile, under the influence of Islâm and Christianity, a number of mixed sects have arisen, such as that of Nânak Shâh already named, and the later Brahmosamâj, which is perhaps destined to give a new direction to Brâhmanism.

To the wives of the three great gods, Durgâ, Lakshmî, and Sarasvatî or Sâvitṛî, Râdhâ, the spouse of Kṛishṉa, must also be added, who is indeed regarded by some sects as the chief goddess.

It is impossible to mistake the striking correspondence between the worship of the Saktis and the primeval nature-worship of the pre-Aryans and pre-Semites, in which the great mother-goddess is the supreme object of worship, and which has left so many traces behind it through the whole of Asia. The Dakshinâchari and Vâmâchâri flow into each other, among other places, at Calcutta. At any rate, the sect of the Right-hand established there follows to some extent the ritual of the Left-hand. On this subject compare *Pratâpachandra Gosha,*

Durgâ pûjâ, with notes and illustrations, announced in the *Theol. Tijdschr.* 1872, p. 344, *sqq.*

The sect of the Brahmo-samâj founded in 1830 by Râm Mohun Roy, and reformed in a liberal spirit in our own time by Keshab Chander Sen, recognises the moral grandeur of Jesus, and the truth of the fundamental Christian principles, but does not absolutely abandon the Hindû tradition. It aims at a religion consisting in the worship of God as the loving Father of all men, and resulting in brotherly love to all. Whether it is destined to exercise any great influence in the future, cannot as yet be determined.

III.

RELIGION AMONG THE ERÂNIAN (PERSIAN) NATIONS. MAZDEISM.

Literature.—General and historical works: F. SPIEGEL, *Erânische Alterthumskunde*, i. *Geogr.*, *Ethnogr.*, *und ält. Geschichte*, Leipzig, 1871, ii. *Religion, Geschichte bis zum Tode Alexanders des Grossen*, ibid., 1873. The third and last vol. is in the press. Id., *Arische Studien*, i. Leipzig, 1874. F. MÜLLER, *Zend Studien*, i. and ii., Vienna, 1863. FLATHE, Art. "Perser, Geschichte" in Ersch and Gruber's *Allg. Encyclopädie*, sect. iii. vol. xvii. pp. 370–434. LASSEN, *Aeltere Geographie*, ibid., pp. 435–443. SPIEGEL, *Erân, Beitr. zur Kenntniss des Landes und seiner Geschichte*, Berlin, 1863. F. JUSTI, *Beiträge zur alten Geogr. Persiens*, i. Marburg, 1869, ii. ibid., 1870 (Universitäts Festschrift).—*Sacred Literature.* Editions of the *Zend-Avesta* by SPIEGEL (with Huzvaresh-translation), Leipzig and

Vienna, 1851, and following years, and by WESTERGAARD, Copenhagen, 1852–54. Of the *Vendidâd Sâde*, by H. BROCKHAUS, Leipzig, 1850. Of the *Bundehesh*, with transcription, translation, and glossary, by F. JUSTI, Leipzig, 1868. Latest editions of the Persian cuneiform inscriptions, SPIEGEL, *Die Altpers. Keilinschriften, im Grundtext mit Uebersetz., Gramm., und Glossar*, Leipzig, 1862: C. KOSSOWICZ, *Inscriptiones Palaeo-Persicae Achaemenidarum, ed. et expl.*, Petropol., 1872. The *Arḍâ-Vîrâf Nâmak*, with translation, &c., by M. HAUG and E. W. WEST, Bombay and London, 1872. Further, M. HAUG, *Die fünf Gâthâ's . . . Zarathustra's, herausgeg., übersetzt und erklärt*, i., Leipzig, 1858, ii., ibid., 1860, to be used with very great caution. The following chiefly depend on Spiegel: *Decem Sendavestae Excerpta, recensuit et latine vertit* C. KOSSOWICZ, Paris, 1865, and by the same writer, *Gâtha ahunavaiti*, Petersburg, 1867; *Gâtha ustavaiti*, ibid., 1869; *Saratustricae Gâthae poster. tres*, ibid., 1871. *Neriosengh's* Sanskrit translation of the *Yaṣna*, edited by SPIEGEL, Leipzig, 1861. F. SPIEGEL, *Avesta, aus dem Grundtext übersetzt*, 3 vols., Leipzig, 1852–1863, with which must necessarily be compared his *Commentar über d. Avesta*, 2 vols., ibid., 1865–1869, as it contains a number of emendations and modifications of the translation. Detached pieces: M. HAUG, *Das achtzehnte Kapitel des Wendidâd übersetzt und erklärt*, München, 1869. HÜBSCHMANN, *Ein zoroastrisches Lied* (*Yaçna*, 30), ibid., 1872. Comp. further, R. ROTH, "Beiträge zur Erklärung des Avesta," i.–iii., and F. SPIEGEL, "Zur Erklärung des Avesta," both in the *Zeitschr. der Deutschen Morgenl. Gesellsch.*, xxv., pp. 1 *sqq.*, 215 *sqq.*, 297 *sqq.* M. BRÉAL, "Fragments de Crit. Zende," *Journ. Asiat.*, 1862 (includes an essay on the first Farg. of the Vendidâd). W. D. WHITNEY, "On the Avesta," *Journ. Amer. Orient. Soc.*, v. 1856, and

Oriental and Linguistic Studies, New York, 1875, and MAX MÜLLER, *Chips from a German Workshop*, artt. v.–viii. (A number of purely philological works cannot be enumerated here.) *Religion.*—TH. HYDE, *Historia Religionis vet. Persarum eorumque Magorum*, Oxford, 1700, still noteworthy. I. G. RHODE, *Die heilige Sage und der gesammte Religionssystem des Zendvolkes*, Frankfort, 1820, founded entirely on the translation of the Zend Avesta by Anquetil Duperron, which is no longer of any use. The confusion of elements belonging to different periods, and the want of a good translation, render K. SCHWENCK'S *Mythologie der Perser*, Frankfort, 1855, useless. C. P. TIELE, *De godsdienst van Zarathustra van haar ontstaan in Baktrië tot den val van het Oud-Perzische Rijk*, Haarlem, 1864, requires revision, especially for the history of the origin of Mazdeism. M. HAUG, *Essays on the Sacred Language, Writings, and Religion of the Parsees*, Bombay, 1862 (to be used with caution). F. WINDISCHMANN, *Zoroastr. Studien, herausgegeben von* SPIEGEL, Berlin, 1863 (contains among other things a complete translation of the Bundehesh and the Farvardin-Yasht). Id., *Die Persische Anahita oder Anaïtis*, Munich, 1856. Id., "Mithra," in *Abhandll. für die Kunde des Morgenl.*, i., No. 1, Leipzig, 1857. I. G. STICKEL, *De Dianæ Persicæ Monum. Grœchwyliano*, Jena, 1856. J. H. VULLERS, *Fragmente uber die Religion des Zoroaster*, Bonn, 1831. J. OPPERT, "L'Honover, le verb créateur de Zoroastre" (*Ann. de Philos. Chrétienne*, Janv., 1862). A. HOVELACQUE, *Morale de l'Avesta*, Paris, 1874. JAMES DARMESTETER, *Haurvetât et Ameretât, Essai sur la Mythologie de l'Avesta*, Paris, 1875. On the Pârsism of the present day, DADHABAI NAOROJI, *The Parsee Religion*, and *The Manners and Customs of the Parsees*, London, 1862.—See further, "Contributions towards a Bibliography of Zoroastrian Literature," in

Trübner's *American and Oriental Literary Record*, July 20, 1865.

99. After the division of the Aryans into Hindus and Erânians, the latter probably remained for a considerable time faithful to the ancient Aryan religion, though not without adopting Turanian elements into it. Mazdeism or Pârsism is a reformation of this religion, ascribed by its confessors to Zarathustra (Zoroaster). Of the history of this reformer, whose very existence even has been called in question, nothing is known with certainty, though a number of legends have been transmitted of his birth, temptation, and miraculous deeds. It is equally uncertain at what time the religion of Zarathustra was founded. It appears from the oldest sources that the religious reformation accompanied the introduction of agriculture and of settled life. The language in which these documents are composed is an East-Erânian, and Bactria, therefore, must have been the fatherland of Mazdeism, though it was certainly raised to the rank of state religion in the Persian empire from the time of Darius Hystaspis, and perhaps even before him. Taking its rise in East-Erân probably before or during the eighth century before our era, it made its way after that date with the Aryan tribes over Media and Persia, and there, it would seem, in the hands of the non-Aryan priestly tribe of the Magi, unknown in Bactria, it underwent not unimportant modifications.

The close relationship of Pârsism to the old-Aryan religion is placed beyond all doubt by comparing it with the Vedic and Brâhmanic religions. Haug and others (including the present writer in an earlier work) have defended the opinion that Mazdeism arose at the same time with the old-Vedic religion, and that both were the result of a schism among the followers of the old-Aryan religion. The grounds on which this opinion is based, appear, however, on further inquiry to be insufficient.

On the question whether Zarathustra must be regarded as a mythical personage, there is as yet no agreement. Kern, "Over het woord Zarathustra en den mythischen persoon van dien naam" (*Mededeelingen van de Koninkl. Akad. van Wetenschappen*, 1867), answered it in the affirmative. On the other side, Spiegel, *Erân. Alterth.*, i. p. 708, and *Heidelb. Jahrbb.*, 1867, No. 43. Justi, *Gött. Gel. Anzeigen*, 1867, No. 51. Cf. Spiegel, "Ueber das Leben Zarathustra's," in *Sitzungs-Berichte der Königl. Baier. Akad. Philos.-Philol. Classe,* January 5, 1867. Even the name Zarathustra has received various explanations.

From the inscriptions of Darius I. it appears that Mazdeism was in his time the official religion of Persia. With the exception of the short sepulchral inscription of Cyrus, no such inscriptions remain from his predecessors. It is not improbable that they also were already Mazda-worshippers.

The selection of the eighth century is not arbitrary. In the narratives given by the Assyrian kings of their military expeditions into Media, it is not till the eighth century and onwards that Aryan names begin to appear, and in the first Fargard of the Vendidad only East-Erânian countries are named, while with the exception of the Median city Ragha, neither Media nor Persia is mentioned. This tradition describes the countries created by Ahura-Mazda, which can have no other meaning than the countries where Mazdeism prevailed. If its origin cannot be brought down later than the eighth century B.C., Mazdeism must by that time have been in existence.

The Magians were certainly a pre-Semitic and pre-Aryan priestly tribe in West Asia, whose head, Rab-mâg, belonged to the court of the Babylonian kings. See Jer. xxix. 3. It is held by some scholars (Lenormant) that, in the form *emga*, "glorious," "exalted," the name is already found in Akkadian as a title of honour borne by the learned and the priests, which seems rather doubtful to me. The Akkadian word *maḥ*, "great, high, principal," has more likeness to the Semitic *Mâg*, the Persian *Magus*, the Bactrian *Môghu*. Of course the Erânians must have derived it from their own *Maz*, "great," or *Maga*, "greatness."

100. Our knowledge of the Zarathustrian religion is chiefly derived from the Avesta (or Zend-avesta), a collection of writings or fragments composed at different dates, the remains of a much richer literature, and from the Bundehesh, a cosmogonic-theological work, written in Pehlevi not earlier than the third century of our era, but preserving many older traditions. The Avesta is divided into *Izeshne* (*yaṣna*), "sacrifices," "sacrificial prayers," *Vispered* (*vispê ratavô*, "all lords") praises to the supreme powers, and *Vendidâd* (*vî-daevadâta*), the law "given against evil spirits," a book which contains, together with ancient traditions, the moral and ceremonial laws, and the prescriptions relating to purity. These three books together, arranged in a peculiar way, constitute the pure Vendidâd (*Vendidâd-sâde*), the Parsee prayer-book. The *Yashts*, sacrificial songs, resembling some which occur in the books just named, form, with some shorter texts, the small Avesta (*Khordah-Avesta*), and are certainly by far the most poetical portion of the Holy Scripture. The greater part of these books are written in the same East-Erânian or Bactrian dialect, but a portion of the Yaṣna, chaps. 28–53, like some ancient prayers, is composed in another dialect, and contains the five Gâthâs or religious odes and a prose-work, the Yaṣna of the seven chapters, —certainly the oldest documents of Pârsism.

The Bundehesh was composed under the reign of the Sâsânidæ, the restorers of Pârsism, whose sovereignty began at the commencement of the third century A.D. By that time Bactrian had already become a dead language. But it is clear that the learned men who wrote this book employed ancient documents in its composition. The Avesta, the Yashts not excluded, must be older, but it is not possible to determine with any certainty the dates of the origin of the different books. Their relative antiquity is all that is settled. Their chronological succession is as follows: the second part of the Yaṣna, the Vendidâd, the first part of the Yaṣna, the Vispered, the Yashts, &c.

101. Far above all divine beings stands *Ahura mazdâo*, the all-wise Lord or Spirit. In the oldest hymns and texts, including, for instance, the confession of faith, he is glorified as the Creator and the God of light, of purity and truth; the giver of all good gifts, and in the first place of life,—his praise and worship transcending everything. He is invested with the same rank in the inscriptions of the old-Persian kings of the race of Hakhâmanis, who profess themselves indebted for their sovereignty to him; and the restorers of the empire and its religion, the

Sâsânidæ, vie with them in his worship. With the extension of the world of divine beings as objects of worship, the homage dedicated to him increased rather than declined. The finest names were devised for him, and the latest representation is perhaps the most exalted. The preaching of this god as the supreme, and, indeed, almost as the only deity, is certainly the new and characteristic element of the Zarathustrian reformation, the adherents of which even called themselves distinctively *Mazdayaṣnan,* worshippers of Mazda. It was an obvious step to identify him with the good spirit (*ṣpeñtô maînyus*), one of the two who, according to the Pârsee doctrine, existed from the beginning, and this identification took place at an early period; but it was not till a very late modification of the system that he was placed on the same footing with the evil one of the two spirits (*añrô-maînyus*), and boundless time (*zrvan akarana*) was set above both.

A large number of Ahura mazda's titles of honour may be found collected in the *Ormazd yasht.* The description given of him by the Bundehesh is more elevated than that in the Avesta.

In the combination *Ahura-mithra* (dual) he takes the place of the old-Aryan Varuṉa; but it would be erroneous on this account to place him on a level with the latter; he stands infinitely higher.

The system which represents Zrvan akarana as the supreme deity, and Ahura mazda and Añrô-maînyus as his sons, is most probably no earlier than the time of the Sâsânidæ, and is an attempt to restore monotheism, which was endangered by the application of dualism to the conception of deity also.

102. Next to Ahura mazda follow six lofty spirits, and these seven make up the number of the sacred immortals (*amesha speñta*). The representation of seven supreme spirits is old-Aryan, but the new system raised one of them above the rest, and inserted fresh figures in the ancient frame. For five of these Amesha speñta (*Amshaspands*) were originally abstract ideas, their personification being only slightly advanced in the oldest hymns. The first three, *Vohu manô*, "the good mind," *Asha vahista*, "the best purity," and *Kshathra vaïrya*, "the desired kingdom," are scarcely more than attributes of Ahura mazda; the last two, *Haurvatât* and *Amĕrĕtâṭ*, "welfare" or "health," and "immortality," are eternal powers conferred by Mazda. *Ârmaiti* alone, an old-Aryan deity, has a more definite personality, and denotes at once the wisdom which protects and fosters the earth and the earth itself. *Vohu manô* became at a later date the genius who protects mankind and receives them into his abode in heaven, as the agent by whom Ormazd's creation is extended; long afterwards, under the degenerate name of Bahman, he appears as the lord of the animal world. As the genius of purity, Asha vahista is, of course, the spirit of fire, the enemy of sickness and death, the adversary of all evil spirits, and he is always, therefore, closely connected with Atar, "fire," the son of Ahura mazda. Kshathra vaïrya soon becomes the genius, not only of the kingdom but also of riches, lord of the precious metals, who teaches their proper employment, and punishes their misuse. Haurvatâṭ and Amĕrĕtâṭ are already in the Gâthas gods at once of health and long life, and of the waters and plants, and, in general, of plenty, and they are, therefore, most closely connected with Ârmaiti. They gradually came to be regarded more definitely as the spirits who provided food and drink, the conquerors of hunger and thirst.

The Amesha ṣpeñta have a general resemblance to the Vedic Âditya's, which were originally six or seven in number, and various epithets are applied to them in common. See Spiegel, *Erân. Altherth.*, ii. p. 31. But in personality they were quite different.

It is remarkable that the names of the Amesha ṣpeñta are half neuter and half feminine. Ârmaiti, in the form Aramati, also occurs in the Veda, and acts among the Hindûs as well as among the Erânians as the genius of wisdom or piety, and also of the earth. Accordingly the founder of Mazdeism has adopted this entire figure from the old-Aryan system.

The relation between Asha and Atar is completely analogous to that between the Babylonio-Assyrian Anu and Ṣamdan, though the two pairs of deities are at the same time separated by great diversities.

J. Darmesteter has endeavoured to prove that the abstract significance of the Amesha ṣpeñta preceded the material, and, in particular, that Haurvatâṭ and Ameretâṭ originally personified health and long life. Not till a later period, so he supposes, were they set over the waters and plants; and it was from their older attributes that their significance as spirits of plenty was derived. Though the essay contains much that is admirable, and the author has accurately expounded the necessary connection between the various functions of these deities, he has failed, in my judgment, to furnish the *proof* that the material significance is the derivative. The question is part of the larger subject of the origin of Mazdeism and its connection with the Vedic religion, an inquiry which is still far from being completed.

103. The general name *Yazata*, "worshipful," served for addressing a number of spirits, partly derived from the Aryan mythology, partly peculiar to the Zarathustrian system. The first named deities, which were probably too deeply rooted in the popular faith to be altogether supplanted by new and more abstract representations, were not, however, adopted among the Yazatas without having undergone some modification, and being made subordinate to Ahura mazda. The chief of them are *Mithra*, the god of light, *Naïryô ṣañha*, the fire-god, *Apãm napât*, the god of the fire dwelling in the waters, *Haoma*, the god of the drink of immortality, and *Tistrya*, the genius of the dog-star. The goddess of the heavenly waters and of fruitfulness, *Anâhita* (old Pers. *Anâhata*), is of foreign Chaldee origin. When, under the government of Artaxerxes Mnemon, the cultus of Mithra, combined with foreign usages, increased in importance, this goddess, also, was worshipped with special zeal, and in entirely unorthodox fashion. The cultus of both deities spread over Western Asia to Europe, and was on the whole more widely diffused than that of any other deity of antiquity.

It was natural that prominence should be given in Mazdeism to that side of the character of the old-Aryan deities which most harmonised with the spirit of the new doctrine. Thus Mithra became more especially what Varuṇa had been in the Vedic religion, the god of truth and right, the guardian of leagues; Naïryô ṣañha, in the Veda Narâ ṣañsa, a surname of Agni and other deities, the messenger between the dwellers in heaven and men; Haoma (the Indian Soma), the genius of life and health, the protector against evil spirits and wicked men—the revengeful and licentious; and Apãm napâṭ was at any rate brought into connection with the genuinely Mazdayaṣnian representation of the heavenly glory. Tistrya alone retained his physical significance pure and simple, like the other star-spirits with *Hvare kshaeta*, the sun-god, and Mâo, the moon-god, at their head, who, however, retire into the background among the Erânians. Moreover, the traditions of the Aryan heroes supplied not a few elements for the Erânian, some of which were even attached to the person of Zarathustra.

The goddess Anâhita bears the genuine Aryan surname *Ardhvî Ṣûra*, and her common name signifies the "unspotted." She is, however, a foreign deity. See my *Godsd. van Zarathustra*, p. 181, where it is shown that she was adopted from the Semites. It was not then known, and has only come to light since, that the Semites must in their turn have derived her from the Akkadians.

104. The genuine Zarathustrian Yazatas are all, like the majority of the Amesha ṣpeñtas, personifications of ideas, as is plain from their very names, such as *Rashnu razista*, "the most perfect justice," *Daena*, "the true faith," or "the law," and others. Even the ancient prayers were elevated into personal spirits of this kind, and the most eminent of these, the *Ahuna vaīrya* prayer, was even turned into a sort of Logos, a divine creative word. But the highest in rank of all the Yazatas is Ṣraosha, who was placed nearly on a level with the holy immortals. He is, as his name proves, a fine bold personification of "hearing," both of invocation and of listening to the sacred prayers, maxims and sacrificial songs, and he thus naturally becomes the founder of sacrifice, the genius

of obedience and watchfulness, who contends against evil spirits with spiritual weapons.

Besides Rashnu razista and Daena, there also deserve to be mentioned among this order of Yazatas *Mãthra ṣpeñta,* the sacred sacrificial rubric or magic formula, and *Damôis upamanô,* the "oath" or "curse," and the Zarathustrian Question. The entire divine revelation, namely, is clothed in the form of answers given by Ahura mazda to the questions of Zarathustra, and these last are then ascribed to the inspiration of a special genius. The well-known *Honover* is simply the later form of Ahuna vaîrya, and was originally the oldest of the Pârsee prayers.

Ṣraosha appears already in the Gâthâs as a personal being; the tendency to anthropomorphism fastened more strongly on him than on any of the other Yazatas of the same order, and at a later date he was for the most part connected with Mithra.

105. From the Yazatas we must distinguish the Fravashis, the divine or heavenly types of all living beings, including the Yazatas and even the Amesha ṣpeñtas. They are at once the souls of the deceased and the protecting spirits of the living, created before their birth, and surviving after their death, and they are sometimes identified with the stars. This doctrine, arising out of animistic representation of the independence of souls or spirits, and of their immortality, and recurring in one shape or another among all nations of antiquity, received among the Erânians—probably under the influence of a native religion—a special development, and, in a higher form, was adopted into the Zarathustrian system from the very beginning.

The Fravashis reappear afterwards in Judaism as guardian angels, and from these they passed into Christianity (cf. Matt. xviii. 10). The meaning of the word Fravashi is uncertain. It probably signifies "the earlier" (*fra*) "grown" (*vaksh*).

106. Pârsism is decidedly dualistic, not in the sense of accepting two hostile deities, for it recognises no worship of evil beings, and teaches the adoration only of Ahura mazda and the spirits subject to him; but in the sense of placing in hostility to each other two sharply-divided kingdoms, that of light, of truth, and of purity, and that of darkness, of falsehood, and of impurity. This division is carried through the whole creation, organic and inorganic, material and spiritual. Above, in the highest sphere, is the domain of the undisputed sovereignty of the all-wise Lord, beneath, in the lowest abyss, the kingdom of his mighty adversary; midway between the two lies this world, the theatre of the contest.

At the head of the evil or dark spirits stands Añro maïnyus, the "attacking" or "striking" spirit, the creator of everything physically or morally unclean, and, as such, the opponent of Ahura mazda. Beneath him stand the *daevas* (the devas of the Aryan and pre-Aryan period), degraded from the rank of good to that of evil spirits. These include some Vedic gods, as well as purely Erânian creations, of which last-named *Aeshma*, "anger," is the chief, or, at anyrate, the best known. To the kingdom of Añro maïnyus there belong, further, the *Drujas* (Nom. sing. *drukhs*), the "liars" or "deceivers," an order of female spirits or monsters, who were already counted as evil spirits before the daevas had become so, and the

Pairikas, another order of female beings, who seduced the pious by their beauty. It was not till later that some amount of arrangement was introduced among these beings, and each of the principal spirits, for example, each of the Amesha ṣpeñtas, obtained his distinct counterpart. The character of Añro maïnyus is opposition, he simply follows the creative activity of Ahura mazda, producing whatever may injure his good creations.

Añro maïnyus becomes in Pârsi *Âharman*, in modern Persian *Âhriman*, among the Greeks Ἀρειμάνιος. His name signifies the "striking" or "attacking spirit." He is also called the "wicked" (*akem*), or the "most wicked" (*acistem*) "spirit" (*manô*). In the Gâthâs he is still a more or less abstract conception, but he very soon comes to be personified.

The Vedic gods enumerated among the Daevas are Indra (*Iñdra* or *Añdra*), Ṣarva (*Ṣaürva*, originally a fire-god, afterwards an epithet of Agni, later still identified with Ṣiva), and Nâsatya (*Nâoñhaïthya*), the prototype of the Vedic Aṣvins. Aeshma daeva was adopted in the form of *Ashmodeus* by the Jews and the Christians. Of the other genuinely Erânian Daevas we must also mention *Aṣto-vîdhôtus*, the "bone divider," a genius of dissolution, and *Apaosha*, the "drought."

Druj, nom. *drukhs*, denotes literally the "deceiver," the "liar," and is really the same word as the old High German *gitroc*, modern Dutch *gedrocht*, both signifying "a monster," "a monstrous conception of the imagination, by which man is deceived." This order of beings includes old-Aryan spirits of darkness, such as *Azhi dahâka*, the "biting snake," the *Ahi* or cloud snake of the Veda, and *Naṣus* (νεκύς), the "corpse-demon;" and purely Erânian spirits, like *Bûshyañṣta*, a genius of sleep.

Païrika is derived from a root (*par*) which, among other meanings, signifies to fight, to contend, and also to go away, to run off. Even pure nature-beings, such as *Duzhyâïra* (old Pers. *Dusiyâra*), the "bad year," "failure of crops," are referred to this group.

The classification of the evil spirits places *Akô manô* ("evil disposition"), for example, opposite to Vohu manô, and Iñdra, the king of the Daevas, opposite to Khshathra vaïrya, the "desired kingdom."

Târic and *Zâric*, the demons of hunger and thirst, or, more correctly, of sickness or death, are the adversaries of Haurvatâț and Ameretâț.

107. This dualism further dominates the cosmogony, the cultus, and the entire view of the moral order of the world held by the Mazda-worshippers. Not only does Añro maïnyus spoil by his counter-creations all the good creations of Ahura mazda, but by slaying the protoplasts of man and beast, he brings death into the world, seduces the first pair to sin, and also brings forth noxious animals and plants. Man finds himself, in consequence, surrounded on all sides by the works of the spirit of darkness and by his hosts. It is the object of worship to secure the pious against their influence. This is of the utmost simplicity, without images or temples: pure fire plays the principal part, and has the power, when combined with the sacred spells and sacrificial songs, to break the might of the evil spirits, and purify men from their pollution. The whole life of the believer is a constant conflict with evil, in which, as is universal in antiquity, little difference is made between physical and moral evil. Agriculture, likewise, and the care of clean animals and

plants are powerful means of weakening the kingdom of impurity. But the love of truth, also, vigilance and activity, are weapons which win the victory in this contest.

The protoplasts of men and animals are the well-known *Gayômart* (modern Pers. *Kayûmarṣ*), *i.e.*, *Gayô maretan*, "human" or "mortal life," and *Gôshurûm*, *i.e.*, *Gêus urvan*, the "bull" or "ox-soul," both of whom were slain by Âhriman. The first men, Gayômart's offspring, are seduced by him to sin. The correspondence between the legends of the fall among the Persians and the Israelites is well known.

108. With this fundamental thought the disposal of the dead, and the representations of the destiny of the deceased and the future of the world, are in accord. Purity inheres especially in fire, earth, and water: the bodies of the dead, therefore, must not be burned, nor buried, nor cast into a river; they are exposed on artificial mounds or towers reserved for the purpose (*dakhmas*), to be devoured by birds of prey. After death the souls of the departed are obliged to cross the bridge Chinvaṭ. For the wicked this bridge is too narrow, so that they fall off, and sink down into the under world (*Duzakh*), there to be tormented by the spirits of evil. The good, however, are welcomed by Ṣraosha or Vohu manô into the Abode of Song (*garô demâna*), the dwelling-place of Ahura mazda and the saints. But the joys of heaven and the pains of hell do not last for ever. Hereafter the sovereignty of Añro maïnyus shall come to nought. Three thousand years after Zarathustra, the conquering saviour (*Ṣaoshyãṣ Verethragna*), preceded by two personages to p ·pare the way, shall be born by supernatural means. The contest reaches its climax. Everything is in flames, but only the wicked suffer; the pious feel nothing more than an agreeable warmth. By this discipline all creatures are refined; the evil spirits are destroyed; the earth is renovated, and the sole sovereignty of Ahura mazda begins, to be continued without end.

The bridge Chinvaṭ, commonly interpreted as the "bridge of the gatherer," an explanation which now appears to me very doubtful, is borrowed from the old Aryan mythology, and was probably originally the rainbow which unites heaven and earth. The Pârsee eschatology represents the judgment of souls as conducted there not only by Ṣraosha, but also by Mithra, the genius of truth, and Rashnu, the genius of justice. Ṣaoshyãṣ (Pehlv. *Ṣôciôsh*, Pârsi *Ṣaosyôs*), the Saviour, is the son of the virgin mother *Eredatfedhri* ("she who possesses a mighty father"), who conceives him in a miraculous fashion from Zarathustra. He renews the world and resuscitates the dead, after having first destroyed everything. Here, also, in spite of the differences, the correspondence with Jewish and Judæo-Christian ideas is striking. The doctrine of the purification of the wicked is peculiar to Pârsism.

109. The old-Aryan theology and cultus are only in part the source of many of the distinctive features of Pârsism. The doctrine of the Fravashis, and the whole system of spirits with the dualism so strictly carried through it, the cosmogony, the special homage offered to fire, some of the sacrificial customs, and other representations, also remind us of the religion of the Akkadians, who were so closely connected with the ancient inhabi-

tants of Media and Elam. It is probable, therefore, that the Zarathustrian religion, especially in its later development, owed its form to the influence of the native religion of the Medians. The Chaldee religion may also have contributed one element or another to the Median and Persian Aryans, for before their settlement in Media and Persia, the Assyrians had reduced a good deal of Erân under their sway. Some other peculiarities again must be derived from other sources. But to all these foreign elements the Aryan mind has given an independent shape, resulting in a religious communion, whose simple creed and pure practical morality preserved it from the extravagances of its sister communion in India, and stimulated its adherents to an active life and valiant deeds. The less luxuriant climate of Erân and the national character may have co-operated in this direction; but this high development, and especially their almost monotheistic conception of deity, must be to a large extent ascribed to the preaching of a reformer, or at any rate to a little circle of thinkers.

After the Greek conquest Mazdeism fell into decline. It was brilliantly restored in the third century A.D. by the Sâsânidae, but it finally succumbed before the fanatical violence of Islâm. In a few districts of Persia it still drags on a miserable existence, but it continues to flourish with some vigour among the Parsîs who emigrated to India, and there it even appears to be not incapable of reforms.

Amid many rash conjectures, F. Lenormant, *La Magie chez les Chaldéens*, pp. 178 *sqq.*, and 191 *sqq.*, has many just remarks on the influence of the old-Median religion on

Mazdeism, and the correspondence between the former and the Akkadian. His idea that the Proto-Medes worshipped a serpent-deity, and that this was Azhi dahâka, and identical with King Astyages, is altogether erroneous. Azhi dahâka is a purely Aryan demon, and Astyages has nothing to do with him.

The strange treatment of the dead, and the great value set on the dog, which distinguish the Erânians from kindred races and from their western neighbours, have been found among Tibetan tribes; and these practices, therefore, they must have adopted from the earlier inhabitants of southern Erân. See among others, Köppen, *Religion des Buddha*, ii. p. 322 *sqq*.

IV.

RELIGION AMONG THE WENDS OR LETTO-SLAVS.

Literature.—See I. J. Hanusch, *Die Wissenschaft des Slavischen Mythus*, Lemberg, 1842, pp. 49–62. The Russian sources are enumerated by W. R. S. Ralston, *The Songs of the Russian People*, London, 1872, pp. x–xii. See further, Ralston, *Russian Folk-Tales;* Id., *Khilof and his Fables;* Id., *Early Russian History*, London, 1874, and *Gottesidee und Cultus bei den Alten Preussen*, Berlin, 1870. The work of Hanusch, though rich in material, is rendered useless by its want of a critical and historical method of comparison. Ralston is a well-informed and careful guide, who may be safely trusted. Comp. also F. J. Mone, *Geschichte des Heidenthums im Nordl. Europa*, 2 vols., Leipzig and Darmstadt, 1822–23.

110. Down to the introduction of Christianity, religion, among the Wends or Letto-Slavs, remained at a

point of development far behind even that of the Vedic and old German religions. It is very probably older, and it is certainly lower, than any of the Indo-Germanic religions with which we are acquainted. It contains the germs both of the polytheism of the Hindus and of the dualism of the Persians, but without the philosophical colouring which distinguishes the one, or the ethical character of the other. Its cosmogony is still purely mythical, the conflict between the divine beings is simply that between the powers of nature, and with this stage of development its cultus and its doctrine of immortality are in accord.

The Letts, who form one of the two great divisions of this race, include the Letts proper, the Lithuanians, and the old-Prussians. The Slavs are divided into East and West-Slavs. Of the first of these groups the principal members are the Russians, of the second, the Poles and Czechs (Bohemians and Moravians). The Slavs of Southern Austria and European Turkey (Servians, Bulgarians, Croats, &c.) form a separate group of Southern Slavs, different from, yet most closely allied with, the Eastern. The name Wends, now limited to the Slavs of the Lausitz, seems to have been originally the most general.

It is probable that the Letto-Slavs, like the Germans, remained united with the Aryans longer than the Kelts, Greeks, and Romans, and they have preserved the religion of this period in its purest form, while it reached a higher and independent development among the Germans.

The proofs of the other statements in the text will be found in the following sections.

111. Like all mythological religions, that of the Wends, also, rests on the doctrine of souls or spirits, which scarcely reaches among them a higher stage than among savages. The soul, of which the ancient Wends formed very different conceptions, though they were such as are found among all other peoples, moves about in freedom, remains for a while after death in the neighbourhood of the body, but then sets off on its journey to the shadow-land, which is sought either in the underworld, or on a happy island in the East, the abode of the sun, or in the sky. The journey is thus either a sea-voyage over the world-ocean, or a journey on foot over the rainbow or the milky-way, or the ascent of a steep and slippery mountain; and the survivors were careful to provide the dead with what they would require on one of these expeditions. The idea of retribution has not yet arisen; the life after death is simply a continuation of the life on earth. The dead, therefore, were furnished with everything appropriate to their condition, even with wives and slaves; for the unmarried a consort was provided at the grave; and second marriages were rare. To the three representations of the kingdom of the dead correspond three modes of disposing of the corpse,—(1), burial, which carried the soul to the underworld; (2), burning, which bore it in the smoke to heaven; and (3), burial or burning in a boat, which transported it to the island of the sun. But the souls of the deceased always continued in relation with the living, and as their return was dreaded, feasts and sacrifices were zealously celebrated to appease them, or all kinds of devices were employed to keep them away.

The soul was represented as a spark kindled by the god of thunder, as a star (as among the Persians), a vapour, a breath of air, a shadow; or, again, as a winged creature, whether an insect or a bird, especially a dove, a crow, or a cuckoo. The butterfly was even called a "little soul" (*dushichka*). It appears also as a mouse, as among other nations; the milky-way is called the "mouse-path."

The sky is named *Rai* (Lithuan. *rojus*, comp. Sanskr. *rāj.* = "to be bright or white"), and the underworld *Peklo*, which is a regular deity among the old-Prussians. It was only under Christian influence that this afterwards became hell. The stories of the island *Buyán* ("the burning") agree in many respects with one of the chief dogmas of Pârsism. The white stone *Alatuir* (electron ?) found there, is the sun. The world of the dead is also called *Nava*, a name which has not as yet received an adequate explanation, but which some writers have connected with the conception of the voyage of the ship (*navis*, *ναῦς*).

Burning and burial were both practised by the Slavs as by all the Indo-Germans; with these correspond the different representations of the realm of the dead.

The same usages are found among the old-Prussians and the Lithuanians.

112. A peculiar richness characterises the doctrine of spirits among the Letto-Slavs, of which that of the old-Russians may serve as an example. They divided the demons into spirits of the house, the water, the forest, and the air. The house-spirits are, properly speaking, fire-spirits, and are the objects, in their two-fold character, of great veneration. The house-spirit watches over and protects the house and its inhabitants, not excluding the

animals, shares all their fortunes, is, as a rule, friendly; or, when he is angry, is easy to be appeased: but, if he is altogether neglected, shows that he is a spirit of might, who rules not only over the beneficent fire on the hearth, but over the lightning as well. All the qualities of water, its fertilising and destructive power, its treacherous beauty and mystic depth, its magic power which sets the mill-wheel in motion, are personified in the beautiful *Rusálkas*, and their male companions; all the terrors of the forest and the dangers which threaten travellers through it, are embodied in the wood-demons, which are naturally at the same time the spirits of the storm. *Koshchei*, the genius of winter, is a very evil being, and so are the contagious sicknesses which wander about in the shape of old women or hideous men, as well as that multitude of wizards and witches, who, during their lifetime, often become were-wolves, and, after death, bloodsucking vampires. All this is purely animistic; but the Slavic demonology is favourably distinguished from that of savages by the poetical guise in which it is arrayed. That it is not mere poetry, but really religious belief, is proved by the awe with which the spirits are regarded, and the often costly sacrifices offered to them.

Domovoy (*doma* = "house"), the house-spirit, stood in the closest connection with the domestic hearth, and, in case of removal, had accordingly to be transferred with great ceremony to the new dwelling. Frequently he assumed the the form of the master of the house. He is found, however, wherever there is fire, even in the lightning. The crowing of the cock, his sacred animal, puts to flight all other spirits, but not him. Only the Domovoy of the same house is friendly: those from elsewhere are jealous and dangerous.

To the *Vodyanuie*, water-spirits, belong the *Rusálkas* (*rus*, old-Slav. = "stream," *rosá*, "dew," Lat. *ros*), much dreaded for their deceitful qualities, and in the summer time solemnly chased away. *Tsar Morskoi*, the water-king, with his fair swan daughters, stands at the head of this realm.

The wood-spirits, *Lyeshie*, bear most resemblance in conception and character to Pan and the Satyrs, and have nothing in common with the clouds, with which a certain school of mythologists attempts to connect them. That they are also wind-gods appears from the representation of the storm as their marriage-procession, and the whirlwind as their bridal dance.

The Domovoy is content with small domestic sacrifices, but the spirit of the mill-stream requires the first swarm of bees, the other water-spirits demand a horse, the wood-spirits a cow, and all exact a portion of the harvest. In ancient times, also, human sacrifices were certainly offered.

113. Religion did not, however, remain stationary at this point among the Wends any more than among other nations. Besides these spirits they also recognised and worshipped real deities, raised above nature, who were called by the Letts *Dêwas* and by the Slavs *Bogu*. At their head there once stood among all the peoples of this race the thunder-god *Perun* or *Perkuns*, the god who smites the demons with his glowing flashes so that the blood pours forth from their wounds in streams upon the earth. In honour of him a perpetual fire of oak-wood was kept up. Among the Lithuanians and old-Prussians, two other gods were placed as his equals by his side, of whom the one, *Patrimpo*, must have been a joyous and

beneficent sun-god, and the other, *Pecollos*, the god of the hidden solar fire in the underworld, both being indisputably of native origin, and not adopted from any other source. Sun-gods were worshipped by the Slavs in great numbers; some being male, such as *Dazhbog*, the god of day, son of *Svarog*, the god of the sky (*Svarozhich*), and *Lado*, always united with *Lada*, counterparts of *Freyr* and *Freya*, and corresponding in character with these German deities; one being female, the spouse of the unfaithful Moon-god, and mother of the stars, who belongs to another mythological formation. Fire-gods also, —of whom one, *Ogon*, bears the same name as the Vedic *Agni*, and another *Kuznets*, is a sort of Vulcan, a cunning smith, but at the same time a hero who destroys demons —and a multitude of other divine beings, were objects of worship. Among these we may further name the Spirit of Life (Polish, *'Zywie*, Russian, *Jiva*), embodied in the cuckoo, the White and the Black god (*Byel bog* and *Czerno bog*), gods of light and darkness, of whom the first is also named *Svantovich*,—representations and names agreeing with some of the Pârsî, but destitute of the ethical significance which they received in the Zarathustrian system, and which none of the Wend deities possesses.

Dêwas in Lithuanian signifies "god," but the unfavourable meaning which the word acquired among the Persians attached itself even amongst the Letts to *deiwys*, "idol," "ghost." *Bogu* is the Sanskr. *bhagha* (Bactr. *bagha*), old-Pers. *baga*, from *bhaj* (Bactr. *baz*), to "divide," to "distribute." In the use of this word again the Slavs agree more closely with the Persians than with the Hindus. Some writers regard *Perun* as a deity adopted from the Scandinavians. Among them he appears under the name of *Fiörgyn*, in a very subordinate position. If there was any borrowing at all, the originalty is not in this instance on the side of the Germans. This is true also of the Lettic triad, which has been supposed to be derived from the Goths. From what source, in that case, came the purely Lettic names of these deities? Comp. *Gottesidee und Cultus der alt. Preuss.* p. 39 *sqq.* *Patrimpo*, the joyous harvest-god, and *Pjecollo*, the ripener of the grain, are both sun-gods, but the latter dwells in the underworld, and is the god of the dead, a part which he also plays in the beautiful Lithuanian myth of *Nijola* (the Letto-Slavic Kora-Proserpina). His name, which is applied among the Russians to the underworld itself, comes from *pjec*, to "bake," to "warm," the Sanskr. *pach*, to "burn," to "cause to ripen." Patrimpo I am inclined to connect with the Sanskr. *ṭrimp* (from *ṭrip*), to "enjoy to satiety."

Svarog comp. with Sanskr. *svarga*, the sky.

Lado or *Did-Lado*, "the great Lado" and his consort, "the great goddess," are, like Freyr and Freya, gods of love, marriage, and fertility.

Jiva, *'Zywie*, comp. Sanskr. and Bactr. *jîv*, "life," old-Pers. *ziv*, personified by the Pârsîs as *Jîsti*, father of the double unity *Ashâhura*. *Byel* and *Czerno bog* are parallel with the two Zarathustrian spirits Ṣpèñtô-maĩnyus and Añrô-maïnyus. *Svanto* or *Sveto* in Svantovid = Ṣpèñtô, being identical in form and meaning (*i.e.*, "holy").

114. The relation between man and the higher powers, also, so far as we know, still stood, at any rate among the Slavs, at a very low stage of development. The spells in which they believed, the amulets which they wore to secure or avert the presence of spirits, the peculiar oracles by which they sought to discover the future, all belong to the animistic view of life. This is also true to a certain extent of their feasts, in which the magic purport was not wholly obscured, and the life of nature was as yet scarcely elevated by any ethical conception, though poetic and dramatic elements were not wanting. The East-Slavs appear to have had neither temples nor priests, nothing but sacred places and wise men and women, a kind of enchanters and enchantresses, who had power over the elements, and were at the same time gifted with prophetic utterance.

The Lettic branch was somewhat more advanced. At least the Lithuanians had a priestly order, and the old-Prussians even a sort of high-priest, who lived apart in a sacred place, surrounded by the veiled images of the gods, and from this retreat issued his commands through his subordinate priests.

The amulets, composed of all kinds of charms, have always the form of a button, a lock, or a net, *nduzui*, which is connected with *uzui*, "bands," and *uzit'*, to "fasten:" these are clearly fetishes, serving to secure the presence of the guardian spirit by binding him, and to keep off hostile spirits. The oracles, both those by which it was sought to learn the coming weather, and the result of the harvest, as well as those concerning the issue of a war or of personal destiny, are marked by the accidental and magical character of the lot, which is genuinely animistic. The feasts also were supposed to possess a magical efficacy on the elements, as in the case of the ceremony of pouring water on a girl decked with leaves at the summer festival of the Servians, "that the heavenly women (the cloud-spirits) may give rain," as they said.

Among the East-Slavs this feast still retained a bacchanalian and even phallic character.

It was customary among them for the head of the family or the tribe to offer sacrifices on behalf of all beneath a sacred tree (an oak was preferred), or on the bank of a running stream. But the *Vyedun*, the "enchanter," literally, the "knowing one" (*vyedat'*, to "know"), and especially the *Vyeshchaya Zhena*, the "wise woman," were held in high honour among them, at any rate in times of prosperity.

The old-Prussian high-priest was called *Kriwe* or *Griwe* (from *krych*, to "hide"?), and dwelt at a place named *Romowe* (*rozmowa*, "conversation"?), which the dead also were obliged to pass upon their journey.

V.

RELIGION AMONG THE GERMANS.

See the *literature* in K. SIMROCK, *Handbuch der Deutschen Mythologie mit Einschluss der Nordischen*, 3rd ed., Bonn, 1869, p. 7 *sqq.*, and L. S. P. MEYBOOM, *De Godsdienst der oude Noormannen*, Haarlem, 1868, p. 19 *sqq.* Indispensable, JACOB GRIMM, *Deutsche Mythologie*, 3rd ed., 2 vols., Göttingen, 1854, and J. W. WOLF, *Beiträge zur Deutsch. Mythologie*, Göttingen, vol i., 1852, vol. ii., 1857. Comparative, W. MANNHARDT, *Germanische Mythen-Forschungen*, Berlin, 1858. For Dutch mythology, L. Ph. C. VAN DEN BERGH, *Proeve van een Kritisch Woordenboek der Nederland. Mythol.*, Utrecht, 1846.

115. Among the Germans religion reached a much higher development than among the Wends, which must be ascribed rather to the richer endowments of their race than to the influence of a more advanced civilisation. With this circumstance is connected the fact that, with the exception perhaps of the Keltic, there is not one of the Indo-Germanic religions which has departed so far, in respect of the names of the chief deities, from its kindred as the Germanic. In doctrine it most resembles the Persian, and, like the Persian, it is inferior in philosophical contemplation to the Vedic religion, though it equally surpasses it in its moral standard. Our fullest knowledge of it is derived from the two Eddas, of which the older contains a collection of very ancient and chiefly mythological songs, while the younger is composed of prose traditions, together with fragments of older poems. They are the sources for the religion of the Scandinavians or Normans, from which, however, that of the Germans proper does not essentially differ. German mythology must be studied chiefly through the medium of oral traditions.

The superiority of the German religion over that of the Slavs is evinced by the fact that it made so much more out of the same materials. The fundamental conception in all the Indo-Germanic religions is the conflict between the higher deities who control nature, and the rude forces of nature, especially between light and darkness. No nations of this race have realised this dualism with such clearness as the Letto-Slavs, the Germans, and the Persians, but while with the first it remained purely physical, the two latter alone, and certainly independently of each other, gave to it an ethical character, and wrought it, as it were, into a sublime drama.

The older Edda ("grandmother," here, however, in a

special sense, as the guardian of the ancient poesy) is ascribed to Saemundr, the wise, and is therefore called *Edda Saemundar hins fróda:* the latter was collected and written by Snorri, the son of Sturla, and bears in consequence the name *Edda Snorra Sturlusonar.* Among the best translations is that of Simrock (3rd ed., Stuttgart and Tübingen, 1863). How much still remains to be done for the criticism and correct interpretation of the Edda-sagas is proved, for instance, by the important dissertation of Barend Symons, *Untersuchungen über die sogenannte Völsunga Saga*, Halle, 1876. In the *Story of the Volsungs and Niblungs*, London, 1870, Morris & Magnússon have reproduced some portions of the elder Edda for English readers.

116. The cycle of the Germanic gods is not entirely deficient in names derived from Indo-Germanic antiquity, but they are not numerous, and the deities which bear them only occupy in the system a subordinate place. The ancient Dyaus still survives in *Tyr*, who is still among some tribes a god of the sky; but in the system of the Edda he is not a little degraded, for he has become the god of the sword and of fraternal strife. The Letto-Slavic Peruns or Perkunos may be recognised in *Fiörgyn* (Goth. *Fairguni*) who has furnished a name to several mountain-forests, but he has seen his sovereignty pass to his son *Odhinn* and his grandson *Thôrr*, who are purely Germanic gods. The very ancient and general name for deity, Deva, is not quite forgotten, but it has been obliged to give way to the more usual designations *Aesir* and *Vanir*, which are found exclusively among the Germans. The deities belonging to these orders, derived probably from different tribes and only afterwards united, opposed the wild powers of nature which were represented as giants. These, under the names of the "eaters" (*jötunn*) or the "thirsty" (*thurs*), were worshipped as powers of violence and terror, and human sacrifices even were offered to them. They were at first neither good nor bad, but they came gradually, and with increasing definiteness, to be regarded as evil beings, foes of the good deities. Between them and the Aesir and Vanir stand the Elves, divided into three classes, two of which consist largely of dwarfs. They are the lower, less dreaded demons of an earlier period, and therefore, though they are at peace with the gods, they often play a very mischievous part. They also, like gods and giants, were the objects of sacrifice.

Tyr, genit. *Tys*, Goth. *Tius*, old high Germ. *Zio*, is the Vedic Dyaus, the Greek Zeus. In compounds it often occurs with the general meaning of "god." Among the Semnones or Suabians Tyr is still the god of the sky, among the Scandinavians the god of the sword and of unnatural war, but the sword was originally the lightning, and the war the strife of the heavenly powers.

Fiörgyn is the Perkunos of the Letto-Slavs, and was probably adopted from them. The elves it has further been proposed to identify with the Vedic Ṛibhavas, and the *Maren* with the Vedic Maruts, but, like Tyr and Fiörgyn, they have no prominent place in the German system.

The plural *tîvar*, "gods," which occurs now and then, corresponds to the Vedic *deva*. The *Aesir* (*Âs*, pl. *Aesir*, Goth. and old high Germ. *ans*) are commonly explained to mean the "beams," the supports of the universe, which seems to me very doubtful. It is far more probable, in accordance with the opinion kindly communicated to me by my friend Prof. Kern, that the word, of which the original form is *ansu*, is connected with the Erânian *anhu* (and thus also with the Ahuras and Asuras), and means, therefore, the "beings," the "spirits." The *Vanir* are originally the "waters," and hence also the "beautiful," the "lovely;" comp. Venus.

The three classes of elves are the *Liös*-("light"), *Svart*-("black"), and *Döck*-("dark") *Alfar;* the two last kinds dwell in the ground, and to them belong the dwarfs. That they were not mere productions of poetic imagination, but beings in whose existence and power men really believed, is proved by the sacrifices dedicated to them.

117. By the union of Aesir and Vanir, the elevation of single attributes of the gods to independent beings, and other causes, the German polytheism grew richer and richer, but it is a mistake to suppose that it issued from monotheism. It was not till afterwards that an approach was made to this in the representation of the highest god as the All-Father. Far above the other Aesir stand Odhinn, Thôrr, and at first also Loki. Odhinn or Wodan was originally a nature-god, the personification of the violent movements of the air, of the breath which blows through the universe. Then, as a deity controlling nature, he was the warlike patron of princes and heroes, whom he gathers after their death into his Walhalla; and finally he rose to be the king of the gods, lord of the world, and god of the soul. Thôrr or Donar, the Âsa *par excellence*, with his wonderful hammer Miölnir, was, as his German name implies, the thundering god of the sky. As such he was the summer-god, who contends with and overcomes the dreaded powers of winter; and, as protector of agriculture, the god of the people and of servants, he was especially a god of civilisation. Loki, probably also a god of the air, was very closely connected in the old myths with these two chief-gods, so that he forms a triad with them, and fights by their side against the winter-giants, whom he generally outwits. In later times he was to acquire a totally different significance. The chief of the Vanir was Freyr or Fro, the Lord, god of the bright sky, source of life and fertility, and therefore, in the system to which he properly belonged, the creator. After his union with the Aesir, he became the god of peace and love. Of the goddesses, who differ little from each other, the Asynia Frigg, wife of Odhinn, and the Vana Freya, "the Lady," sister of Freyr and spouse of Njördr, the god of the sea, occupy the highest rank. Subsequently Freya entirely supplants Frigg, and even takes her place as Odhinn's consort. Originally a personification of the earth, then of the moon, she becomes the goddess of beauty, fertility, and love. The doctrine of the three Norns or goddesses of destiny covers a deeper thought, which the Greeks embodied in their Moirae, and the Romans in their Parcae, each in their own way.

All-Father, originally (as early as *Hrafnag.* 1) an epithet of Odhinn. Odhinn, O.H. Germ. *Wuotan*, New Germ. *Wodan*, Fris. *Weda*, from *watan* = to "wade," *meare*, connected with the German *wuth* ("wrath") and *muth* ("courage"). — Thôrr (for *Thonar*, *Thonr ?*), O.H. Germ. *Donar*, is the *Âsabrâgr*, the Asa-prince. The representation of him contains non-German (Turanian) elements, such as the epithets *Atti* or *Etzel* (Attila), *i.e.*, "grandfather." Loki, whose name is connected by Simrock with *lux*, λεύκος, Sanskr. *lûg*, and by Grimm with *lukan*, to "shut," to "close," seems rather, as his name *Loftr* implies, to have been a god of the air (*luft*). In the myth in which he outwits the winter-giant with his horse Svadilfari (the cold wind), he is the cool spring-breeze.

The triad of the three highest gods corresponds curiously with the three chief heroes of the Finnic epos, and so with the three principal deities of the ancient Finns.

The meaning of the name Norns is uncertain. They are three, *Urdhr*, the "past," *Verdhandi*, the "present," and *Skuld*, the "future." The Greek Moirae and the Roman Parcae are both of another character, the dominant idea being, in the one group, that of death (μόρος, *mors*), and in the other that of production (*partus*). The Norns have it for their function to accomplish destiny, *scöp* (cf. *scheppen*, *schaffen*, to "shape," to "create"), *örlög* ("fate," still surviving in the Dutch word *oorlog*, "war").

118. The moral standard of the Germanic religion is shown forth, among other indications, by the history of the Âsa Loki and of the goddess Hel. The first gradually sinks lower and lower beneath the rank first occupied by him by the side of the two highest gods, and he finally becomes an evil being. As the god of fire he was not to be trusted; for however beneficent he might be, he was at the same time dangerous and treacherous. While the myths were still nothing more than nature myths, this caused no difficulty: but when the attempt was made to detach the Aesir from nature, and measure their character by a moral standard, it was inevitable that Loki should sink and finally be thrust out. Hel encounters the same fate, though she was originally no other than the dark

underworld, properly speaking the twilight, both darkness and light, the goddess of death and life.

Loki, who was first of all the brother, then the bosom-friend of Odhinn, was the contriver of frequent tricks by which he brought the Aesir into danger, but he always rescued them again by his cunning. He counsels an alliance with the winter-giant, the architect (*Smidhr*, "smith," *Vind og Veder*, "wind and storm"), with his horse Svadilfari, which was to overthrow the god, but he manages to frustrate it. He carries Idunn to Thrymheim, but he brings her back, and is one of those who go thither to recover the stolen hammer of Thôrr.

When, however, the conflict of the powers of nature came to be transferred to the domain of ethics, he became the father of the destructive powers, the wolf Fenrir, the serpent of Midhgardh, and Hel, and it was he who instigated the murder of Baldr. He abuses the gods as their evil conscience, he is pursued, chained, then he breaks loose again in the last contest, only to be finally altogether overthrown. The myth is exactly parallel to the Prometheus myth, which is, however, worked out in a completely opposite sense, with sympathy for the hero.

Hel (Goth. *halja*, connected with the Sanskr. *kâlî*, the "black"), has an equally ambiguous meaning as "twilight," but the further she can be traced into antiquity, the higher is the position which she occupies.

119. The clearest manifestation, however, of the ethical character of this religion is seen in the description of the great drama of the world, which corresponds both in general and in some detail with the Persian, and, like its parallel, rests upon ancient nature-myths. Its chief features are as follows. In the beginning innocence and

freedom from care everywhere prevail. But lying and sin soon make their appearance, and even steal within the circle of the gods. The gods are indeed constantly victorious in the conflict with the giants; but the adoption of giantesses into their community, the birth of violent monsters, children of Loki, his falsehoods and deceptions, are all the forerunners of a future fall. The death of Baldr, the best and wisest of the Aesir, one of the disasters brought about by Loki, is the great turning-point of the drama, for it proves the mortal nature of the gods. The wicked god and the dangerous monsters are for a time subdued and put in chains, but at last they burst their bonds. The break-up of all institutions and ordinances (*Ragnarök*, commonly the "twilight of the gods") begins. For three years there is winter, and an unnatural war rages. The gods wrestle with the collected forces of cold, fire, and darkness, and in this strife they perish with their adversaries. Then, however, everything renews its life; the chief of the Aesir are now hallowed and purified; mankind lives again, no longer subject to the miseries of existence; and the earth recovers its power of growth. Baldr returns from the underworld, and beneath the sway of the supreme but unnamed god, all beings in the renovated world lead a life of freedom from care, and peace.

The basis of this representation in nature may still be clearly traced. Like all ancient nations, the Germans made at first no sharp distinction between moral and physical good and evil. But for the study of the development of religion, it is of the highest interest to observe how the same nature-myths underwent an ethical transformation among both Germans and Persians, quite independently of each other, and with characteristic differences among each people; and how, consequently, while the forms remain the same, the development of religion advances with that of the nation.

The myth mentions three female Thurses, or giantesses (Old Engl. *thurst*, goblin or wood-demon, A. S. *thyrs*), which were adopted into the circle of the Aesir, and thus became the primal cause of their fall. These three are not the three Norns (Simrock), but *Angurbodha*, *Gerda* and *Skadhi*, the wives of Loki, Freyr, and Njördhr. Beneath these three there lay originally (1) a thunder-myth (Loki, the god of fire, by Angurbodha ["messenger of fear"], the thunder-cloud, begets Fenrir and Hel, *i.e.*, darkness, and the serpent of Midhgardh, the shower); (2) a myth of the sunset (Freyr, the sun-god, sinks into the arms of Gerdha, the earth-girding sea); and (3) a winter-myth (Njördhr, the god of the sea, is married to Skadhi).

Baldr is *Bäldäg*, the white god of day, the Byelbog of the Slavs, having probably been adopted from them. *Hödhr*, his blind brother, who slays him, agrees in that case with Czerno bog,. and was originally the god of darkness.

Ragnarök, interpreted by Grimm as Götterdämmerung "twilight of the gods," and formerly translated by others "elementorum dissolutio," in connection with *Aldar log*, "ruptura sæculi," is properly the break-up or dissolution of the ordinances and regulating powers in nature and the world. All the chief Aesir take part in the contest, and each has his special adversary, whom he overcomes, though he himself is in his turn overthrown. Odhinn fights against Fenrir, Tyr against Managarm, Thôrr against the serpent of Midhgardh, Heimdall against Loki. Vidhar alone, the god of the forest and of revival, survives Fenrir, whom he slays.

The same myths which at first expressed simply the conflict between light and darkness, night and day, and were afterwards transferred to the succession of the seasons, became then blended into one whole, and were applied to the entire course of the history of the world. It was the necessary consequence that they were at the same time elevated by moral conceptions.

120. It is remarkable that while the conception of the gods among the Germans stands so much higher than that of the Letto-Slavs, their psychology, their doctrine of immortality, and their cultus, are in the same backward condition. The representation of the soul and its destiny after death is still largely animistic, though the idea of retribution after death is not wholly wanting. Magic was still very general. The cultus was on the whole exceedingly rude; even human sacrifices were not infrequent. It was conducted among the Germans chiefly in sacred groves, or at least in very small and simple temples. But some progress is, nevertheless, to be traced. The Normans had larger sanctuaries, and among them some of great celebrity. The cultus of animals and trees was only kept up because it had been brought into connection with the worship of the higher deities, and a deeper significance began to be sometimes attached to sacrifice. The priests acquired a very high rank. They belonged, among the Germans at any rate, to the nobility, and had peculiar influence as heralds and judges. Even their names indicate rather an exalted conception of their office.

All these considerations prove that the Germanic religion was in a state of transition and temporary decay when Christianity began to make its way to the North. The new faith was itself no longer entirely pure, as it was already mingled with a number of Greek and Roman elements, and it was unable wholly to supplant the ancestral religion, but it blended with the popular beliefs, and breathed a new spirit into the old forms. And it is certainly not a matter of chance that it was among these same Germans, who, even in barbarous times, had introduced moral conceptions into their theology, that the reformation was most earnestly taken to heart, and most triumphantly carried out, and that its prevailing character was not intellectual, but ethical.

The reception of the heroes in Odhinn's Valhöll implies already the passage from the theory of continuance to that of retribution. For though they continue there the occupations of their past lives, their reception is a reward for their valour. There are, moreover, traces of a place of punishment.

Human sacrifices consisted not only of criminals and prisoners of war, but even of widows and slaves. In epidemics even children were offered, and they were also immured in the foundations of new buildings, in regularly animistic fashion, with food and toys.

In the development of religion, the forms of worship, which are very tenacious, are the slowest and the last to undergo modification.

An O.H. Germ. title for priest was *Êwarto*, from *Êwa*, the "divine and human law." Another, Old-Norman, was *Godi*, fem. *Gydja*, from *Gudh*, "god." Among the Normans the priests exerted influence even over war, and indeed the priesthood and the kingship were combined among them.

In the fusion of Christianity with the popular beliefs, the myths and traditions became legends; the place of Wodan was occupied by Christ, St. Michael, or St. Martin; for Donar appeared Christ or St. Peter; Fro was supplanted by St. Andrew, *mitissimus sanctorum*, St. Stephen, or St. Nicholas; the place of the goddesses was taken by Mary; St. Gertrude represented Gerdha, &c. Loki, of course, became the devil.

CHAPTER V.

RELIGION AMONG THE INDO-GERMANS UNDER THE INFLUENCE OF THE SEMITES AND HAMITES.

Literature.—M. W. HEFFTER, *Die Religion der Griechen und Römer*, 4 vols., Brandenburg, 1845. W. H. ROSCHER, *Studien zur Vergleich. Mythologie der Griechen und Römer*, I. *Apollon und Mars*, Leipzig, 1873. II. *Juno und Hera*, ibid., 1875 (deficient in exactness of method, the conclusions, therefore, being insufficiently confirmed). A. PREUNER, *Hestia-Vesta*, Tübingen, 1864, a monograph of great importance. EMILE BURNOUF, *La Legende Athénienne, Étude de Mythol. comparée*, Paris, 1872 (sets forth a doubtful and improbable theory). W. GRIMM, *Die Sage von Polyphem*, Berlin, 1857 (also in the *Abhandll. der Kaiserl. Akad. zu Berlin*, 1875, p. 1 *sqq.*).

I.

RELIGION AMONG THE GREEKS.

Literature—History.—G. GROTE, *History of Greece*, 8 vols., London, 1862, vol. i., describes the Greek religion objectively, without any attempt to explain it. E. CURTIUS, *History of Greece*, transl. by A. W. Ward, 5 vols., London, 1868–73, admirably adapted for exhibiting the connection between the history of the people and the development of its religion. J. P. MAHAFFY, *Social Life in Greece from Homer to Menander*, London, 1874, ingenious but one-sided. Comp. further SCHÖMANN'S *Griech. Alterthümer*, 2 vols., 3d ed., and A. H. G. P. VAN DEN ES, *Grieksche Antiquiteiten*, 2d ed., Groningen, 1873.

Mythology and Religion.—F. G. WELCKER, *Griech. Götterlehre*, 3 vols., Göttingen, 1857–62. J. A. HARTUNG, *Die Religion und Mythologie der Griechen*, 4 vols., 1865–73. L. PRELLER, *Griech. Mythologie*, 2 vols., 2d ed., 1860–61 (a 3d ed. of vol. i. has since appeared). J. W. G. VAN OORDT, *De Godsdienst der Grieken en hunne Volksdenkbeelden*, Haarlem, 1864. Id., *Grieksche Mythologie. Eene schets*, 's Gravenh., 1874. For the older works comp. Preller, i. pp. 19–24.

Important Monographs.—J. OVERBECK, *Beiträge zur Erkenntniss und Kritik der Zeusreligion*, Leipzig, 1861 (also in the *Abhandll. der Sächs. Gesellsch. der Wissensch.*, iv. No. 1). NÄGELSBACH, *Die Homer. Theologie*, 2d ed. by Autenrieth, Nürnberg, 1861. J. GIRARD, *Le Sentiment Religieux en Grèce d' Homère à Eschyle*, Paris, 1869. F. LEITSCHUH, *Die Entstehung der Mythologie und der Entwickelung der Griech. Religion nach Hesiods Theogonie*, Würzburg, 1867. E. BUCHHOLZ, *Die Sittliche Weltanschauung des Pindaros und Aeschylos*, Leipzig, 1869. E. ZELLER, *Die Entstehung des Monotheïsmus bei den Griechen*, Stuttgart, 1862. J. MÄHLY, *Die Schlange im Mythus und Cultus der Classischen Völker*, Basel, 1867. H. F. PERTHES, *Die Peleiaden zu Dodona*, Moers, 1869. E. DÖHLER, *Die Orakel*, Berlin, 1872. H. D. MÜLLER, *Ares, ein Beitrag zur Entwickelung der Griech. Religion*, Brunswick, 1848. J. RUSKIN, *The Queen of the Air* (Athênê), 2d ed., London, 1869.

121. The Greek religion, which was destined one day to attain a higher development than the other Indo-German religions, was not at first separated from them by any great differences. The proof of this may be found in what is still known of the religion of the Pelasgi, whose name denotes rather a period than a race. The statement that they worshipped the God of heaven on their sacred mountains without images and under no definite name, does not warrant the inference that their cultus was purer than that which succeeded it and was monotheistic, but simply means that they still regarded and worshipped their gods, even the highest of them, as nature-beings, and if they made no images of them, they were nevertheless not without fetishes. Some sanctuaries of this Pelasgian Zeus continued to exist in later times, and one, that at Dodona in Epirus, even remained in high honour. There, the will of the deity of the sky was learned from the rustling of the sacred oak, his fetish, or by other purely animistic methods. In Arcadia and Messenia, human sacrifices even were offered to him. It was not till afterwards that the institution of the Olympic games, and the protection of Sparta, gave to the ancient Zeus-worship in Elis the high significance which made this region itself a holy land, and raised the temple to be one of the principal sanctuaries of all the Hellenes.

It appears that Asia Minor was the last place in which the Greeks, the Phrygians, and the later Italian races were united in one people. Phrygian worship and arts were naturalised in Hellas from the remotest times.

The Pelasgians were not a special Greek race, but the name denotes all the first settlers in Greece who were found already in the new fatherland by tribes which entered it subsequently, such as the Dorians and Ionians. They were not, therefore, regarded as barbarians, and their gods were invoked together with the Hellenic. The attempt (made by P. Volkmuth, among others, *Die Pelasger als Semiten,* Schaffhausen, 1860) to prove that they were Semites, and more specifically, Phenicians, must be treated as a complete failure. The points of agreement between the Syro-Phenician and the Greek religions, which are called in to support this conclusion, must be viewed in quite another light (see below).

A deity without name or image, belonging to the remotest times, denotes a nature-power which has as yet received no human form. The Pelasgic cultus cannot have advanced to monotheism, for by the side of Zeus there was certainly a female deity, whose place was occupied at Dodona by Dionê, who was brought from elsewhere, and at Olympia by Hera; and it is equally certain that the Pelasgi also worshipped other gods, such as Pan, the god of pastures, an ancient deity of light.

The fetishes remaining from this remote period, besides the oak at Dodona and other trees, consisted in sacred stones, such as that of Delphi, sticks, like the so-called sceptre of the Pelopidæ at Chaeronea, the most ancient Hermæ, and various animals, subsequently dedicated to the gods, but originally regarded as their incarnations, as the eagle of Zeus, the wolf of Apollo, the owl of Athênê, &c. Metamorphoses are an attempt to bring the oldest representation of the gods into harmony with the later.

Zeus revealed himself at Dodona by his breath, or rather by his voice, heard in the rustling of his oak or in the thunder, the latter being imitated in a peculiar way. It was the oracle of an agricultural people. His servants were the sacred *Selloi,* from whom the name Hellenes, even, has been derived. At the time when Dodona flourished, the people still called themselves *Graikoi,* Greeks.

In Arcadia the chief ancient sanctuary of Zeus was on Mount Lykaion, and in Messênê on Mount Ithômê. In the former locality and at Elis, the sacred mountain bore the name, as in Thessaly, of Olympus.

122. But whatever be the resemblances of the Greek religion in origin and character to kindred religions, especially to the Vedic and Germanic, and though in the Pelasgian period, at any rate, it reached no higher level, it soon advanced in development beyond them all. The ancient nature-deities are replaced more and more by gods endowed not only with the shape of men, but with real humanity, who continually rise in moral dignity and grandeur, and to whom the Greeks transferred the divine element in man. The causes of this development are the same as those of their great progress in general civilisation, which was due (among other circumstances) to the nature of the country which they inhabited, their splendid natural gifts, and the many-sided intercourse of the several tribes both among themselves and with the representatives of an older and very rich culture. The last of these may indeed be regarded as the foremost cause of all. In the Greek religion we see the first fair fruits of the fusion of the Indo-Germanic and Aryan with the Semitic and Hamitic elements,—the dawn of a new era.

Herodotus, i. 131, draws a distinction between the Egyptian and Hellenic gods, the former of whom he designates ἀνθρωποειδεῖς, the latter ἀνθρωποφυέας.

The peculiarity of the countries occupied by the Greeks, which consisted chiefly of coasts and islands, has been rightly specified as a cause of their advanced civilisation.

But it is necessary to avoid the one-sidedness which derives everything from this circumstance. That the genius of the people was another factor, is proved by the low stage occupied by the later inhabitants of the same regions.

A highly important stimulus to the development of religion among the Greeks came, however, from the active sea traffic to which their country gave occasion, and which brought the backward Greek races into contact not only with their more advanced kinsmen, but also with the Semites and Hamites. Besides this, they were obliged in some cases, as in Asia Minor, in Crete and Cyprus, to divide the country with the Phenicians and Syrians already settled there. Although it is supposed from the evidence of the Egyptian monuments, that they took part as early as the fourteenth and thirteenth centuries in military expeditions against Egypt (which still appears very doubtful, at any rate), the influence exerted on them by the inhabitants of this country seems to have been mediate rather than direct.

Wherever the Phenicians established their colonies, they at once founded a sanctuary for their national deities, whom the native Greeks then either adopted or blended with their own gods. *Melkart* of Tyre was naturalised as *Melikertes* or *Makar*, or was combined with Herakles. The luxurious Sidonian Ashtoreth was transformed into Aphroditê, and the stern Tanith was united with other goddesses. Under the influence of Baal-Shalam the Pelasgian Zeus of Salamis became Zeus Epikoinios, &c. The Greeks were further indebted to the Phenicians for the cultus of the planets and the doctrine that the stars are deities which rule the world, both these, as we know, having been in their turn derived from the Akkadians. We may refer also to the Samothracian gods. The worship of images, likewise, passed from the Semites to the Greeks.

The elements received by the Greeks from their own kinsmen have been to a large extent personified by tradition, in the band of gods and heroes who came from the East into the later civilisation of Hellas, such as Herakles, Dionysos, Danaos, Argos, Agenor, and others, while Kadmos, the brother of Kilix or Phoinix, represents rather the Semitic civilisation. It is probable that the worship of the sea-god Poseidon (an Ionic name), and certain that the cultus of Apollo, was introduced among the inhabitants of Greece proper by their kindred in Asia Minor.

The history of the Greek religion is one of the most striking examples of the great law that the richness and elevation of religious development are proportional to the opportunities of intercourse on the part of one nation with others, and the completeness of the fusion of races.

123. It is often possible in the myths and forms of the Greek gods still to distinguish very clearly between the national and the foreign elements. Thus in the myth of Zeus, his contest with Kronos, like that of Kronos with Ouranos, his absolute victory over the powers of nature, his unlimited sovereignty, are of Semitic origin; while his contest with Prometheus and his human passions and attributes come from Indo-Germanic sources. The beneficent Dêmêtêr, the fruitful mother-earth, with her daughter Korê, the blooming spring begotten by Zeus, protector of agriculture and giver of abundance, is genuinely Greek; while the sombre queen of the under-world, who becomes by Poseidon the mother of Persephonê, goddess of death, must be a foreign deity.

In the same way Greek theology also possesses two representations of the world of the dead. According to one, the Semitic, it lay within the earth, and there the departed led a life of shadows without spirit or consciousness, which was, however, a melancholy continuation of their earthly careers. The other, the Indo-Germanic, placed it in the west, at the setting of the sun, where the privileged were admitted to Elysium or the islands of the blessed. These different representations it was endeavoured as far as possible to combine.

In some cases the union of these dissimilar elements was never successfully effected. The difference between the chaste maidenly Artemis, protectress of innocence and modesty, hostile to everything savage and lewd, and the blood-thirsty and sensual goddess of Tauris, Asia Minor, and Crete, was always vividly felt even by the Greeks. Generally, however, the fusion is so complete that it is hardly possible to separate the foreign from the national elements. This is the case, for example, with Dionysos, Apollo, and Athênê.

What we have designated briefly Semitic, is strictly speaking only north-Semitic, after it had been modified by intercourse with the oldest occupants of Mesopotamia. The myths adopted by the Greeks from the Semites were as a rule Akkadian, but they reached the Greeks in the form given to them by the Northern Semites.

Whatever be the meaning of the name Kronos (to the unfortunate derivations which have been proposed Kuhn has recently added another by the suggestion of a doubtful Sanskrit word *krâna*, "creating for himself," *Ueber Entwickelungsstufen der Mythenbildung*, Berlin, 1874,

p. 148), it is certain that he has nothing to do with Chronos, "time," and that the god who mutilates his father and eats his children is of genuinely north Semitic origin. A satisfactory explanation of his myth is still wanting, but that he is a god of the dark, and particularly of the nightly sky, is proved by the representation that he eats up his own children, all of them light-gods. The stone, the form in which he devours his son Zeus, is supposed by some scholars to be the sun, which the god of night is afterwards obliged to vomit forth again, after which the other gods whom he swallowed, also return to life.

The Indo-Germanic character of the Prometheus myth has been shown by Kuhn, *Die Herabkunft des Feuers und des Göttertranks bei den Indogermanen.* The spirit of the myth also, as it was worked out by the Greeks, is completely non-Semitic.

The world of the dead beneath the earth with the shadows that cannot feel, is obviously Sheôl with the Rephaîm. For this reason (if for no other) the rape of Persephonê and her descent into hell must be a non-Greek myth; and accordingly we find the exact parallel to it in the old Akkadian epos.

Perhaps even the chaste Artemis is not a Greek goddess at all; but she is, in any case, Indo-Germanic. Her name points to a Phrygian origin. *Artamas*, comp. the Erânian *arta, areta,* "perfect," *arethamat,* "lawful," "legitimate."

In Dionysos lurks an Indo-Germanic deity of the drink of immortality and the vintage, with which is connected the myth of his birth from Semelê. The god of the seasons, to whom a festival was celebrated in the winter, is probably a foreign sun-god. On the Lycian god, Apollo, see below. If the name of Athena really corresponded to a Sanskr. *ahanâ*, the "dawning," and Athenaia to *ahania*, the "day-bright," as Max Müller supposes, we should have to regard her also as an Indo-Germanic goddess. The adoption of foreign elements into the conception of her becomes probable when it is considered that a Phenician Athênê was worshipped on the Isthmus, and that she came from Salamis to Attica, and it is made further evident by a comparison of her attributes and cultus with those of the Phenician Tanith.

On the whole subject of this section compare the very interesting essay of E. Curtius, "Die Griechische Götterlehre vom Geschichtlichen Standpunkt," in the *Preuss. Jahrbb.*, July 1875, though some of the conclusions must be accepted with reserve.

124. The poetic and philosophical feeling of this richly-endowed people, the creative power of the Greek mind, is displayed, for instance, in their treatment of the myth of Prometheus, which became in their hands the vehicle for profound and elevated thoughts, or in the manner in which they raised the nature-myths of Dêmêtêr and Persephonê to be the expression of a genuine human feeling, and ennobled the mystic significance which had already been attached to it in other lands. But it nowhere comes more clearly into view than in a comparison of deities such as Hermes or Aphroditê with the divine beings of Indo-Germanic or Semitic origin, from which they have sprung. Hermes or Hermeias, once the hound of the gods, the god of the wind and the changes of light and darkness which it produces, the great enchanter and conductor of souls, becomes among the Greeks the messenger and right hand of Zeus, the mediator between him and men, the ideal herald, the god of graceful speed, of

music, of eloquence, and philosophy. Aphroditê is no other than the Phenician and Mesopotamian Astartê ('Ashtoreth, Istar), but while it was the aim of philosophy to infuse a deeper meaning into the naturalistic myths of her birth out of the waters, her sovereignty over the monsters of the ocean, and her intercourse with Adonis, they were transformed by Greek poetry and art into the loveliest of images, and she herself, though retaining many features which recalled her origin, was raised to be the goddess of beauty and grace, of spring and flowers, of family peace and social harmony.

Hermeias is identical with *Sârameyas*, the name of the two dogs of Yama, the god of death, the mythic watch-dogs in the Veda. Max Müller doubts whether *Saramâ*, their mother, the messenger of Indra, who goes to fetch back the stolen cows, was a dog. But the *Sârameyau* certainly were so. Hermes possesses no Semitic trait. His original physical significance as a god of wind perfectly explains all the myths about him, such as the stealing of Apollo's cows, the slaying of Argus, his combat with Stentor, and all his attributes, as guardian of the flocks (the clouds), guide of the shades, herald of the gods, god of music and eloquence, his magic power, his swift-footedness, &c. As god of eloquence, he naturally became in Greece the god of philosophy as well.

That the Greeks originally possessed a goddess of spring, beauty, and love, of their own, whose name, however, disappeared, is highly probable; indeed, the Latin Venus may be said to prove it. Aphroditê, however, whose name is perhaps a corruption of 'Athar'atha, is certainly the Phenician goddess of Cyprus and Cythera, who passed from there to the Greeks, bringing with her Kinyras, Adonis, and Pygmalion. But all these myths, which were once coarsely sensual, and for the most part cosmogonic, were touched with the magic wand of their poetry.

125. The first-fruits of this mingling of the Phenician, Phrygian, and Hellenic elements was the brilliant civilisation which preceded that of Greece proper, and spread over the whole of the west coast of Asia Minor and Crete. It was the era when the old Lydian supremacy flourished, together with Troas and Lycia, and the powerful kingdom in Crete named after Minos. There it was, and then, that the Greek mind first gave signs of possessing sufficient strength to appropriate the Semitic elements independently, and endow them with a new form. Then it was that the myth of Zeus received its shape in Crete, and his cultus was established, in the mode which soon became the property of all Hellenes, and supplanted that of the Pelasgian Zeus. Then it was that the Greek Herakles arose, probably in Lydia, out of the Assyrian Ṣamdan, brought thither by conquest. Then it was that the knightly people of the Lycians, kinsmen of the Greeks, and their forerunners in civilisation, after coming under the influence of the Semitic spirit, wrought out the noble figure of Apollo, the god of light, the son and prophet of the most high Zeus, saviour, purifier, and redeemer, whose cultus, lifted high above all nature-worship, spread thence over all the lands of Greece, and exerted on the religious, moral, and social life of their inhabitants so profound and salutary an influence.

In Crete, several forms of Phenician cultus still prevailed. This is the scene of the chief myths of Zeus, which have a Semitic origin. This does not prove that Crete was also the place of their rise, but simply that they there attained the form which became dominant among the Hellenes.

The mingling of various elements may still be very clearly traced in the Trojan tradition. By the side of the Assyrian names Ilos (*Ilu*) and Assarakos stand Phrygian, like Kapys, Dymas, Askanios, and Kasandra, and pure Greek names such as Andromachê, Astyanax, and others. Some heroes even bear double names—Paris-Alexandros, Dareios-Hektor—of which only the second are Greek. The first have a pure Erânian form (Paris, from *par*, "deserter"), but they are doubtless really Phrygian, as this language was connected alike with Erânian and with Greek. On this subject see further Curtius, *History of Greece*, vol. i. pp. 47–68.

126. Last of all, the higher civilisation made its way to Hellas, Greece proper, both by direct colonisation on the part of the Phenicians, and to a greater extent by Greek settlements from Asia Minor and Crete. The point attained by the religious development of the Acheans, before the supremacy of the Dorians, is shown by the Homeric poems. The gods are no longer half-conscious nature-powers; they are beings possessing moral liberty and freedom of action like men—they are in the same way subject to pain and grief, and they are obliged to support life by food. But their food is of a heavenly kind, which secures them immortality; in theory, at least, all things are known and possible to them, and the chief of them rule no more over a limited realm. Although they are not themselves raised above passions and selfish desires, they are nevertheless the guardians and avengers

of the moral order of the world, the violation of which excites their wrath more than an injury offered to themselves. The world of the gods is arranged after the pattern of the households of earth. To the council (βουλή) of the kings, mustered round their leader, corresponds the assembly of the high Olympian gods, under the presidency of Zeus, their superior, not by privilege of birth, but, like the chief of the princes of the earth, by his greater power and ability. The popular assembly (ἀγορά) has its heavenly counterpart in the convocation of all divine beings on certain occasions to learn the will of the king. Their supremacy is established; the contest with the rude powers of nature has long been finished, and they have been subdued for ever. In this respect they have advanced beyond the Vedic and Germanic gods.

On this and the following sections compare Nägelsbach, *Homerische Theologie.*

Between the religion of the Acheans and their adversaries, the Dardanians, there is no essential difference. But the gods which protect the latter stand, like their heroes, at a perceptibly higher level than those of. the former, which correctly commemorates the fact that the inhabitants of Hellas were still behind those of Asia Minor in civilisation.

The difference between gods and men is very naïvely indicated, among other signs, by the doctrine that it is no human blood, but a peculiar fluid (ἰχώρ), which runs in the divine veins.

127. High above all the other gods stands Zeus, whose power is unlimited, who is not bound by any recognised restraint, and is alone not subject to the will of the

majority. Even his consort Hera, who generally opposes him, can effect nothing but by and with him. Vainly does his brother Poseidon strive to establish similar prerogatives. Most closely connected with him are Athena and Apollo, who constitute with him a supreme triad.

As Athena is the personified Mêtis, the "reason," the wisdom of the divine Father, who withstands him, yet to whom he always yields, Apollo, no less beloved of Zeus, is his mouth, the revealer of his counsel, the son, who, ever and in all things, is of one will with him. For it is one of the features which distinguishes Zeus from the other gods, that he never communicates directly with men, but only through his messengers, Iris or Hermes. In reality, all the gods are little else than representatives of Zeus, each in his own realm which he has received from him. Thus, monarchism has touched the borders of monotheism.

The dependence of the gods and of the whole world on Zeus is finely described in the well-known passage, *Iliad*, Θ. 1–27.

The circumstance that Dionysos and Ḍêmêtêr have but little significance in the Homeric poems does not warrant the conclusion that their worship was not yet generally diffused. But they were chiefly popular gods, worshipped by the tillers of the soil, and they did not, therefore, figure in the aristocratic Homeric society.

128. The conviction that the world was not ruled merely by an arbitrary will, was expressed by the doctrine of destiny (*αἶσα, μοῖρα*), though the representation of it was deficient in clearness, and the question whether the supreme god determined the course of destiny, or whether he, like all the other gods, was subject to it, so that he had only to consult and to execute it, was answered now in one way and now in another. The deity makes known his will to men by personal revelation, by miracles and signs, or by inspiration and dreams, but most clearly of all by his works. Yet the trustworthiness of signs is already called in question, and once even the noble sentiment is uttered that they are insignificant compared with the divine voice in the heart of man, which commands him to do right without thought of the consequences. Morality and religion are already in intimate connection, but psychology and the belief in immortality still stand on the animistic level.

Zeus and Moira frequently coalesce in the description of the poet; what she does is also ascribed to him and to the other gods; good and evil gifts are allotted by him. On the other hand, he is represented as knowing nothing of the will of destiny by himself; he is obliged to consult it with his scales, and is bound to fulfil it completely.

In the Homeric psychology a noteworthy separation is made between the understanding (φρένες) and the soul (ψύχη), the former of which dies with the body; an idea which we also meet with among the Hindûs.

Retribution after death is as yet scarcely mentioned. The shades continue the occupations which they discharged during their lifetime: in the kingdom of the departed, Teiresias is still a soothsayer, Minos a judge, Orion a huntsman.

129. The rise of Delphi marks a new and important era in the history of the Greek religion. Dodona continued to be spoken of with reverence, but its influence had long been limited to a small and backward portion of the country. The other religious centre, also, the Thessalian Olympus, was gradually abandoned by the more gifted tribes which had surrounded it, and lay in the midst of a land of barbarians. At Delphi, lying at the foot of Parnassus, there was in existence already before Homer a famous oracle, first of the Earth-goddess, afterwards of the Pythian Apollo; and it was located in a temple where Zeus and Dionysos were worshipped together with the deities already named. When the Dorians had quitted Thessaly to seek new homes, they attached themselves as ardent worshippers of Apollo to the Delphic sanctuary, and wherever they settled they established the cultus of the Pythian deity. Delphi became the chief seat of a new Amphiktyonic league, and was, in fact, for a considerable time, the centre of the nationality of the Hellenes. The power exercised by the Delphic priesthood in the centuries between the Doric migration and the Persian wars was very great. No new political institutions, no fresh cultus, no additional games, were established without the sanction of the Pythian oracle, and it was carefully on the watch against the neglect of the old and the introduction of new gods, while it strove to maintain peace between the different Hellenic states. It had its representatives and exponents in the chief cities of the principal states, and foreign princes or states which sought to enter into relations with Greece applied to the Delphic Apollo, who spoke all languages. The colonies, whose despatch was always determined and directed by him, spread his worship far and near. It was not a new religion, destined to replace the worship of Zeus, for Apollo was simply the revealer of his holy will; it was a higher stage of the development of this same religion, by which some bounds were set to polytheism, and the ethical took the place of the physical. It accepted no outward actions as satisfactory; only with a pure heart might the deity be approached, and self-examination and self-knowledge were the first and loftiest of his demands. The false and double-minded gained no light from Apollo, the evil-doer no help; but on the weak he bestowed protection, and on the repentant grace. Truth and self-control, without self-mortification or renunciation of nature, a steady equilibrium between the sensible and the spiritual, moral earnestness combined with an open eye for the happiness and the beauty of life, such were the characteristic features of the Delphic Apollo-worship, in which the Greek religion almost reached the climax of its development.

Other places besides Delphi served as the centres of these leagues of states; for example, the sanctuary of the Ephesian Artemis.

The legislation bearing the name of Lycurgus originated in Delphi, and received its sanction from there. When the sanctuary at Olympia in Elis had acquired a higher significance by the protection of Sparta, it was consecrated by the Delphic oracle, and Apollo was placed beside Zeus as the guardian of the Olympic games and institutions.

No Hellenic state might consult the oracle with hostile intentions against another Hellenic state. The memory of a civil war might not be perpetuated at Delphi by any permanent trophies. It was not till the period of decline after the Persian wars that this principle was infringed.

It is well known that the Pythian oracle was consulted by Phrygian and Lydian princes, and by Italian peoples, amongst others, even by the Romans. Foreign nations were regarded at Delphi as guests.

For him who approached with a pure heart, so it was said, a single drop of the consecrated water of the well of Castalia sufficed; but he who came with an evil mind could not wash away with a whole ocean the pollution of his sin. It was a mark of the ethical character of the Delphic religion that the doctrine of retribution after death accompanied it. This doctrine never, it is true, became really a matter of popular belief among the Greeks, but it was promoted by men of earnest views, and it was proclaimed by poets and sages connected with Delphi, such as Hesiod, Solon, Pythagoras, and Pindar.

130. The general diffusion of civilisation and knowledge among the Greeks, which resulted from their splendid gifts, their love of freedom, and other accessory causes, prevented the rise of a dominant class of priests or *literati*, like that which existed among the Brâhmans. Moreover, the priesthoods were generally in the hands of the nobles, and were not mutually dependent on each other. Priests and prophets (*μαντεῖς*), however, received high honour, for it was they who expounded the signs of the divine will, interpreted the utterances of the deity, and bestowed forgiveness of sins. Above all, however, the Delphic priests contrived to maintain their position at the head of civilisation, and of everything which went on in Greece and the neighbouring states. The form of the ancient oracle uttered by the Pythia in ecstasy was retained, but the real answer was given by them, and as their decisions were as a rule wise and practical, they were largely

invoked. This in itself secured them great power over the actual course of affairs. But they also contrived to give a definite direction to literature, philosophy, and art, though they did not themselves take part in them. They formed an intellectual aristocracy, which stood in relation with all the foremost men of different countries, which pointed out who were the best and the wisest of their time, which led the way in a certain edifying style of history and in the composition of sacred songs, which encouraged the authors of didactic and lyric poetry, and thus proved itself the active ready representative of the god who led the band of the Muses. The system of Pythagoras, who founded a real religious community in a thoroughly Delphic spirit, the poetic school of Hesiod, whose Theogony was even regarded as a book of revelation and a rule of belief, were called into existence by the influence of the priesthood of Delphi. The festive games, also, which were of so much importance in this period for the national life of the Hellenes, were regulated by them, and the Pythian games were favourably distinguished from the others by the prominence given in them not to bodily exercises, but to the musical contest.

The real cause which prevented the rise of a hierarchy in Greece was not its polytheism, for that proved no obstacle in India, but chiefly the general civilisation of the whole people, which made theology in the hands of priests and philosophers not an obstacle, but a means of development, and was in its turn a result of the active intercourse which the position of their country enabled the Greeks to maintain.

It was by Delphi that the seven famous Sages were

enumerated, whose teachings were framed, like the Hebrew, in short maxims. It is well known that at a much later time still the oracle, in reply to a question by his disciple Cherephon, declared Socrates to be the wisest of all mortals.

The festival games at Olympia were at first solely gymnastic. The Nemean and Isthmian were founded with the sanction of the Delphic oracle, on condition that they should be open to all Hellenes. This specification was characteristic of the Delphic policy.

131. About the end of the sixth century B.C., the influence exercised for three hundred years by Delphi began to decline. This was in part to be ascribed to circumstances, especially to the lessening interest of Sparta, which found a new religious centre in Olympia, and to the rivalry between this state and Athens, which, together with Sikyon, now attached itself more closely to Delphi. But it was to a still larger extent their own fault that the priests of Apollo lost their power. They ceased to be faithful to their own principles; they exchanged their sound statesmanship for a narrow-minded and temporising policy; they no longer followed the pure moral aims of earlier days, but pursued particular interests; they strove to maintain their position by craft and intrigue; and they even sold themselves for Asiatic gold. In the great conflict with Persia, Delphi no longer represented the national spirit; it wavered, and led others to waver, and thus injured the common cause. The great god was still an object of reverence, but the people began to despise the oracle. The aristocratic spirit of the Delphic priesthood, also, was no longer in harmony with the pre-

vailing spirit of the time. The era of the democratic Dionysos-worship, which at Delphi only occupied the second place, had begun.

The contest with the Persians had not only a national, but a religious character as well. In spite of the vacillating attitude of the oracle, the allies resolved to dedicate a tenth part of the spoil to the Delphic god.

132. The national religion of the Hellenes, however, was not to succumb without breaking forth into a splendour hitherto unknown. Involved in a struggle for very life with the increasing unbelief, it put forth all its powers, and then, even when decline had already set in, it attained the fulness of its glorious stature. It was at Athens that this last conflict was fought out. The Doric migration had brought together in Attica a number of Achean and Ionic tribes, and had fused together several religions, with that mingling of elements which is always productive of rich development. The teacher of Athens was Delphi, to which it was faithfully attached, and it was by Apollo-worship, which became the popular religion under Solon, that the foundations of a higher civilisation were laid, but the special contributions made by Athens itself were called forth under the impulse of the cultus of Dionysos and the worship of Athena. The first of these was favoured by the tyrants, Peisistratos and his successors, owing to their readiness as demagogues to promote a cultus which had proved more acceptable than any other to the masses of the people. To the myth of the Thracian god, who was worshipped at Eleusis by the side of Dêmêtêr, Onomakritos, by a new mystic system, imparted a higher significance.

The Bacchic choric-song, the dithyramb, was developed into a separate art by Lasos and his disciple Pindar, who was initiated into the Eleusinian mysteries, and made it the vehicle of the most elevated religious thoughts. These choric songs and dances grew into dialogues and performances, which were in their turn the source of tragedy and comedy. By slow degrees a greater freedom was attained in the choice of dramatic subjects, and tragedy, in the hands of Eschylus and Sophokles, became the means of bringing forth in living forms to general view the kernel of religious truth hidden in the mythologic shell. Both were men of their time, with an open eye for all advance, but at the same time earnestly devoted to their ancestral religion. The deep religious feeling which characterised the Dionysos-worship—the fruit of the Semitic spirit, and the genuinely human element contributed by the Hellenic —were fused by them into a noble unity.

Curtius, *History of Greece*, i. p. 304, has called attention to the number of great men in Athens who were descended on the father's or mother's side from noble Messenian families who had emigrated thither. Such were Kodros, Solon, Peisistratos, Kleisthenes, Perikles, Plato, Alkibiades.

The most ancient local deity of Attika was Zeus Herkeios. Eleusis was the seat of the worship of Poseidon and Dêmêtêr, with which that of Dionysos was united. The contest between Athena and Poseidon at Athens is well known. Apollo was early worshipped at several places on the coast.

When the chief families at Athens were burdened with blood-guiltiness, Solon sent for the prophet Epimenides, a man of impressive character, from Crete. He purified and atoned for everything in the name of Apollo, who then, under his influence, became the national god.

Eschylus was himself born at Eleusis, and belonged to a family which was very closely connected with the sanctuary. He grew up beneath the influence of the grave rites performed there. The union of the religious and humanist elements is nowhere more strikingly displayed than in the Titan Prometheus, as he is represented by Eschylus—proud and noble, unwearied in thought and endeavour, unsubdued in conflict and humiliation, but the victim of his own self-exaltation and wantonness, which made him forget that the only true wisdom has its source in Zeus, and in the heart of genuine piety.

133. The spirit which was promoted by poetry was fostered also at Athens by sculpture. It was most closely connected with the worship of Athena, the goddess of art, the "workmistress" (*Erganê*), and shed most glory on her cultus and that of her father Zeus. Its greatest genius, Pheidias, flourished in the time of Kimon and Perikles. While the more advanced no longer found in the ugly old images to which the people continued to pay a superstitious reverence, the deity whom they mentally conceived, and many a philosopher ridiculed the worship of images, Pheidias wrought statues which were not intended to be worshipped, but were designed to furnish a purer idea of the deity, and to be dedicated to it as worthy offerings. This was especially the case with his two masterpieces, the virgin Athena of the Parthenon and the Zeus of Olympia. In these two works of art, and in the ancient Tragedy, the religion of the Hellenes reached the climax of its development. The ideal humanisation of deity, for

which the way was prepared by the cultus of the Delphic Apollo, was perfected at Athens by Eschylus, Sophokles, and Pheidias.

> The family of Pheidias was hereditarily devoted not only to art, but also to the worship of Athena Erganê.
>
> In the *Athena Parthenos* Pheidias succeeded in combining chastity with gentleness, victorious strength with calm peace, profound wisdom with clearness; while the Zeus of Olympia united the greatest and most impressive sublimity with clemency, supreme dominion and power with graciousness. Both works, the productions of the highest art, were at the same time the expression of a profound religious idea.

134. But not even the miracles of art, which always hastens to the aid of a dying form of religion, can save it from ruin, when it no longer answers to the wants of a new generation. It was impossible for poets and sculptors to arrest the increasing decline of the Hellenic religion. The causes of that decline lay in the triumph of democracy, which weakened the reverence for lawful authority, the great disasters which befell the state and excited doubts of the power of the protecting deities, the boldness of philosophical speculation which questioned the personality of the gods, the genuineness of their signs, the validity of their tradition, and set unintelligent powers in the place of the living gods of Olympus, while sophistic, the bastard-daughter of philosophy, undermined both faith and morals. The proof of this is furnished by the constant increase of superstition. Men sought satisfaction for their religious cravings in all kinds of foreign worships, from dirty mendicant priests, who promised atonement for money,

and ventriloquists who professed to be inspired. Secret associations replaced the state mysteries. Vainly did a poet like Euripides strive to unite the religious aspirations which filled his mind, with the claims of thought. He himself was too much affected by doubt to be able to harmonise the traditional belief with the ideas of his time, and he died, gloomy and dissatisfied, far from his native land. Had it been possible for any one to reconcile these conflicting elements, it would have been effected by a man of prophetic nature, like Sokrates, the opponent of the Sophists, an acute inquirer into existing systems, a profound and original thinker, but at the same time endowed with a heart of childlike piety, and a lofty moral character, which wrought his faith, his doctrine, and his life into complete accord. In him the reconciliation of religion and philosophy was accomplished. But the authorised representatives of religion rejected his aid, like that of all the noble thinkers of their days. Their fanatical zeal, a new sign of decline, was not directed only against the philosophers and the sophists, including even the religious Anaxagoras; it pursued Alkibiades, it did not spare Perikles and Pheidias, and it endeavoured to establish a regular inquisition. Sokrates, also, became their victim. Condemned for apostasy from the ancestral religion, for introducing new religions, and for corrupting youth, he was forced to drink the poisoned cup. A religion which thus murders its noblest thinker, who has been declared by deity itself to be the wisest of all mortals, has closed the path to all further advance, and has no other future before it than lingering petrifaction or death.

The rich activity of religious art, just at the period of a religion's decline, is a common phenomenon. Instances abound in the splendid temples of Nebukadrezar in Babylon, in the revival of sacred art in Egypt under the Saitic princes, and even under the Ptolemies, in Rome under the early emperors, and in the Italy of the Renaissance.

Among the foreign religions which now found great acceptance in Greece may be named the Phrygian worship of Sabazios and the Mother of the gods, the Thracian cultus of Kotytto, and the Syrian of Adonis, which was already widely diffused in the East. Between the adoption of these foreign forms of worship in a state of decay, and the independent working of lofty religious ideas and conceptions, to which the Hellenic religion was indebted in the period of its growth for its advanced development, there is a vast difference.

Sokrates was diligent in sacrificing; he revered the oracles, and loyally held fast to the religion of his fathers. The Apollo-worship won his greatest sympathy; the guiding principle of each was the same. He gained his belief in deity by the path of inward experience, and he heard within him the voice of his good spirit, which was with him no figure of speech, but an intense conviction. The miserable nature of the charges brought against him is clearly indicated by the description of this as the introduction of new gods. The close affinity between the persecutors of Sokrates and the Sadducees who put Jesus to death is well illustrated by their hypocrisy in postponing his execution for thirty days, to prevent the desecration of the city while the Athenian festival-ship was on its voyage to Delos.

The persecution of Pheidias, who died broken-hearted in prison, was also inspired by religious zeal: he was accused of having perpetuated his own likeness and that of Perikles on the shield of the Parthenos. Alkibiades was perhaps not so innocent of ridiculing the Eleusinian mysteries, which was the charge brought against him. His guilt, however, was never proved, and the mutilation of the Hermæ, which was also laid at his door, was probably the work of his enemies themselves. The fury of the zealots knew no bounds. Every honest man was in danger of being accused of atheism. Open liars were praised and honoured; noble citizens were laid on the rack. So untrue is it that intolerance was alien to the Greek religion.

II.

RELIGION AMONG THE ROMANS.

Literature.—T. MOMMSEN, *History of Rome*, translated from the German by W. P. Dickson, 4 vols., London, 1867 (6th Germ. ed. 1874). A. SCHWEGLER, *Römische Geschichte im Zeitalter der Könige*, Tübingen, 1853. I. A. HARTUNG, *Die Religion der Römer*, 2 vols., Erlangen, 1836. L. PRELLER, *Römische Mythologie*, Berlin, 1858 (2d ed. 1865). For the earlier literature comp. PRELLER, *ibid.*, pp. 41–43.

135. The religions of the Greeks and Romans were originally, like their languages, very closely connected, as the names of some of the chief gods prove. The traces of agreement would certainly be still more numerous, had not the difference in national character and in outward circumstances led each of the two religions to develop itself for a considerable time in exactly opposite directions, till the nations came once more into contact with each other, and their religions blended together. The aim of the Greek was towards a more and more complete anthropomorphism, which Attic sculpture wrought out to perfection; but to this the Roman felt an instinctive aversion. He was too little of an artist, and had also too deep a reverence for the higher powers to represent them as beings resembling men. The powers of nature, so far as they had not yet in an earlier period become personal deities, remained spirits to his view, or became personifications of abstract ideas. This is the character likewise of the new gods whom they created, beings who only possess a nebulous existence, rarely uniting in marriage or forming amorous connections, and remaining for the most part childless. The remains of the old Roman mythology are therefore extremely scanty. But the ideas which were elevated to the rank of spirits are innumerable. Not only has every man his Genius, and every woman her Juno, but every deity, also, together with every being, every object, every action or function, every moral quality even, has its own spirit, which is limited to its own province. If the dominant elements in Greek mythology are personality, freedom, and the richest diversity, the Roman theology is characterised by the abstract idea, by necessity, by the severest order and monotony. The difference between the two corresponds exactly to that between the Hindû and Persian religions, to the latter of which the character of the Roman affords a complete parallel.

Identity of name subsists between *Jupiter* (*Diovis*) and *Zeus*, *Zeus pater*, *Vesta* and *Hestia*, and probably between *Juno* and *Dione*. *Janus*, it has been suggested, is connected with the Greek form *Zen*. *Mars* and *Ares* are regarded by recent investigators as entirely different deities. I am not only of the opposite opinion, but I even believe the names have originally the same significance. *Neptunus*, a name which disappeared among the Greeks, is certainly the *Apãm napaṭ* of the ancient Aryans.

The intercourse with Eastern nations, which can be traced back among the Greeks to the earliest times, did not begin among the Romans till after their national life had developed, and it consequently produced a much deeper impression on the religious ideas of the former than on those of the latter.

There is a characteristic difference between the Greeks and Romans in prayer. The Greek looked towards the deity with uncovered head, the Roman veiled his face.

The nebulous character of many Roman deities also appears from the formulæ: "*Sive Deo, Sive Deae*," "*Sive Mas, Sive Femina*," "*Sive quo alio nomine te appellari volueris*," employed concerning the gods or addressed to them.

It appears that the marriages of the gods, and their children likewise, were much more numerous in the earliest times, but that such representations were afterwards rejected by the strict Romans. One of the most important survivals of genuine Roman or rather of Italian mythology, is the myth of Hercules and Cacus, the old Indo-Germanic conflict between the god of light and the cloud demon; but it is noteworthy that the Greek Herakles has already stepped into the place of the national god, and that Cacus (the "burning"? or the "blind"?) was brought into connection with the Greek word κακός.

The term Genius is employed for the spirits of female beings also, *Genius Junonis Sospitæ*, *Genius Famæ*, *Genius*

Forinarum. The fertility in the creation of special genii which distinguished the Roman religion particularly, may be estimated from the fact that not only every condition of social life, but every operation of agriculture, ploughing, sowing, harvesting, down to the opening of the barns,—nay, even the annual supply of corn in the market (*Annona*), and the healthy flesh of the human body (*Carnia*, properly speaking a demon who kept off blood-sucking vampires), had their special representatives in the world of spirits.

The peculiarity here indicated as attaching to the Roman religion is connected with the Roman national character, which Mommsen finds in the profound sense of the existence of the general in the particular, in the devotion and self-sacrifice of the individual to the whole, and which he regards as the basis also of the political unity and the universal dominion of the Roman Empire.

The resemblance of the Roman and Persian religions is indeed striking. In both the ethical rises above the mythological elements; in Pârsism abstract ideas become in like manner immortal saints (*amesha spènta*) and ministers of Ahuramazda, and there also, just as among the Romans, everything, including even the gods, has its own spirit or Fravashi, a word which does not differ very widely in meaning from Genius (connected with *genus*, *gigno*).

136. In spite of the complete modification of the Roman religion subsequently by the adoption of foreign elements, particularly those of Greek and Oriental origin, it remained true to this character during every period of its existence, and continued to develop itself in this direction until the end. When silver coinage was introduced, about the middle of the third century B.C., Aescu-

lanus, the ancient genius of copper money, immediately begot a son, Argentinus. The first Greek gods whom the Romans made their own received new and intelligible names in place of their former Greek designations, which had ceased to be understood, or they were modified so as to represent some abstract conception. Thus Mercurius, the god of trade, was imitated from the Greek Hermes; Minerva, the "thinking," from the Greek Athena; while Proserpina was the Greek Persephonê. The number of genii who were mere abstractions continued to increase. Terror and pallor in battle, peace and freedom, hope and good fortune, became the objects, as spirits of dread and blessing, of a real worship; and if in ancient times only *Fides*, "good faith," was venerated as a separate deity, altars and sanctuaries were soon erected for several other virtues, divine or moral attributes, such as *Concordia, Pudicitia, Mens, Pietas*, and *Aequitas;* at a later date to *Constantia, Liberalitas, Providentia;* and finally even to the *Indulgentia* and *Clementia Cæsaris.* From this last phenomenon to the deification of the emperors themselves, which also, indeed, originated under the influence of the East, there was but a step.

The designation of Greek gods by Latin names, so that the Romans could better understand their meaning, has nothing to do with the fusion of Greek with old Italic deities, like that of Aphroditê with Venus, of Bakchos with Liber, of Dêmêtêr with Ceres, and of Artemis with Diana.

The *Virtutes*, which were the earliest to become Genii, were originally attributes of distinct deities, as Fides of Jupiter (comp. *Dius Fidius*), Concordia of Venus, Pudicitia of Juno, Mens of Fortuna.

A most remarkable example of personification is found also in that of the divine voice, as *Aius Locutius.*

137. The religion of the Romans stands at first at about the same point of development as the Pelasgic. The number of spirits or genii is unlimited, and they are worshipped with more zeal than any others. Among them may be named the *Lares,* or Lords, who were at first, at any rate, only worshipped in private; the *Penates,* or hearth-spirits, to whom, together with Vesta, public adoration was paid; the *Manes,* the *Larvae,* and the *Lemures,* all of whom were souls of the dead, the first being good and pure, properly spirits of light, while the two last wandered about as ghosts, not having as yet come to their rest, and at a later period were regarded definitely as evil spirits. No sharp lines were drawn to distinguish these spirits, to whom other groups might be added from one another, for they were in fact only different representations of the same idea. Nevertheless, it is incorrect to name even the oldest Roman religion polydaemonism. The decisive step which leads to polytheism had been already taken. The term *Dei, Divi,* was no longer applied exclusively to the spirits of the sky; it became, just as among the Greeks, the generic name for personal and intelligent beings belonging to the earth and the under-world as well as to the sky, and ruling nature by their will (as *numina*). The transition was still in progress. The evil deities who were dreaded, such as Vediovis, were still worshipped equally with the good. Their number, moreover, was still small. Some, like *Robigo,* the god of the corn-rust, *Consus,* probably the god

of the hidden germs, *Carmentis,* the deity of the magic incantation, and others, were not yet much more than spirits; but others, such as the good shepherd's god, Faunus, the god of sowing, Saturnus (*Saëturnus*), with his joyous festival, the fire-gods, Vulcan and Vesta, and especially the three most eminent of all, Jupiter, Janus, and Mars, were personal deities in the fullest sense, possessing supreme power not only over the realm of nature, but also over society and morals.

The genius was also called *Cerus* or *Kerus,* a word connected with the Sanskrit root *kṛi,* "to make," "to do."

The Lares do not differ much in character from the Greek heroes. If their name is identical with the well-known Etrurian word *Lars* (which is, however, declined differently), they must be the "lords," the "potentates." The term *Penates* is derived from *penus,* the domestic "hearth," connected with *penes* and *penitus.* The name *Manes,* allied with *mane,* "early in the morning," denotes the "bright ones," the "pure." The Silvans and Fauns bear more resemblance to the bands of Hindû deities. They are the spirits of the forest and the field.

Besides the deities specified in the text, the oldest Roman festival calendar also mentions *Tellus,* the nourishing earth; *Ceres,* the goddess of growth; *Pales,* the deity who gave fruitfulness to the flocks; *Ops,* the goddess of the harvest; *Terminus,* the boundary-stone of the land; *Neptunus, Tiber, Mater* (*matuta*), the morning goddess, a sort of dawn; and *Liber* and *Libera,* regarded by some as the "deliverers" from bondage and sorrow, by others as the gods of the blessing of children. It is noteworthy that Juno, Minerva, and Diana, though they were very early worshipped in Rome, the two first on the Capitol, the last on the Aventine, have not as yet appeared.

138. Here, as elsewhere, it is by a fusion of different elements that a higher development has been reached. The religion of the earliest inhabitants of Rome had not advanced beyond that of shepherds and tillers of the soil; it was from the Sabines that higher religious conceptions, together with a certain patriarchal-hierarchic polity, were first introduced. As Rome became more of an Italian centre, the number of gods who received its citizenship increased, and if this caused a loss of the old simplicity, the horizon was at the same time enlarged. After the union of Latins and Sabines, three gods were raised far above the others; Jupiter was the highest, Mars the most worshipped, and Janus the most characteristic of the people. Jupiter, the good father, source of blessings and of creation, sustainer of good faith and honesty, was still, as the severe requirements imposed on his priest evince, and as results from his whole character, pre-eminently the god of purity and holiness. Whatever Mars may have been in an earlier period, whether sun-god or spring-god, he had certainly by this time become, *par excellence*, the god of war, protector of the flocks of his people, champion of the citizens, who received as his spring-harvest the *Ver Sacrum*, the young men sent forth to conquer for themselves a new abode, and whose priests, from their magic war-dance, were called the *Salii*. Janus (*Dianus*, the "light one," the "bright"), with his two faces, the god of the summer, who opened the day, and afterwards also the year, gave his name to the month which succeeded the winter month, was the opener of all life, the beginner of all movement, and almost became the Creator, but the soldierly Romans connected him likewise with war.

Even the Palatine Mars, before the coming of the Sabines, was still more of a nature-god than of a god of war, and only acquired this latter significance by his union with Quirinus, the war-god of the Sabines. Different derivations are assigned to his name, which would make him either the god of death (*Mavors, Maurs, Mors*, so Mommsen), or a sun-god (from *mar*, to "shine," to "sparkle," Roscher). The proposal of Roscher to identify him with Apollo, on the ground of some external correspondences, seems to me to ignore the vast difference between the character of the two deities. In the opinion of Preller, Mars is the same as *Mas*, "the male power" (comp. *Maspiter, Marmar*, and his marriage with *Nerio*, whose name is connected with the Sabine *Nero*, "strong," and with the root *nṛi, nar*, "the male element"), and in this capacity he would be the god of new life, of re-awakening fruitfulness, and the genius of war. Mommsen and Preller may at bottom be both right, for *mors* and *mas* probably both have the same root (Sanskr. *mṛi*) signifying death (comp. Sanskr. *marya*, "man," "warrior," *marta, martya*, "man," and the Maruts, the Vedic gods of storm and war). The *Ver Sacrum* was a sacrifice of men and cattle to the god of war, in the hope that this propitiation would induce him to spare during the year the rest of the warriors and the flocks of the community. The practice of opening the temple of Janus Quirinus at Rome at the outbreak of war, and closing it again when peace was established, has been variously, but not yet satisfactorily, explained. I look for its origin in the old animistic notion that it was needful to give the deity an opportunity of accompanying the troops.

139. Much greater weight was attached by the practical Roman to the cultus than to the doctrines of religion.

This was the one point of supreme importance; in his view the truly devout man was he who punctually performed his religious obligations, who was pious according to law. There was a debt to be paid to the gods which must be discharged, but it was settled if the letter of the contract was fulfilled, and the symbol was given in place of the reality. The animistic conception that the gods might be employed as instruments for securing practical advantages, lies at the basis of the whole Roman cultus. In the earliest times, therefore, it was quite simple, so far as regards the absence of images or temples, but it was at the same time exceedingly complicated and burdened with all kinds of ceremonies and symbolic actions, and the least neglect destroyed the efficacy of the sacrifice. This necessitated the assistance of priests acquainted with the whole ritual, not to serve as mediators, for the approach to the deity was open to all, but to see that the pious action failed in no essential element. Each god had his Flamen or "fire-kindler" (literally "blower"). Of these there were twelve, the three principal ones (*majores*) being the priest of Jupiter, the *Flamen dialis*, who was bound by rigid obligations, and the two priests of Mars, the *Flamines Martialis* and *Quirinalis*, the heads of the two Salian-Colleges. The wives of these *Flamines* performed the cultus of the corresponding goddesses. No special deity claimed the services of the *Pontifices*, the bridge- or road-makers, a priesthood whose head, the *Pontifex Maximus*, was rising higher and higher in authority, though at this period, at any rate, the three *Flamines majores* were still his superiors; the Augurs, also, who discerned the will of the gods from the flight of birds, and other sacred orders, were likewise unconnected with any particular deity. Everything was regulated with precision by the government; and the fact that the highest of the priests was always under the control of the state prevented the rise of a priestly supremacy, the absence of which in Greece was due to other causes; but the consequence was that the Roman religion remained dry and formal, and was external rather than inward. Even the purity (*castitas*), on which such great stress was laid, was only sacerdotal, and was attained by lustration, sprinkling, and fumigation, and the great value attached to prayer, so that a single error had to be atoned for as a neglect, had its basis in the superstitious belief that it possessed a high magic power. Such a religion was certainly intelligible to all; it was not without a favourable influence on political and social life, and it was admirably adapted to form a well-organised army of conquerors, a nation that could rule the world, but to spiritual life it contributed nothing, and it did little for the advancement of speculation, poetry, or art.

It was not necessary to offer to the thundering heaven-god or to the river-god of the Tiber any human sacrifices, but to the former onions and poppy-heads were offered for his lightning to strike, instead of human heads, while thirty puppets made of rushes were annually cast into the latter.

Varro regrets the days when the gods were worshipped "*sine simulacro.*" In fact the little "houses of the gods" (*aedicula*), which came into use in early times, were regarded as departures from the law of Numa. It is erroneous to quote this circumstance in proof of the purity of the primitive cultus; it only indicates the low stage at which that cultus stood. The sacred trees, stones (*Jupiter lapis*), and animals (the wolf of Mars, and his woodpecker, *Picus*, who even becomes in tradition a pre-historic king, *Picumnus*), prove that it was originally nothing more than fetishism.

The *Flamen dialis* might not touch anything unclean, nor hear the lamentations for the dead, nor tread upon a grave. He might not put away his wife, nor marry a second time, and the thoroughly patriarchal character of his priestly functions is revealed in the rule that on the death of his wife he must lay down his office.

Human sacrifices were not uncommon among the Romans also in early times. It was said that they were abolished by Numa. But even down to the days of the emperors a human victim, though he was a condemned criminal, was put to death, and slaughtered enemies and those who suffered capital punishment were regarded as offerings to the gods. The self-sacrifice of individuals (*devovere se*) on occasion of plagues or disasters was also prompted by the same idea.

It was an instance of the favourable influence exerted by the Roman religion upon social life that certain crimes which were not dealt with by any law, such as the sale of a wife or of a married son, the beating of a father, or the violation of hospitality, were subject to the curse of the gods, that is, involved a kind of excommunication, of which men stood in great dread.

The anxious care for purity, and the belief in the magic power of prayer, are further points of concord between the Roman and the Parsee religions. Scrupulous adherence to forms, which frequently led among the Romans to a repetition of the sacrifices, on some occasions even as many as thirty times, was common to all ancient priestly religions, but was seldom so strongly developed as in the case before us.

140. The Tarquinii and Servius Tullius gave an entirely new direction to the state religion, which was pursued without interruption after their fall, and in fact until the decline of pre-Christian Rome. They founded a splendid temple on the Capitol for Jupiter, as the mightiest and greatest of the gods, *Optimus Maximus;* others placed Juno and Minerva by his side. With this temple splendid games and a brilliant cultus were associated. The ancient patriarchal god of light and purity thus became the powerful ruler, of whose citadel it was said that it should become the head of the whole world; he was the divine personification of the conquering Roman state. Such he continued to be. Into his temple the great Scipio Africanus the elder, went every morning to prepare himself by quiet prayer for his daily work, and all his triumphs he ascribed solely to the protection and aid of this great god. Jupiter O. M. is the expression of the belief of the Romans, to which they remained faithful even in that age of decline when they ridiculed the rest of their ancestral religion. While the Roman empire continued to extend over the world, it was impossible to doubt his power. The nations trembled before him more than they had ever done before Asur or Maruduk. Even a stranger, like Antiochus Epiphanes, founded a sanctuary to him in his capital, and endeavoured to spread his worship with fanatical zeal. The Jewish people alone claimed for their deity

the same sovereignty, and accordingly offered the most steadfast resistance to the attempts of Antiochus and of the Romans. But the Jews were conquered, and a temple of the Capitoline god was erected under Hadrian on the ruins of the temple of Yahveh, until at last Christendom, which issued from this same Jewish people, drove Jupiter O. M. out of his Capitol for good.

Optimus, in the formula Jupiter O. M., possesses no ethical significance, at any rate in the earliest times, but simply denotes the "mightiest," the "strongest."

The changes brought about by the Tarquinii affected both the representation of the god and the mode of his worship. Temples and images of the gods in human form, hitherto scarcely known among the Romans, were now introduced.

141. It soon became evident that a cold formal state religion of this kind, though it was now surrounded with great pomp, and was raised to be a symbol of a bold political idea, while it might satisfy a few statesmen and patricians, could not meet the wants of a whole people. This deficiency was perceived by the same kings who modified the native cultus, and they endeavoured to meet it by the introduction of foreign deities and usages. A sanctuary was erected on the Aventine for Diana, who was here really identical with the Artèmis of Massilia, and consequently with the Ephesian goddess; while the books containing the records of the oracular utterances of the Sibyl of Cumae, were brought to Rome, and intrusted to the care of two officers and two interpreters. These were the first traces of Greek religion at Rome. But they were not left to stand alone. One Hellenic god after another, at first with the substitution of a Latin name, at last even without that, received citizenship at Rome. What the last kings had done voluntarily, though certainly with the view of meeting the wishes of the people, the Senate was afterwards obliged to permit, in consequence of the demands of public opinion, though it rarely resolved to do so without hesitation. The Greek deities were followed by the Asiatic, such as the Great Mother of the gods, whose image, consisting of an unhewn stone, was brought at the expense of the State from Pessinus to Rome. On the whole, it was not the best and loftiest features of the foreign religions that were adopted, but rather their lower and sensual elements, and these, too, in their most corrupt form. An accidental accusation brought to light, in the year 186 B.C., a secret worship of Bacchus which was accompanied by all kinds of abominations, and had already made its way among thousands. Five years later an attempt was made, by the aid of some supposititious books of Numa, to substitute a certain semi-Greek theosophy for the State religion, but this proved too much for the sober sense of the Romans.

For the guardianship of the Sibylline books *duoviri sacris faciundis* were appointed.

It has been conjectured that even the Capitoline triad, especially Minerva, shows an imitation of Greek models, and in the institution of the *Ludi Romani* this influence cannot be mistaken. The novelty lies in the introduction of Greek deities; Latin and Sabine gods had been admitted long before. The worship of the Massilian Artemis was quickly followed by the rites of

Dêmêtêr, of Persephonê, and of Dionysus, which were amalgamated with the native worship of Ceres, Liber, and Libera; then came Castor and Pollox, Apollo, Esculapius; with the garden-goddess Venus, the Greek Aphroditê was identified, and the luxurious cultus of the Erycinian Venus, the mother of Eneas, soon rose to be the national worship.

The Bacchic mysteries, introduced at Rome by a couple of Campanian priests, were not the pure Eleusinian rites, but the fanatical and immoral performances which prevailed in Greece after the Peloponnesian wars. They afforded the Romans a welcome means of secretly practising unchastity, poisoning, falsification of wills, and other crimes, as well as of forming political conspiracies. P. Ebutius, who very nearly became their victim, brought the scandal to light.

The supposititious books of Numa consisted of seven Greek books on theosophy, and seven Latin on the *jus pontificium;* the fabrication, however, was so clumsy that the fraud was detected immediately, and the Senate gave orders that they should be burnt.

142. The current of the age was, however, too powerful to be turned even by any Roman authority. It was in vain that the philosophers, the soothsayers, and the priests of foreign gods were from time to time expelled; the first had become indispensable for the higher classes, many of these being also equally devoted to the last, who were, however, in especial request among women and among the lower classes. The state religion, undermined by philosophy, fell more and more into decline. As early as the first Punic war, a general ventured to ridicule the auspices, and the augurs soon did the same. Priestly offices were no longer secured to the worthiest occupants, but were sold to the wealthiest, and the highest of all sometimes remained vacant for years. Incredulity was followed by the usual result—the rank growth of superstition. Astrology and necromancy made their way even among the cultured and the learned, and went hand in hand with the grossest abuses. The eyes of the multitude were always turned towards the East, from which deliverance was expected to come forth, and secret rites brought from there to Rome were sure of a number of devotees. But they were only bastard children, or, at any rate, the late misshapen offspring of the lofty religions which once flourished in the East, an un-Persian Mithra-worship, an un-Egyptian Serapis-worship, an Isis-worship which only flattered the senses and was eagerly pursued by the fine ladies, to say nothing of more loathsome practices. Yet even these aberrations were the expression of a real and deep-seated need of the human mind which could find no satisfaction in the state religion. Men longed for a God whom they could worship heart and soul, and with this God they longed to be reconciled. Their own deities they had outgrown, and they listened eagerly, therefore, to the priests of Serapis and of Mithra, who each proclaimed their god as the sole-existing, the almighty, and all-good, and they felt especially attracted by the earnestness and strictness of the latter cultus. And in order to be secure of the eradication of all guilt, men lay down in a pit where the blood of the sacrificial animal flowed all over them, in the conviction that they would then arise entirely new-born.

After the death of L. Merula, in the time of Marius, the office of *Flamen dialis* remained vacant for seventy years, as no one was willing to submit to the great self-denial which it demanded.

The practice of astrology and magic was a return to the ancient civilisation of the proto-Babylonians. The astrologers at Rome were always called Chaldeans. They found credit even with learned persons, like Varro and Nigidius Figulus; under Sept. Severus they were publicly recognised, and under Alexander Severus they even received a sort of professorial chair at Rome. Magic had a more mixed character, for the aid of northern priests, especially of the Druids, was also invoked. As early as 97 B.C., it was found necessary to prohibit human sacrifices instituted in accordance with magical dogmas. Emperors, like Nero, and even Hadrian, were not disinclined to it.

Besides the deities named in the text, a number of others were also introduced into the Roman Empire, especially from Syria, such as *Atergatis, Maiuma,* the goddess of Gaza, *Deus Sol Elagabal* (the god of Byblus [Gebal] worshipped at Emesa), &c. On Serapis, see above, § 37. The most interesting of all these deities was the old-Aryan Mithra, whose worship had attained a high ascendency as early as Artaxerxes Mnemon, and, in conjunction with all kinds of un-Parsee usages, had spread through the East. His cultus, which always remained relatively pure, was brought to the West by pirates. By the Romans he was identified with their *Sol invictus,* to whom not only Julian, but also Constantine, even after his conversion to Christianity, is said to have been devoted. How far this Mithra was, moreover, from being the pure Zarathustrian god of light may be inferred from the fact that the highest—and, properly speaking, the only—god of the system, compared with whom Mithra is nothing more than a genius, remained entirely unknown in the West.

The *Taurobolia* and *Kriobolia* must also have been derived from the East, though their origin is unknown.

143. It was natural that the policy of Augustus should include the restoration of the national worship, but it was only the outward institutions which he re-organised; he could breathe no life into its dead forms. Two important religious innovations characterise the age of the empire —the deification of the emperors, and the growing power of universalism. Not only was the emperor on the Capitol made the centre of worship, which was to be expected in a state religion, but men now began to follow also at Rome the example set centuries before by the Egyptian princes, and in later days by the Ptolemies and Seleucidæ, for which the worship of genii afforded the means of transition, and the prevailing Euhemerism which explained the gods themselves as princes deified in ancient times, supplied the justification. Even during his lifetime Cæsar was honoured as a deity, and after his death he was enrolled among the gods by the Senate with great formality. All the emperors, with a few exceptions, followed him in turn, although Augustus and Tiberius still offered some resistance to the practice, and a Vespasian ridiculed it. Men talked of their majesty and eternity; their head was surrounded with a crown of rays and a nimbus; sacrifice was offered to their images, and they had the sacred fire carried before them. They were designated by the names of the gods—Hadrian was the Olympian, Nero Zeus, the liberator, and even the saviour of the world. Empresses thought it not beneath them to serve as priestesses

in the temples of their dead consorts, in expectation that they themselves would be deified, and cities esteemed it an honour to be temple-guardians (properly "temple-sweepers," *νεωκόροι*) of the Imperator. Thus this new cultus became a regular instrument of propaganda among the non-Roman nations, alike of the religion and of the supremacy of Rome. For Augustus and Roma were placed side by side as symbols of the restored empire with all its civilisation and its belief.

The second innovation was that Jupiter O. M. was now not only raised with the loftiest titles to be the chief of all the deities in the world, but was also identified with all the highest gods of other nations, and the provinces witnessed everywhere the rise of imitations of the Capitol. The relation was thus reversed. Men had begun by honouring the foreign gods, as mysterious powers, above their own; now that they knew them better, they saw that they stood no higher, and were essentially the same; each chief god was in fact a Jupiter, and the cultus of this Jupiter in different forms, combined with that of his incarnation upon earth—the emperor—now became the universal religion for the great universal empire.

The deification of Cæsar under the name *divus Julius* had proceeded so far that his image was not allowed to be carried in procession at family obsequies among the images of the ancestors of the house. The cultus of the emperors was pursued with such zeal that games were actually instituted in their honour, temples were built, and special priesthoods appointed; the Greek usage in the first case, and the Egyptian in the second, supplying the model. Even by the Christian Tertullian the emperors were called, though in a modified sense, *a Deo secundi, solo Deo minores.*

Jupiter now received the splendid titles of *summus excellentissimus*, or *exsuperantissimus*, *pacator* or *praeses orbis*, and others of the same kind. The inscriptions of the period speak of a *Jupiter O. M. Heliopolitanus* (Baälbek), *Damascenus*, *Dolichenus*, and even of a *Pœninus* on the St. Bernard, and a *Culminalis* in Styria. See Orell. *Inscript. lat. Collectio*, No. 228 foll., and Henzen (vol. iii. *Collect. Orellianae*), No. 5642. Cf. Grimm, *Deutsche Myth.* p. 154.

144. The Greco-Roman civilisation was the most composite, and consequently the highest, of antiquity. It soon far outgrew the ancestral religion, and men sought anxiously for the satisfaction of their religious wants. Fresh elements, therefore, were constantly being added to those which had already coalesced from Greece and Rome, and the whole mass continued to seethe and ferment. But an inspiring idea was necessary to draw forth from this confusion a new form of religion which should answer the needs of the civilised world. This idea was brought by the Gospel, the latest and most precious gift of the East to the West. But the West contributed its share, for it was here that the Gospel found its way prepared; here alone was it possible for it, though after long struggles, to prevail. The Eastern nations had retrograded; the Slavic and Germanic peoples were still backward. It was not till later that the era of the Germans dawned. The first form which Christianity assumed as an established religion was Roman. The Roman Catholic Church is simply the Roman universal empire modified and consecrated by Christian ideas. It left the old forms for the most part standing, but it ennobled and elevated them by the new spirit; its organisation and its efforts after unity which controlled all its development were inherited from the Romans, and it was by their means that it was enabled to become the teacher of the still rude populations of the North, to preserve rather than to diffuse the treasures which it had received from the Ancients and from Jesus.

THE END.